Decrypting Political Theology

Decrypting Power and Coloniality: Philosophical Perspectives from and through the Global South

Series Editors: Ricardo Sanín-Restrepo, Marinella Machado Araujo, Angus McDonald, and James Martel

The theory of encryption of power (TEP) proposes a fresh understanding of how the use of language monopolizes and hides power, preventing access to it through the denial and neutralization of differences based on class, race, and gender. It argues that coloniality exists because it encrypts power; hence the theory develops insights alongside and in parallel to decolonial theory and critical and subaltern studies. The central claim exposes how, in the name of the people, the people are made vulnerable to dispossession and exclusion, and how in the name of democracy, democracy is undermined and potentially destroyed. Theorizing encryption challenges the linkages between liberalism and colonialism, capitalism and sovereignty, constitution and economy, and their claims of necessity. The insights produced can be brought to bear on such phenomena as information circuits of disinformation on social media platforms, artificial intelligence, weapons, technologies of surveillance, and data mining.

Titles in the Series

Decrypting Political Theology: Genealogy, Tendencies, Antagonisms, by Andityas Matos

A Hopeful Political Imagination: Courage and Fantastic Critique in the Age of Meltdown, by Oscar Guardiola-Rivera

Decrypting Justice in and through the Global South, edited by Ricardo Sanín-Restrepo, Marinella Machado-Araujo, and Sabelo J. Ndlovu-Gatsheni

Decrypting Political Theology

Genealogy, Tendencies, Antagonisms

Andityas Matos

BLOOMSBURY ACADEMIC
NEW YORK • LONDON • OXFORD • NEW DELHI • SYDNEY

BLOOMSBURY ACADEMIC
Bloomsbury Publishing Inc, 1359 Broadway, New York, NY 10018, USA
Bloomsbury Publishing Plc, 50 Bedford Square, London, WC1B 3DP, UK
Bloomsbury Publishing Ireland, 29 Earlsfort Terrace, Dublin 2, D02 AY28, Ireland

BLOOMSBURY, BLOOMSBURY ACADEMIC and the Diana logo are trademarks of Bloomsbury Publishing Plc

First published in the United States of America 2025

A catalog record for this book is available from the Library of Congress.

ISBN: HB: 978-1-6669-7865-0
ePDF: 979-8-2162-5358-7
eBook: 978-1-9787-6881-9

Series: Decrypting Power and Coloniality: Philosophical Perspectives from and through the Global South

Typeset by Deanta Global Publishing Services, Chennai, India

For product safety related questions contact productsafety@bloomsbury.com.

To find out more about our authors and books visit www.bloomsbury.com and sign up for our newsletters.

Παιδία, ἐσχάτη ὥρα ἐστίν.

Filioli, novissima hora est.

Little children, it is the last time.

1, *John*, 2, 18.

Contents

Introduction

Why Political Theology Today?

The Kingdom is spread upon the earth, but men do not see it.

(*Gospel of Thomas*, 113)

Historically, law and politics have often been characterized as secular domains, particularly since the Modern era. Yet, even though contemporary States may formally disregard religion, their fundamental structures – sovereignty, political representation, people, Constitution, state of exception, tripartite division of powers, ministry, mission, hierarchy (these last three structure angelology) and so forth – are deeply rooted in theological concepts, models and experiences. Traditional political theory and philosophy often overlook the extent to which the legitimacy of political power is grounded in what has been conventionally termed *political theology*. This is a key to philosophical readings capable of overcoming encryption and the resulting uncritical lack of knowledge of the intricate relationships between religion and politics, seeking a profound understanding of complex phenomena in which power and faith are intertwined.

My aim, of course, is not to defend the necessity of a religious basis for politics, but rather to highlight that, despite denials, such a basis exists and cannot be fully understood through purely quantitative analyses so germane to Political Science, Sociology and other disciplines. While I do not dispute the validity and usefulness of these disciplines, I argue that their data can be interpreted in a richer and more comprehensive way by abandoning the liberal and unrealistic dogma that religion has no influence or importance in a secular State. Instead, as I have already explained in other texts,[1] I propose that all political power, however technical or rational it may seem, is rooted in what Montaigne, in opposition to the Enlightenment discourse that would soon become the only acceptable social narrative, called 'the mystical foundation of authority'.[2] This perspective was radicalized by Jacques Derrida (1989–90), for whom, ultimately, obeying the law corresponds to an act of faith. Thus, one obeys the law because it has *credit*, a word that shares the same root as the Latin term for 'belief', *credere*. This credit/belief engenders debt, an obligation that is virtually impossible to fully discharge, and consequently, a sense of perpetual guilt. From this perspective, Giorgio Agamben is categorical when he states that current political philosophy will not be able to escape its contradictions if it does not become aware of its theological roots (2018b: 295).

From this horizon, I commence this book with a concise GENEALOGY of the idea of political theology, examining its main theories and authors, both classical and contemporary. However, this is not merely a historical analysis but rather a critical-philosophical inquiry. To this end, I draw upon the theory of the encryption of power, which, according to Ricardo Sanín-Restrepo and Marinella Machado-Araujo, involves 'the imposition of institutional simulations of difference that condition, neutralize or prohibit political agency (action), reducing it (difference) to static and solid models of identity that present themselves as the only form of power' (2020: 2). Indeed, political theology may be the most prominent example of the encryption of power, a metaphysical process that substitutes immanence for transcendence, multiplicity for unity and *potentia* for *potestas*, resulting in centralized and self-contained political institutions. Thus, 'to encrypt (power) is to simulate power (democratic, constituent) and to prohibit or condition Being while collapsing political agency (constituent power, resistance) within fixed, final, transcendent and solid structures (constituted power, the law)' (Sanín-Restrepo and Machado-Araujo 2020: 2). Within this context, I initially ask what exactly political theology encrypts throughout its development in the Middle Ages, Modernity and Contemporary times. The central theme of this first approach revolves around Carl Schmitt's proposal, which defined political theology as a legitimate field of study for philosophers and jurists concerned with the phenomenon of legitimizing modern political power. Schmitt asserted that all the primary definitions of State theory secularize theological concepts. Furthermore, I delineate brief yet essential conceptual distinctions between the idea of political theology and related theoretical constructs, such as theocracy, dual sovereignty and political religion. The latter is often associated with totalitarian scenarios, which, contrary to a common belief, is not necessarily the case of political theology.

In the second chapter, I explore the critical potential of various TENDENCIES within political theology. To accomplish this, I present some proposals for reconfiguring and overcoming Carl Schmitt's political theology, which has dominated theological-political studies for much of the past century. While theoretically refined, Schmitt's political theology is notably authoritarian and conservative, centring on the concept of sovereignty, which, as I will discuss, constitutes one of the primary apparatuses for the encryption of power. Even during Schmitt's time, this orientation faced criticism, particularly from Walter Benjamin and Jacob Taubes. Notwithstanding, alternative theological-political systems only emerged from the intersection of political theology with new theoretical proposals – such as those of Derrida, Foucault and Deleuze – and with new social movements and identity struggles, including Black and feminist ones. Therefore, by considering both the theoretical and practical processes of decrypting power, numerous spaces are now opening up for democratic and libertarian theological-political visions capable of challenging the traditional vision centred on the ideas of sovereignty, omnipotence, obedience, patriarchy and hierarchy. This is the domain of the new political theologies that I term radical-democratic, as they reject representative democracy, the quintessential form of the encryption of power, and are constructed with a focus on the democratic potentialities that arise from recognizing the *an-archic* nature of all power, a central topic of my argument to which I dedicate an important subsection. I also explore themes such as the death of God, the interpretative openness of the Scriptures and the valorization of the *mikrói* (the oppressed), creating a rich backdrop that enables us to re-examine the entire modern political-legal tradition.

In the third chapter, dedicated to Antagonisms, I analyse contemporary phenomena such as the empowerment of authoritarian religious groups, Christofascism, economic theology and the rise of Neo-Pentecostalism in politics. Expanding upon the themes of the previous chapter, I highlight how the theological-political landscape has become a significant arena of social conflict that cannot be dismissed as merely 'pre-modern'. Instead, it is one of the primary dimensions where fundamental political decisions are debated and implemented. To this end, I demonstrate how the encryption of power by traditional political theology led to the emergence of extremely authoritarian economic theologies that, while claiming to be non-political or neutral, ultimately generated significant political effects of domination. An example of this is the strengthening of neoliberalism as a social metanarrative with a religious bias. Themes such as individualism, unbridled competitiveness and subjectivation through guilt/debt create an atomized and uncritical society, which is reflected in the United States and Brazil – a privileged field of my analysis due to decolonial reasons that will be clarified – in the capture of politics by sectarian, violent and fundamentalist religious visions.

The book concludes with an invitation to rebuild a life in common, that is, a reconstruction of politics. The so-called 'crisis' of politics largely stems from a limited conception of the nature of political power, which fails to consider historical, transcendent and 'irrational' elements linked to its metaphysical-religious foundation. These elements appear increasingly influential in our contemporary world.

In this sense, there arises the need to transcend the liberal conception of politics, which appears as the only possible one in the contemporary horizon, understanding that life in community is not reduced to the technical-institutional aspects that have captured it today, but rather involves continuous existential decisions translated into true vital wagers. To this end, a proposal that emerges subtly – *in aenigmate* – throughout this book will be discussed in the conclusion. This is the call made by Paul – and later by Heidegger and Agamben – to (de)constitute our forms-of-life deemed 'normal' and unchangeable by adopting a psychic structuration related to potency and messianic futurability. From this perspective, it is a matter of living the current life not as an unchangeable reality given once and for all. Instead, considering the dynamics of transformation and ontological indeterminacy that continuously act within the so-called 'objective' reality, these authors invite us to live this life *as if it were another*, (re)inserting into the real the potency that, in fact, (de)constitutes and sustains it. Thus, traditional political theologies centred on sovereignty and encryption can, finally, not be destituted – such would be nothing but naïve idealism – but, in some way, decrypted, problematized and antagonized.

The central thesis of this book is that only a critical-philosophical analysis that examines the encryption of power and the strategies for its decryption can reveal the profoundly theological nature of our institutions, centred on concepts such as hierarchy, debt, guilt, homeland, work, sovereignty, representation, person, Good and Evil. Therefore, this critical work of clarification can reveal how political institutions *actually* function, rather than merely how they *should* function according to normative and rationalist models – that is, encrypted models – often based on 'classical' authors and outdated social realities that do not accurately reflect the complex and multifaceted contemporary reality in which power, faith, belief and law are intertwined.

I reiterate that my aim is not to judge whether the existence of a theological-political dimension in current social practices of power is appropriate – a fact that seems self-evident to me – but rather to investigate the reasons behind this phenomenon, which has been overlooked by specialized literature. This inattention is paradoxical given the significant role of religion in contemporary political-legal practices. I believe it is crucial to critically debate the politicization of religion and the sacralization of politics, particularly in light of the agendas of the extreme right. These agendas emerge as symptoms of a political theologization that is often contradictory and incoherent and can only be addressed through a serious and internal examination of this reality, which will not vanish simply by being denied.

1

Genealogy

Truth came not into the world naked, but in images and figures.

(*Gospel of Philip*, 115, 9–11)

1.1. What is political theology?

According to the 2012 report *The Global Religious Landscape* published by the Pew Research Center in Washington, based on demographic analyses conducted in 230 countries, eight out of ten people worldwide identified as religious. In the United States of America, another report published by the same institution indicated that 29 per cent of the population declared no defined religious affiliation in 2021. This represents a relatively substantial increase compared to 2007, when only 16 per cent of Americans identified as religiously unaffiliated (Pew Research Center 2021). In 2023, the number of non-religious people fell to 28 per cent. However, these data should be interpreted cautiously. Of the total 28 per cent of 'nones' – those who identify as 'atheists, agnostics, or "nothing in particular" when asked about their religion' – only 17 per cent actually describe themselves as atheists; 20 per cent identify as agnostics, while 63 per cent state that they have no particular religious affiliation (Pew Research Center 2024). This implies that less than 0.05 per cent of the American population identifies as atheist, revealing the enduring influence of ideas related to God, transcendence and religion in the world's most powerful nation.

In my country, Brazil, the data is similarly striking, with nine out of ten Brazilians reporting belief in God or a higher power. This places Brazil, alongside South Africa, at the top of the ranking in the *Global Religion* survey conducted by the Ipsos Institute (2023). Official data from the Brazilian Institute of Geography and Statistics (IBGE) from 2010 corroborates these findings, showing that only

10 per cent of those surveyed declared no religious affiliation, and only 1 per cent confessed to being atheist. Religious Brazilians are divided as follows: 65 per cent Catholics, 13.4 per cent Pentecostal/Neo-Pentecostal Evangelicals, 4.9 per cent undetermined Evangelicals, 4.1 per cent Missionary Evangelicals, 2.7 per cent other religions, and 2 per cent Spiritualists (IBGE 2023). The recent 2022 census revealed a significant increase in the number of Evangelicals, who now represent 26.85 per cent of the population. Catholics remain the largest religious group, though in decline, with 56.75 per cent. Other religious groups recorded in the census included Spiritists (1.84 per cent), Umbanda and Candomblé (1.05 per cent), Indigenous traditions (0.06 per cent) and other religious affiliations (4.01 per cent). The number of people with no religion remained virtually unchanged, at 9.28 per cent (IBGE 2025). Given these statistics, it is not surprising that Brazil has a higher number of religious establishments (579,800) than combined educational (264,400) and health institutions (247,500), as reported by *Folha de S. Paulo*, a leading Brazilian newspaper, on 2 February 2024, based on the 2022 census. Finally, while avoiding excessive citation of raw data, it is noteworthy to mention a survey conducted by the same newspaper on 15 October 2022, just two weeks before the second round of the most contested presidential election since Brazil's redemocratization in 1988. In this survey, 59 per cent of respondents indicated that the religion of the presidential candidate was important in determining their vote (49 per cent considered it *very* important), whereas 21 per cent reported that the future president's religion was not a relevant factor in their voting decision.

These numbers alone underscore the centrality of religion in the contemporary political and social landscape. However, if, like me, you are sceptical of purely quantitative analyses, I invite you to conduct a brief experiment. Recall all the individuals who, within the past week, in conversations with you or in collective settings – such as online forums, television programmes, schools, workplaces or supermarkets – made references to God, faith, salvation or religions in general. I attempted to conduct this experiment and quickly lost count, as nearly everyone I interacted with last week, from my Uber driver to my university colleague, from my dentist to the plumber who came to fix my sink, from the gas station attendant to my grandmother, had something to say on the subject. Moreover, all of their religious perceptions were undeniably political, even though none of them seemed to recognize this fact.

All of this – research, data and subjective experiences – should prompt us to reconsider the arrogant self-classification of so-called 'postmodern' societies as secular and rationalist. Instead, they highlight the importance that religion still has today in various fields, from art to law, from economics to politics and in many others. This study is limited to one of these fields, which involves the intersection of belief and power or, if you prefer, religion and politics. Well, there is an approach in political philosophy specifically aimed at studying the relationships between these realities: *political theology*. I seek to present it in the most accessible way possible in this book, which necessarily involves some simplifications and methodological choices, given that the theological-political material, in addition to being very ancient, is marked by enormous and growing complexity.

Perhaps the initial consideration to grasp is that political theology has at least two distinct meanings. Broadly speaking, it refers to the relationships and reciprocal influences between religion and power. This was the prevailing understanding from the Greeks until the early twentieth century, when Carl Schmitt, a controversial and brilliant German jurist, introduced a significantly different and specific meaning. With Schmitt's influence, the notion of political theology came to represent almost the opposite of its original connotation.

Indeed, for centuries, political theology aimed to demonstrate the influence of religious powers within the political sphere. However, from Schmitt's 1922 work onward, the expression began to indicate the impossibility, characteristic of the Modern Age, of basing political power substantially on religion. This gap leads to a process of intense and escalating delegitimization of power, resulting in a corresponding exponential increase in state violence. According to Schmitt, the only viable political theology in the contemporary era is functional rather than substantial. This implies that political powers have merely assumed the functions and forms of religious authorities, which explains their perceived lack of legitimacy and their reliance on violence to assert themselves. Schmitt's position is part of a broader debate on the so-called 'legitimacy of Modernity' that, in the second half of the twentieth century, involved prominent intellectuals such as Hans Blumenberg, Karl Löwith, Eric Voegelin, Odo Marquard and others. This debate not only profoundly questioned the meaning of Modernity but also significantly reshaped our understanding of what political theology is and what it can be in the twentieth and twenty-first centuries. In subsection 2.1.1, I revisit the key participants, arguments and controversies of this debate. Now, it seems more crucial to present a general and 'traditional' perspective on the central concepts of political theology.

It is already clear that political theology is a *field of study* and not a political or religious doctrine. In other words, it is not an ideology or a 'practical' stance that recommends or condemns any specific relationship between politics and religion. Political theology accepts the connections between power and faith as a given reality and tries to understand it, taking Marx's observation seriously: '[. . .] the critique (*Kritik*) of religion is the preliminary condition of all critique' (1956: 378).[1]

In summary, political theology can be characterized as a form of *critique*, as conceived by Michel Foucault, who does not see in it a privileged access to any origin,[2] cause or truth. Critique, present not only in philosophy but also in politics, literature, law, morality, science and, I would add, in theology – that is, in the discourse (*lógos*) about the divine (*theós*) – is an *attitude*, a type of 'virtue in general' that articulates the dimensions of knowledge, power and subjectivation (Foucault 2015: 35). Therefore, critique represents a stance that perpetually questions the field within which it operates, acknowledging an external perspective from which such a field can be evaluated. Critique is always a critique of something – an *epistéme*, an institution, a discourse – that should not be equated with itself (Butler 2004a). I believe it is essential to highlight that this presupposition of an exteriority, a space where critique can occur, distinguishes it from ideology (Adorno 1984 and Galli 2022). Ideology, incapable of perceiving something different from itself, presupposes no outside. Consequently, all ideological discourse is totalizing. Foucault asserts that the critical attitude, while a problematic heir of the Enlightenment,[3] opens up the possibility of an art of not allowing oneself to be governed in a particular way. This is a form of 'voluntary inservitude', a 'reflected indocility' that does not manifest as a general rejection of the current political-legal system, but rather as historically constituted resistances aimed at dissubjection within the games of the 'politics of the truth' (2015: 39).

From this perspective, to comprehend the notion of political theology, it is essential to immediately dispel the misconception that this expression relates to theocratic governments. While the supposed secularism of Western democracies is, at best, problematic and, at worst, a farce, it does not imply that they are theocratic. In fact, theocracy should not be conflated with political theology. Theocracy denotes a form of *direct divine governance* in relation to humanity, without representative bodies. As such, it has existed (and continues to exist) in rare instances, with the classic example being the Jewish people before the reign of Saul. In contrast, political theology involves *representative dynamics*, not allowing for any direct experience – whether individual (mysticism) or social (theocracy) – of the divine. Based on these initial ideas, it is worthwhile to delve deeper, even in a schematic manner, into the models of relationships between politics and religion.

According to Wolf-Daniel Hartwich, Aleida Assmann and Jan Assmann (2007: 149), these relationships can take three basic forms: political theology, theocracy and dual sovereignty. *Theocracy* occurs when it is believed that a God directly governs the world of human beings without the mediation of a specific political class. On the contrary, in *political theology* the spheres of religion and political power are separate, requiring them to interact through certain encryption apparatuses, such as political representation. When these spheres completely coincide – for example, when the political leader is also the religious leader of a community – we have a theocratic model. As I will discuss later, Walter Benjamin similarly understands theocracy as having exclusively a religious meaning, not a political one. Carl Schmitt and Ernst Bloch also understand theocracy in the same way, that is, as a structure that does not participate in the duplicated nature of the theological-political model (Taubes 1987, 2007: 173).

The most radical definition of theocracy originates with the Dutch philosopher Baruch Spinoza (1632–77). In his *Theological-Political Treatise* – a book that, according to his detractors, was forged in hell[4] – Spinoza asserts that this form of government arises from a direct pact between human beings and God, admitting no intermediaries or representatives. The distinction from the Hobbes-Schmitt theological-political scheme is evident. Unlike these models, which theorize the necessity of the State representing God on Earth – whether as a mortal God (Hobbes) or as a functional one (Schmitt) – Spinoza posits that in the genesis of the Jewish theocratic State, 'the Hebrews decided not to transfer their right to any man, but only to God' (2021 [17, 3, 7]: 1039). Interpreting Spinoza's ideas, the Italian philosopher Donatella di Cesare (2014: 82) differentiates between theocracy and hierocracy. Hierocracy is understood as the government of priests, while true Spinozian theocracy is identified with the direct and immediate governance of God. At the concrete political level, this translates into a form of anarchy, as no human political power can be considered legitimate in the face of God's direct sovereignty, which manifests as absolute democracy. Contrary to the claims of most theorists, theocracy and democracy are not mutually exclusive concepts in Spinoza's philosophy.

Finally, the third model can be considered a variation of the theological-political scheme. As described by Rodney Needham (1980), it is *dual sovereignty*, in which religious and political authorities are separated so that, although both are legitimate, neither can interfere with the other's domain of action due to techniques of power division. In the dual sovereignty model, it cannot be asserted that religion influences politics – or vice versa – but rather that both coexist, peacefully or not, mutually recognizing each other as necessary

1.2. Brief conceptual and historical overview

The term 'political theology' does not have a definitively established origin date, but it is undoubtedly an ancient concept. Consequently, its meaning has evolved over the centuries.[5] A perplexing question that arises almost immediately echoes the classic chicken-and-egg dilemma: When discussing political theology, are we referring to religion as the original phenomenon that determines politics or, on the contrary, is politics the initial data that shapes religion? Many of the authors I cite in this book, both ancient and contemporary, lean towards the former interpretation, viewing religion as the birthplace of politics.

However, there are respected scholars who hold differing views. Perhaps the most notable example is the German Egyptologist Jan Assmann (1938–2024), who, inspired by Jacob Taubes and through meticulous analysis of ancient sources from Egypt, Israel and Europe, argues that religion derives from politics (Assmann 1992, 2000). In a deliberately provocative manner, Assmann inverts Schmitt's famous dictum to assert that 'the significant concepts of theology are theologized political concepts' (2000: 20). In a similar context, but strongly influenced by Carl Schmitt, the German historian Christian Meier (1980) discusses 'theological politics' in his analysis of the Greek tragedy *Eumenides*. According to his interpretation, it is the political – embodied by the rational argumentation of the goddess Athena – that, in a certain sense, controls the ancient Hellenic religion represented by the Erinyes, who persecuted Orestes for his matricide. Through the internal pacification of the city, symbolized by the transformation of the Erinyes into the 'Benevolent Ones' thanks to Athena's discursive strategies, a Schmittian political dimension is established, separating the interior (friends) from the exterior (enemies) of the *pólis*. Some scholars even propose the term 'legal theology'. Despite the official secularist discourse, we can observe a contemporary movement toward closer integration between law and religion, particularly in the field of Constitutional Law. This has led to the fetishization of the legal form and the capture of religiosity by the culture of legality, a process evident in both Western countries and the Middle East (Comaroff 2009).

Of course, a third alternative exists. It is a more complex approach that avoids determining which came first – religion or politics – assuming this to be an undecidable question. Instead, it focuses on studying the relationships between these two fields without establishing a hierarchy. This is the approach taken by Merio Scattola (2009). Based on Reinhart Koselleck's (1923–2006) semasiological method, Scattola analyses political theology in terms of its historical mutations, expansions and contractions. I follow a similar approach in this book, albeit in a more concise manner due to the extension limitations of my work. However, unlike Scattola's purely historical study, my analysis is genealogical. Drawing inspiration from Nietzsche, Foucault and Agamben, I aim not only to present a simple evolution of the concept of political theology throughout history but also to identify its points of insurgency (*Entstehung*) that, by modifying certain social, legal or economic dynamics, reverberate into the present day, since genealogy is defined as an investigation of the past that is reflected in the present. Therefore, the objective of this book is not only to provide elements for a better understanding of some philosophical constructs but also to examine the *effects of power* that have derived and continue to derive from them. In other words, I want to analyse how these constructs are situated in contemporary reality and to what extent they can be utilized not only for describing but also for transforming it.

The expression 'political theology' already appears in Antiquity. Varro (116–27 BC) taught in his *Antiquities of Divine Things* that the Greek Stoic philosophers distinguished three theologies: mythical, responsibility of poets; physical, entrusted to philosophers; and political, related to magistrates and princes. The Romans translated these concepts as legendary theology (*theologia fabularis*), natural theology (*theologia naturalis*) and civil theology (*theologia civilis*). In this initial, ancient sense, which was rather unspecific and fluctuating, political theology regulated the proper and ethically required actions of citizens in community life, with particular emphasis on the role of priests (Varro 1976 [VI, 12, 319]: 334–5). While the expression 'political theology' was not commonly used in the language of the ancient and medieval worlds, theological-political practices were abundant and intense during both periods. This is a typical characteristic of these eras, as for the ancients and medievals, every 'theological' reality was inherently political, rendering the term unnecessary because there was no need to name the obvious. In fact, considering that for the ancients political theology was not a problematic or scandalous idea – as it is for us – it was believed that all political power was ultimately grounded in a transcendent basis. Consequently, there was no specific concern with investigating the relationship between power and faith, which seemed entirely natural and inevitable to them. Moreover, it is important to highlight that the theological-political model of the sacred king, symbolizing the mono-theo-logical encounter between Heaven and Earth, emerged in the West only with Constantine and had limited influence among the Greeks and Romans.

Thus, political theology functioned in Antiquity and the Middle Ages as a 'historical *a priori*', a seemingly contradictory expression used by Edmund Husserl and subsequently employed by Michel Foucault, but never fully explained by him. In any case, a historical *a priori* can be understood as a set of ideas characteristic of a particular era – hence, 'historical' – that are not debated or questioned but rather taken for granted. These ideas form the foundation of a specific experience of reality and enable a particular regime of meaning (*epistéme*), deriving from this its *a priori* character. The concept of historical *a priori* is complex and evolves throughout Foucault's work. He developed it during his archaeological phase through various, more or less general approaches, some of which were inspired by Husserlian phenomenology. In *The Birth of the Clinic*, the expression is defined as a type of 'original distribution of the visible and the invisible insofar as it is linked to the sharing of what is expressed and what is silenced' (1963: VIII). In *The Order of Things*, Foucault concisely defines historical *a priori* as an experience of the order through which knowledge is constituted (1966: 13). In a subsequent work, *The Archaeology of Knowledge*, he further elaborates on this concept, stating that the historical a priori 'must account for statements in their dispersion' (1969: 167). It appears that the historical *a priori* proposed by Foucault constitutes a preconceptual articulation. Ironically, while borrowing the Kantian idea of an *a priori* – knowledge independent of empirical experience – Foucault suggests that each and every *epistéme*, functioning as a preunderstanding of a certain reality, is necessarily linked to the determinations, openings and limits imposed by the historical period in which it emerged.[6] In short, the historical *a priori* is something that is not explained but that, at a given time, explains everything, exactly like political theology in the ancient world and, even more so, in the medieval period. Political theology became a subject of inquiry – and began to be named and studied – only in the Modern Age, when the demand for separation between the religious and civil spheres emerged. This phenomenon is reflected in the idea of secularization, a topic discussed in subsection 2.1.1.

Regarding the contemporary world, many scholars mistakenly claim that Carl Schmitt created the term 'political theology' (e.g. Peterson 1994b: 81), which is not true, although it was only with the German jurist that this idea broke out of the circle of specialized university research and reached a wider audience. Carl Schmitt himself, in a letter dated 14 April 1952 and addressed to Armin Mohler, reveals that the coinage of the term 'political theology' was due to the Russian anarchist Mikhail Bakunin, a figure both loved and hated by Schmitt, who admired the intensity and the radicality of his thought without, however, accepting its revolutionary dimension (Taubes 2007: 178). In fact, Bakunin, author of the famous pamphlet *God and State*, written in 1871, would have been the first to use the expression 'political theology' in contemporary times, specifically in the essay *Mazzini's Political Theology and the International*, published in the same year. But the question of the expression's paternity remains complex. As Carlo Galli demonstrated (2015), the term 'political theology' appears as early as the 1843 *Note on the Hegelian Conception of the State*, a work by the young Karl Marx (1818–83) dedicated to critiquing Hegel's idea of the State. Galli also cites its use in an 1887 article by Friedrich Engels (1820–95) and Karl Kautsky (1854–1938), referenced by Hans Kelsen in *The General Theory of Law and Materialism* of 1931. It seems that the doubt will never be definitively resolved, given that the origin of the expression 'political theology' can even be traced back to the works of authors older than Bakunin, Marx and Engels, such as the writers Ugo Foscolo (1778–1827) and Louis Veuillot (1813–83), even appearing in the famous *Encyclopédie* by Denis Diderot (1713–84) and Jean d'Alembert (1717–83), who define political theology as 'the theory of the political use of religion' (Galli 1996: 421).

Regardless of its precise origin, whether anarchist, Marxist or encyclopaedist (indefiniteness that is intriguing), the contemporary understanding of political theology is fundamentally Christian and perhaps also Jewish, according to certain interpretations that I will explore in the second chapter. This is because political theology can only exist within the context of monotheism and political representation. While ancient Greco-Roman and Eastern peoples developed portentous and complex systems intertwining politics and religion, the idea of transcendence did not pose a challenge for them, as polytheism was integrated into all aspects of their lives, both private and public. Thus, these cultures did not experience transcendence as such, considering that the gods inhabited the human world and interacted with it, indicating an experience of 'immanentized transcendence' that became impossible after the radical separation between the spiritual and temporal dimensions socially necessary for the establishment of Christianity.

Within the context of Christianity, there are two major historical periods of political theology: the 'ancient' and the 'modern'. These terms should not be interpreted in a strictly technical-historical sense but rather in a conceptual-structural one. The first period, which is significantly longer than the second, extends from Paul of Tarsus to the seventeenth century. While I will not delve into this initial era in detail, I will make some references to relevant elements and events.

Within the context of ancient political theology, it is essential to emphasize the two primary theoretical frameworks that were prevalent during this extended period: the idea of representation and the doctrine of the two swords formulated by Pope Gelasius I (410–496) at the end of the fifth century. This last theory was made possible by Constantine (272–337) who, in 313, elevated Christianity to the status of the official religion of the Roman Empire, and was further entrenched by Theodosius I (346–395) in 380, when he issued an edict (*Cunctos Populos* or *De Fide Catolica*) making Christianity the exclusive sanctioned religion within the imperial domains. According to this theory, power is constitutively divided between religious and secular authorities, forming a kind of diarchy that, while subject to various forms, transgressions and reinterpretations over the centuries,[7] has consistently represented the obvious horizon – the historical *a priori* – within which medieval religious and secular authorities should operate.[8]

Regarding representation as a specific theological-political strategy of the Middle Ages, it emerged in the first century of the Christian era to address the multiplicity of biblical interpretations and overcome the Church's originally headless character. One of its earliest formulations, understood as an evocation of something that takes the place of God to *re-present* him, is found in the *Letter to the Christians of Magnesia*, written between 88 and 107 by Ignatius (*c.* 30/35–*c.* 98/107), bishop of Antioch. However, it is important to exercise caution here. Contrary to the claims of some scholars,[9] the prefix *re-* in the Latin word *repræsentare* does not imply a new presentation of something that no longer exists or is invisible. Instead, it serves as an intensifying particle capable of indicating the very process of immediate presentification of a certain reality. To represent, therefore, means to make something present here and now.[10] From this derives the famous concept of representation coined by Carl Schmitt, for whom representing means making an invisible being visible through a public presence that possesses adequate *dignitas* (2002: 35–6). In fact, while Schmitt's political theology is distinctly modern, his concept of representation clearly has medieval roots (Hofmann 1974: 187).

The origin of Schmitt's formulation can be traced back to authors such as Eusebius of Caesarea (265–339), who viewed Emperor Constantine as a 'type of universal bishop' ('οἷά τις κοινὸς ἐπίσκοπος'), that is, a supervisor or director representing God and the *lógos*. This established a perfect correspondence between Heaven and Earth, especially after Constantine assassinated the three emperors who formed the Roman tetrarchy with him. According to Eusebius, it is the Emperor's responsibility to ensure the unity of the divine kingdom throughout the Empire. This idea may have been influenced by Paul, who believed that those endowed with superior political powers must fulfil the role of God's ministers (*Romans* 13:4).

It is no coincidence that Eusebius created with the same gesture the classical political theology and the notion of Christian history which, quite different from Greco-Roman history, is still the one that characterizes our world. The ecclesiastical history that Eusebius was the first to write is not merely a collection of occasional reports. Instead, it is a narrative with an inherent meaning, progressing towards a destined fulfilment. The most significant political moment within this narrative occurs with the encounter between the earthly empire of Augustus (which would soon be inherited by Constantine) and the heavenly empire of the Christian God. In Eusebius' words: 'when the Lord and Savior appeared and, at the same time as his advent, Augustus, first of Romans, became king of the nations, pluralistic polyarchy was dispersed and peace covered all the Earth' (*Commentary on the Psalms*, 71). From this perspective, Peterson concludes: 'After Constantine defeated Licinius, political monarchy was restored and, at the same time, divine monarchy was secured [. . .] the *single* king on Earth corresponds to the *single* king in Heaven and the *single* sovereign *nómos* and *Lógos*' (1994b: 50).

Furthermore, Eusebius – whom Franz Overbeck (1837–1905) ironically labelled Constantine's theological hairdresser (Agamben 2014a: 27) – was the author responsible for introducing a theology in which a 'kingdom without a church' prevailed. Unlike the later developments in Catholic Christian theology with Isidore of Seville (*c.* 560–636), Thomas Aquinas (1225–74) and Dante Alighieri (1265–1321), Eusebius' theology did not envision a coordinated opposition between the secular and the spiritual dominions, as articulated in the theory of the two swords. According to Eusebius, the church and the kingdom merged within the person of the Emperor. Only later did theologians such as

Augustine of Hippo (354–430) separate these two instances, drawing upon the authority of Paul of Tarsus (*c.* 5–67). It was with these thinkers – Augustine, Isidore, Aquinas, Dante and others – that political theology emerged in a strict sense, since in Eusebius' theory the theological and the political elements were amalgamated.

Notwithstanding, for the German theologian Erik Peterson (1860–1960), it was with Eusebius that Christian political theology truly began. Peterson argued that Eusebius successfully established the analogy between the coming of Christ and the establishment of Roman imperial power by Augustus, leading to the idea that the Church and medieval emperors inherited this divine monarchy, thus affirming the unity between Heaven and Earth through the unification of the human and divine realms. However, this process ultimately ended with the officialization of the trinitarian doctrine. As Peterson contends, Catholicism subsequently ceased believing in a single God, disrupting the correspondence between the divine monarchy – which would no longer be unified – and the Empire. According to Peterson (1994b), from that moment on, Christian political theology would have ceased to exist, being a stillborn idea, a thesis that Schmitt vehemently rejects (Agamben 2014a: 27–8). I discuss this debate in subsection 2.1.1.

In any case, before the 'end' of political theology, Eusebius stated that the Emperor-Pontiff is the mediator between humanity and God and that he, and not any priest, no matter how high his position in the ecclesiastical hierarchy, is the one who effectively represents divinity on Earth (Scattola 2009: 50–4). This representational scheme, which emerged in the Eastern Church, became fundamental for Roman Christianity, in which the role of the Eastern Emperor would eventually fall to the Pope, giving rise to many problems regarding the relationship between the Empire and the Church, as posed by the various versions of the theory of the two swords. But these problems are not relevant to verifying the formal structure of Christian theological-political representation, which can refer to either the Pope or the Emperor, depending on the historical and political conditions that present themselves to the interpreter.

Following Eusebius, Flavius Vegetius (fifth century–450) asserted that the Emperor must be worshipped and venerated, as having received the title of Augustus, one must dedicate unlimited submission to him, *as if he were* God physically present. Even Emperor Constantine himself, in a letter to the bishops of the Council of Nicaea in 325, stated that the decisions taken at the synod should be attributed to the will of God (Dogliani 2014: 10–13). It can thus be observed that representation emerged early in the history of the medieval West as a central apparatus of theological-political encryption, simultaneously uniting and paradoxically maintaining the distinction between Empire and Church, or Kingdom and Glory, as interpreted by Giorgio Agamben (2011: 68–108).

From a genealogical perspective, it should be noted that the concept of representation raised when the initial Christian belief in the irrepresentability of a God who would directly govern humanity collapsed. This belief was deeply rooted in Judaism and is fundamental to the notion of theocracy, which, as previously discussed, should not be confused with political theology. Beginning in the first centuries of Catholicism, representative thinking translated the presence of the unrepresentable God into intense and extensive iconological practices. This culminated in Eusebius of Caesarea's *Life of the Great Constantine*, a work in which Constantine is presented in the opening pages as immortal, and his elevation to Emperor is portrayed as the 'testament of God' given to Christians to alleviate their earthly torments (Rizzi 2002).

With respect to *modern political theology*, the subject of this book, it is generally acknowledged that its emergence can be attributed, on the political level, to the establishment of the modern system of international law at the conclusion of the Thirty Years' War and the Treaty of Westphalia in 1648. On the philosophical level, it is due to the disappearance and subsequent 'death' of God, an event that occurred not solely with Nietzsche or Postmodernity but was articulated as early as the dawn of Modernity by authors such as Hobbes. Therefore, contemporary political theology can be characterized as a theology of absence (Scattola 2009: 128), a concept I will delve into further in Chapter 2. For now, it suffices to remember that this absence originates precisely from the representational nature of political theology. It manifests in the form of a structural element, as even after the representative process the absence cannot be entirely overcome (Duso 2012: 26–7). In fact, the absence – which, as I will discuss in section 2.2, corresponds exactly to the *an-archic* space of power that representative political theology encrypts – appears insurmountable.

Representative apparatuses diversify in tandem with the historical transformations of human societies' political-legal and cultural institutions, forming various representative discourses. Despite their differing functions, foundations and relationships between representatives and represented, these discourses will always confront the incommensurability of an original void. This absence is filled through processes that transition from an *an-archic* multiplicity to the unity of an order that encrypts it in the form of *potestas*. It is evident that this is not an order of equals but rather a hierarchical and stratified structure, organized to support the dynamics of power whereby many are subjected and few dominate (Costa 2004: 15–16).

1.3. The legitimacy of contemporary political theology

In his interpretation of Schmitt's Political Theology, Paul W. Kahn asserts that defending political theology is equivalent to defending philosophy, the sole discipline capable of critically examining the problem of evil and free will. According to Kahn (2011: 153), political theology opposes the reductionist tendencies that were already evident in Schmitt's time within the fields of law with Kelsen and sociology with Weber. In this sense, political theology preserves a kind of knowledge that, although essential to humanity, is being lost and rapidly forgotten, thereby challenging the optimistic thesis of Geminello Preterossi, for whom political theology is inextinguishable (2022: 3), even though he refers to a particularly broad version of this mode of thought, one sufficiently comprehensive to encompass not only Schmitt and Hobbes but also Hegel and Gramsci. Nevertheless, if we adopt – as this book does – a more restricted definition of political theology, one that does not suffice with merely unveiling the dimension of transcendence within power but instead seeks to examine the reciprocal and archaeological relations between faith and politics, then we must take into account the incisive words of Merio Scattola:

> The discourse of reason [. . .] transforms the problem of coexistence into discursive procedures and dialectical arguments, but it never fully accomplishes its task. Logical calculation never closes in a perfect circle; rather, at its extreme limit, after having traversed all the materials of argumentation, it remains open to something that it presupposes as a condition of its rationality but that cannot be defined within a procedure. If the ultimate limit of reflection is a rational point that, nevertheless, cannot be represented in the form of discourse, we can call this extreme, paradoxical, and aporetic moment the foundation and origin of reasoning about politics. Due to its particular constitution, the origin is not a beginning in space and time that the development of discourse leaves behind as it progressively unfolds. Rather, it is its own condition of possibility, something that the argumentation of reason always carries with it and that, in fact, lies at its very center, perpetually suspended. It is evident, however, that the question of the origin or foundation of politics is also the problem of its essence, and this is an intrinsically philosophical question. This question finds its truth solely within

> political philosophy. Consequently, while political theology, to the extent that it addresses the problem of origin, is undoubtedly political philosophy, its various versions can be understood as interpretations, manifestations, or approximations of this fundamental philosophical-political problem. (2009: 14–15)

Indeed, the living centre of power cannot be fully understood or accessed through simple quantitative operations, which are often deemed 'rational' and 'scientific'. If political power is intrinsically linked to the possibility of experiencing a certain social normativity as the most preferable option among those available or imagined, it is essential to acknowledge the inherent element of *chance* or *risk* present in every act of political foundation. This involves beliefs and desires directed toward the creation of social narratives to justify power. The English historian Edmund Morgan demonstrated how the legitimization of political power depends largely not on fear or coercions imposed on subjects but on the assumption of shared fictions through the suspension of disbelief, giving rise to processes of 'make believe' remarkably similar to those that shape the various political theologies, both right-wing or left-wing, conservative or revolutionary. Morgan uses the idea of 'make-believe' to explain the emergence of the idea of 'people' in England and in the United States, thus indicating that fictionalization processes are essential not only for autocratic governments but also for formally democratic ones, since such processes are generally structuring factors of all political-legal experiences (1988: 13).

From this perspective, the terms 'theology' and 'politics' should not be viewed as mutually independent. Without assuming any origin of one in relation to the other, they only acquire meaning within the theological-political game, where each obscures the other with the same gesture that reveals it (Esposito 2013: 79). This dynamic applies to the Middle Ages, Modernity and our contemporary era, even as there are ongoing attempts to deny this relationship. Giacomo Marramao (1996) is correct to highlight, as one of the unresolved conceptual cores of democratic culture, the disregard of the sacred as an inescapable symbolic aspect of power. In this respect, a totally desacralized society would correspond to a completely depoliticized society, that is, an impossible society. Although a completely autonomous sphere of politics in relation to theology is not conceivable, it is possible to consider politics in relation to a *different theology*, one distinct from the Catholic-Schmittian paradigm, as I discuss in the next chapter.

A theological-political reflection does not entail a simplistic reduction of politics to theology, nor a reversal of the Schmittian equation whereby theology is derived from politics. Rather, it recognizes that any political practice is inherently shaped by an ideal framework that transcends empirical reality. To overlook this ideal dimension and focus solely on the immediate data of power is to obscure and render political action incomprehensible. As Giuseppe Duso (2012: 27) argues, all human collective action must be understood through the lens of an idea that surpasses empirical evidence and the arbitrariness of the will that informs it.

In this context, it is crucial to note that a theological-political perspective does not necessarily entail a belief in metaphysical entities that must be actively empowered in society. Instead, it emphasizes the movement of transcendence inherent to human thought and praxis (Duso 2012: 28), developing, as Foucault (1970) teaches in his famous review of Deleuze's work, a theory that is not the translation of a practice into words, being itself – in this case, political theology – a practice among others. Despite this, it is reasonable to question why such a theory-practice must necessarily be framed within a theological context rather than adopting a transcendental (Kant), discursive (Habermas) or phenomenological (Gadamer) approach, three prominent contemporary philosophical orientations that are generally sceptical of political theology. To address this query, I propose that all political power is grounded in an intrinsic transcendent dimension that cannot be reduced to its empirical manifestations. Consequently, the concept of political theology – whether explicit or implicit – appears to be an integral component of all theories of power, regardless of their political orientation (conservative, revolutionary or radical), historical context (medieval, modern or postmodern) or organizational structure (imperial, multitudinous or *an-archic*).

As I will elaborate in Chapter 2, the challenge is not to eliminate political theology but to engage with it critically, exploring its various manifestations while avoiding its dominance. The Italian philosopher Roberto Esposito (2013) offers a valuable example of this approach. He acknowledges the historical limitations and oppressive tendencies of traditional theological-political frameworks. Yet, rather than rejecting them outright, he proposes to think in relation to them. Esposito observes that the Western philosophical tradition has evolved in close conjunction with political theology, even though one of these two concepts – politics or theology – has often overshadowed the other. This symbiotic relationship is a defining characteristic of the theological-political apparatus, which divides reality into two spheres and prioritizes one over the other to strengthen its own position.

In a reading similar to that of Giorgio Agamben in *The Use of Bodies*, where he describes the bipolar anthropological machine that restricts and negates the common through the alternation of dyads, Esposito argues that the theological-political machine operates by separating what it purports to unite and unifying what it divides. This results in an exclusionary inclusion that, upon closer examination, can be seen as a reversal of the figure of the exception outlined by Agamben as inclusive exclusion (2018a: 34). This dual structure pervades Western thought, such that modern and contemporary attempts to evade political theology ultimately reaffirm its synthetic-disjunctive logic.

Drawing upon Heidegger's closely related concepts of 'machination' (*Machenschaft*) and 'disposition' (*Gestell*), Esposito identifies political theology as a purely procedural mechanism that amplifies a particular phenomenon through its ostensible negation. This negation, however, is merely superficial (2013: 22–9). Thus, the pursuit of a discourse 'outside' or 'after' political theology requires the presupposition of an 'inside' and a 'before' that is, precisely the dual reality from which one seeks to escape. Consequently, liberating oneself from the constraints of political-theological thought can only be accomplished through a radical approach, operating from within its own framework to render it ineffective and unproductive, as Agamben proposes. This seems feasible only by dismantling the Schmittian theological-political apparatus through the deactivation of the sovereign figure.

Following Esposito, I contend that all enlightened, liberal or postmodern efforts to assert immanence in opposition to transcendence are ultimately futile. To summarize, I believe that political-philosophical thought grounded solely in itself is inherently limited, as it dismisses any consideration of transcendence as superstitious, obscure or pre-modern (Esposito 2013: 16). Adopting such an approach, as some contemporary political science does, involves an unconscious immersion in the traditional theological-political apparatus, perpetuating the separation of the world into two realms. One part (the theological) is seemingly forgotten and overcome to make way for the other (the political), which is presented as 'emancipated' thought. However, this 'new' political thought remains trapped and limited by what, forgotten and repressed, constitutes its secret foundation. The Hungarian writer László Földényi observed that the modern imperative to reject religious myths is comparable in its universality and compulsion to the very myths it seeks to dismiss. In essence, the myth is mythically negated (2006: 42). Due to this denial – a repression, in the psychoanalytic sense – contemporary political-scientific thought often fails to fulfil the most fundamental task of thinking: transcending the merely empirical and pointing to the radical nature of power, its multiplicity and difference.

The theological-political machine that divides reality cannot be challenged from an external perspective, as there is no such vantage point. For Deleuze, contemplating immanence is synonymous with recognizing that nothing exists beyond thought, not even transcendence, which can and should be understood within an immanent framework, provided it is interpreted from an impersonal, non-subjective standpoint. As he stated in his last published work, immanence is not the immanence of something but the immanence of itself, not belonging to a subject or an object that can establish limits between the inside and the outside (Deleuze 2003). If the verbal and mental operatives 'inside' and 'outside' are themselves theological-political products, an immanent thought is then that of flux and encounter, of process and relationship, a thinking that indeterminates what the traditional theological-political machine intends to separate and hierarchize (Agamben 2014b: 143). Hence, it appears imperative to institute new political theologies and dismantle the longstanding support for their classical forms. This involves embracing the potential of a novel approach to transcendence-immanence that is grounded not in sovereignty and strength, but in poverty and weakness; not in the person, but in the hidden people; not in destiny and guilt, but in contingency and openness; not in identity, but in singularity; and not in the repetition of the same, but in the repetition of the different, all without reifying or substantiating any of these concepts

In order to effectively address the theological-political machine, it is necessary to engage with its traditional mechanisms, understand its logic and ultimately render it inoperative. This involves more than simply deactivating political theology as Esposito intends or attempting to reform it. What is crucial today is to avoid being trapped by the dual mechanisms that inform it and propose instead democratic-radical political theologies capable of filling the *an-archy* of power, which is never absent in concrete political practices.

In this sense, Jeffrey W. Robbins is right to state that the complete domination of social relations by economic forces ended up eclipsing the political, which could not be adequately considered by liberal theories, incapable of understanding the central question regarding the transcendent foundation of power and violence. Schmittian political theology, a critical current of thought that rejects liberal tenets, has historically borne the responsibility of interrogating this complex issue in contemporary times. This intellectual movement positioned itself as the 'guardian of politics', a role it assumed in response to the perceived failures of political liberalism. As we shall observe, Schmitt's political theology emerged from the disillusionment that followed the shortcomings of liberalism, which the constitutionalist tradition erroneously equated with democracy, a misconception that Schmitt himself never embraced (Robbins 2014: 20). Notwithstanding, contrary to the prevailing view, political theology is not a unified doctrine. While Schmitt and his intellectual associates envisioned it as a specific mode of thought rooted in Roman Catholicism and focused on the divine unity of God and political authority, a broader perspective recognizes the diversity of political theologies, mirroring the multifaceted nature of human religious and political experiences. A pluralistic approach is indispensable for envisioning democratic and libertarian political theologies, as it provides a more robust foundation for democracy than the dogmatic and monolithic secularism that artificially separates politics and religion (Robbins 2014: 138). These emerging political theologies, rooted in democratic multiplicity, do not offer prescriptive normative frameworks for the interaction between political power and religious beliefs. Instead, they provide nuanced epistemological accounts of the experiences of power and faith, identifying the points of tension and convergence that exist within these realities, transcending any rigid secularist boundaries.

While radical political theologies have proliferated, exemplified by the works of Dietrich Bonhöffer, Rudolf Bultmann, Paul Tillich, Gabriel Vahanian and Charles Winquist,[11] these perspectives, though distinct from Schmitt's and often critical of capitalist hegemony, nevertheless demonstrate a limited emphasis on the political. In contrast, the political was a central preoccupation for Schmitt. Moreover, these theological approaches maintain a conservative orientation, failing to engage in the distinctive task of radical-democratic political theology, that is, assume the responsibility to think the places of the new de/ins/tituting multitudinous power to reveal democracy as the political instantiation of God's death. To achieve this goal, it is imperative to begin with theological models grounded in the concepts of *exodus*, understood as a liberation from domination, and the *weakness of God*, a vision that challenges the notion of omnipotent sovereignty, as I elaborate in the concluding chapter of this work. Forms of popular self-organization can be democratic only when they assume the dispersion and diffusion of political power as a non-negotiable objective, not allowing themselves to be captured by apparatuses that encrypt plurality by subjecting it to the theopolitical rule of the One (Robbins 2014: 5–6).

At this point, certain scholars – as Rita Fulco (2024) – advocate for a shift away from political theology in favour of a 'political spirituality', a concept coined by

Foucault in his controversial 'reports of ideas' on the Iranian revolution. This notion encapsulates a practice of disinsubordination that defies conventional religious or rational frameworks and enables a profound transformation of the self. In a 1979 interview with *Le Nouvel Observateur*, Foucault sought to elucidate the concept of 'political spirituality':

> I think it's a certain practice by which the individual is displaced, transformed, disrupted, to the point of renouncing their own individuality, their own subject position. It's no longer being the subject that one had been up to that point, a subject in relation to a political power, but also the subject of a certain mode of knowledge [*savoir*], subject of an experience, or subject of a belief. It seems to me that that possibility of rising up from the subject position that had been fixed for you by a political power, a religious power, a dogma, a belief, a habit, a social structure, and so on – that's spirituality, that is, becoming other than what one is, other than oneself. (2020: 124)

Despite Foucault's limited use of the term 'political spirituality' in his Iran reports – appearing only once in the penultimate line of a concise journalistic piece (2001: 694) – the vehement criticism he faced for this perceived transgression against the secular norms of French academia and public discourse is striking. This underscores the enduring discomfort surrounding the complex interplay of religion and politics, revealing that this issue remains far from resolved.[12]

In any case, Fulco swiftly abandons the contentious Foucaultian term to concentrate on the work of Simone Weil (1909–43), who introduces the concept of 'spiritual politics' (Weil 1949), a notion distinct from political theology. According to Weil, 'spiritual politics' does not seek to justify the powers of this world but rather embodies the exact inversion of what they sustain. She refers to justice, a supernatural and impersonal horizon that no human legal system can reach, thus functioning as a critique of power whose symbol is the cross, a kind of stylized scale that mediates between the human and the divine. From this perspective, it is possible to contrast the Christ of glory with the Christ of the cross, which evokes a provisional power, destined to vanish and delegitimize the absolute claims of human authorities (Fulco 2017, 2024).

Weil's proposition categorically distances itself from law and all forms of violence, turning instead to an impersonal, sacred and ethically – though not morally – unenforceable realm, as outlined in her masterful essay, *The Person and the Sacred*. In this work, Weil contrasts the legal construct of the person with an almost mystical concept of impersonality. Her first move consists of a sharp

– and unanswerable – critique of law, which is something of the commercial and quantitative order, presupposing as its foundation not only the complaint and the process but also the organized violence capable of making them effective (1957: 23–7). She subsequently introduces the central tenet of her 'spiritual politics', focusing on the concept of impersonality, an inner existence that, by transcending the crimes committed or endured by the 'person', reveals the sacred nature inherent in every human being as such (1957: 11–16). This idea echoes Deleuze's (2003) notion of 'a life' (*une vie*), referring to a human presence devoid of qualifications and impervious to political or legal capture, a life that simply *is* (*homo tantum*), thereby collapsing the classical ontological distinction between essence and existence, presented in its Heideggerian version with the dyad Being and entity (being).

While constructions like Weil's hold significance and warrant further exploration, I contend that they are fundamentally flawed by their attempt to abandon the ground of political theology in pursuit of ethereal concepts such as 'spiritual politics'. Instead, I firmly believe that the struggle must be waged not only *within* the realm of political theology but primarily with the objective of *taking* that terrain. Not all political theologies are destined to serve the purposes of separation, hierarchy and domination. It is feasible to articulate dimensions that challenge the transcendence of power without either hypostatizing it and making it sovereign or, conversely, dissolving it into a depoliticized and merely charitable experience, as Weil does.[13]

According to the French philosopher and theologian René Girard (1923–2015), instead of denying theology *en bloc* and in an abstract manner – a procedure that, in fact, means accepting it docilely – it is necessary to access it through critical approaches (2005: 7). This is even more true in regard to political theology, since power constitutes one of the inescapable facets of the universal phenomenon of human violence. From this standpoint, all violence requires legitimization to be subsequently organized into power structures. Absent this, there would be no differentiation between the various forms of violence – legitimate and illegitimate – employed by humans. Girard posits that only violence legitimized through transcendence can be socially accepted and regulated, thereby preventing its uncontrolled proliferation within the social fabric (2005: 25). Nonetheless, the current political-economic system legitimizes violence in an ineffective and contradictory manner, encrypting the elitist and authoritarian nature of capitalist law – separated, proprietary and hierarchical – on which it is based, as will be discussed in subsection 3.1.

Radical-democratic political theologies must also legitimize – and, to some degree, regulate – the violence that will inevitably persist within human societies. However, they approach this task from a distinct paradigm, a genuinely political order rather than a deceptively neutral one, as espoused by liberal economics and politics. To achieve this, not only alternative political paradigms are necessary, but also novel political theologies that emerge from the patient process of decrypting political-religious power, as explored in the following section.

1.4. Encryption and political theology

1.4.1. Cryptophilosophy and glory

Encryption is a linguistic process intimately connected to the idea of philosophy, making it justifiable to consider *cryptophilosophy* as a fundamental aspect of this field of knowledge. Political theology constitutes a significant milestone in its development and legitimation, tracing its origins to the early Greek philosophers, often mistakenly referred to as pre-Socratics.

A pivotal figure within this tradition, Heraclitus of Ephesus (*c.* 535–475 BC), declares in his fragment nº 123: 'φύσις κρύπτεσθαι φιλεῖ' ('nature loves to hide itself', DK 22.123). He uses the Greek verb *krýptesthai* (κρύπτεσθαι), which means, according to *Liddell, Scott, Jones Ancient Greek Lexicon*, 'be in hiding', 'lie in concealment'. This is a middle form of the verb *krýpto* (κρύπτω), 'to hide', which is present in the word 'encryption'. However, unlike Parmenides and Plato, Heraclitus does not speak of a concealment of reality but of a process of *self-concealment* that simultaneously reveals and hides. This distinction is crucial, as Katherine Withy (2022) argues, because by conflating concealment and self-concealment, a prominent figure like Heidegger may have committed several errors in his enigmatic interpretation of the 'veiling of Being'.

Thus, while Heraclitus acknowledged a distinction between reality and its phenomenic perception, he did not formulate a theory of encryption in the strict sense. The opposing forces that constitute the interplay of veiling and unveiling reality are themselves part of reality, not presupposing something more 'real' or 'original' than it. Heraclitus twists the language to express his ideas: 'ὁ θεὸς ἡμέρη εὐφρόνη, χειμὼν θέρος, πόλεμος εἰρήνη, κόρος λιμός' ('God is day night, winter summer, war peace, surfeit hunger', DK 22.67). Note the deliberate absence of the conjunction 'and' (*kai*) between the words. God is not day *and* night, winter *and* summer. Rather: he is day night, winter summer. There is no alternation of opposites or predominance of order. God – the One – is everything at the same time, here and now; his order reigns in disorder, he is the nest of both Apollo and Dionysus. There is no alternation and, consequently, no authentic encrypting apparatuses. There is not *this* at one moment and *that* at another, now night and then day; rather, there is this-that-night-day. The One of Heraclitus is indivisible and complete within each partial moment, embodying the unity within plurality that generates plurality within unity.

Parmenides of Elea (*c.* late sixth century–fifth century BC), who can justifiably be considered the first philosopher of encryption, proposes a markedly distinct perspective, distinguishing between the true path, that of Being – the way of things that Are – and the illusory path of non-Being – the way of things that Are not – which yields no genuine knowledge. He writes in his dense poem:

II	II
Εἰ δ' ἄγ' ἐγὼν ἐρέω, κόμισαι δὲ σὺ μῦθον ἀκούσας, αἵπερ ὁδοὶ μοῦναι διζήσιός εἰσι νοῆσαι· ἡ μὲν ὅπως ἔστιν τε καὶ ὡς οὐκ ἔστι μὴ εἶναι, Πειθοῦς ἐστι κέλευθος – Ἀληθείῃ γὰρ ὀπηδεῖ –, ἡ δ' ὡς οὐκ ἔστιν τε καὶ ὡς χρεών ἐστι μὴ εἶναι, τὴν δή τοι φράζω παναπευθέα ἔμμεν ἀταρπόν· οὔτε γὰρ ἂν γνοίης τό γε μὴ ἐὸν – οὐ γὰρ ἀνυστόν – οὔτε φράσαις (DK 28, II).	Come now, I will tell thee – and do thou hearken to my saying and carry it away – the only two ways of search that can be thought of. The first, namely, that It is, and that it is impossible for anything not to be, is the way of conviction, for truth is its companion. The other, namely, that It is not, and that something must needs not be, – that, I tell thee, is a wholly untrustworthy path. For you cannot know what is not – that is impossible – nor utter it (Burnet 1892);

By rejecting the path of non-Being, Parmenides becomes the inaugural philosopher to distance himself from primordial nothingness, thereby suppressing *an-archy*. His condemnation of non-Being can therefore be interpreted as a prohibition against contemplating the *an-archic* void, which, as we will explore further, is also understood as the non-substantial, self-transcending Without-End (*Ayin Sof*) in Jewish Kabbalah. In any case, Parmenides' dualistic scheme, distinguishing between what is (Being) and what is not (non-Being), was adopted and further developed by Plato (427–348 BC). In his confrontation with the relativism of the Sophists, Plato championed the primacy of a concealed knowledge known as philosophy, surpassing the limitations of mere sensory perception and opinions. Plato extends Parmenides' postulates to their logical radical conclusions, intensifying his paradoxes in an almost mystical manner. It was not until Aristotle (384–322 BC) that a satisfactory – that is, 'rational' – resolution was found for the problem of Being and non-Being. Recognizing that Parmenides' inquiry pertains to motion and becoming, to emergence and decay, Aristotle addresses it by establishing the ontological distinction between actuality (Being) and potentiality (non-Being), a topic I will explore in the subsequent section. Nevertheless, with Plato, particularly in Book V of *The Republic*, the distinction between true knowledge (*epistéme*, ἐπιστήμη) and the opinion (*dóxa*, δόξα) that encrypts it is firmly established, as well as the division between philosophers and ordinary human beings, the former being the sole individuals capable of attaining the truth.

However, it is crucial to highlight that the distinction between *dóxa* and *epistéme* in Plato's philosophy is one of its most intricate aspects and cannot be reduced to a simplistic and scholastic dualism, as it is characterized by subtleties, interconnections and contradictions (Szaif 2007). In numerous instances, Plato presents *dóxa* not as a synonym for false knowledge but rather as a transitional state between complete ignorance and philosophical knowledge (*Symposium*, 202a; *Republic*, 477a–478d). Similarly, Heidegger (1992) compares the opinions of the prisoners in the allegory of the cave not to falsehood but to a lesser degree of openness to truth, understood as *alétheia* (ἀλήθεια), an ontological dimension that, through remembrance, reveals itself. Ultimately, Plato acknowledges that the philosopher, like all human beings, may possess opinions about reality (*Theaetetus*, 189e–190a; *Sophist*, 264a). But, unlike others, the philosopher is not confined to this type of uncertain cognition, continually striving for self-improvement by directing cognitive efforts toward *epistéme*. Therefore, in *The Republic*, the opposition is not primarily between the philosopher and the ignorant but rather between the philosopher and the 'philodoxer', the lover of opinions who restricts himself to *dóxa*, granting unwavering credence to appearances (*The Republic*, 479e–480a). Even so, given the limits of this work, it is reasonable to assert that a clear distinction exists between true knowledge and opinion within a significant (and influential) portion of Platonic thought – for instance, in *Gorgias*, *Parmenides*, *The Republic* and *Timaeus* – which is explicitly translated into the absolute separation between the sensible and the intelligible realms. At least in Plato's writings that have come down to us, there is no bridge between these two spheres.[14] As Sanín-Restrepo interprets through Deleuzian lens, Plato divides the world into the unified order of ideas and the simulacra that distort them, establishing an adversarial ontology between the Unity that governs reality and the difference, conceived as mere appearance that must be eliminated (2016: 48). This construct is simultaneously metaphysical, ontological and epistemological, as the two realms are separate, with one encrypting the other.

Aristotle addresses the distinction between *epistéme* and *dóxa* within a more relative and non-idealistic approach, rejecting the Platonic theory of ideas, which, in addition to failing to resolve the challenges of this world, merely duplicates – or, in my interpretation, encrypts – it. Despite this, Aristotle differentiates between *epistéme*, akin to our scientific knowledge, and *dóxa*, an expression of simple opinions: 'Τὸ δ' ἐπιστητὸν καὶ ἐπιστήμη διαφέρει τοῦ δοξ αστοῦ καὶ δόξης, ὅτι ἡ μὲν ἐπιστήμη καθόλου καὶ δι' ἀναγκαίων, τὸ δ' ἀναγκαῖον οὐκ ἐνδέχετι ἄλλως ἔχειν' ('Scientific knowledge and its object differ from opinion and the object of opinion in that scientific knowledge is commensurately universal and proceeds by necessary connections, and that which is necessary cannot be otherwise', *Posterior Analytics* [I, 33, 88b]: 30–31).

Nevertheless, there is an alternative interpretation of Aristotle, suggesting that, with a single gesture, he may have distanced himself from Plato's cryptophilosophical dualism and, simultaneously, paved the way for future political theology. Indeed, in the concluding lines of Book Lambda of *Metaphysics*, Aristotle rejects political authority to the duality – and even to the mathematical plurality of principles – proposed by Plato, affirming that things do not want to be badly governed, concluding that 'the government of many is not good; let there be one ruler' ('οὐκ ἀγαθὸν πολυκοιρανίη· εἷς κοίρανος ἔστω', *Metaphysics*, 1076a, 3).

This idea can be interpreted as a precursor, albeit at a different level, to the cryptophilosophical dualism initially conceived by Parmenides and Plato. However, in Aristotle, this dualism is no longer grounded in the distinction between *epistéme* and *dóxa*, idea and shadow, but rather, in a manner that foreshadows political theology, in the relationship between transcendence and immanence secured by a singular power both in Heaven and on Earth. Thus, for example, as Eusebius of Caesarea observed in his immoderate defence of Constantine's actions, the latter had fulfilled the will of God by slaughtering his three fellow emperors who comprised the Roman tetrarchy, as a unique heavenly authority should correspond to a singular imperial power on Earth.

Regardless of the accuracy of interpretations of Plato's work, the notion of a mental or spiritual reality superior to sensory perception has been a decisive legacy of Western thought. In his *Seventh Letter*, Plato asserts that 'the soul seeks to know not the quality but the essence', with the latter being separate and hidden (343c).

The development of this cryptophilosophy – initially proposed by Parmenides, further structured by Plato and politically reconfigured by Aristotle – culminated in medieval theology. This tradition affirmed not only God's integral transcendence over the world but also His governance, which often operates through mysteries beyond human comprehension. As Paul states, humans see only a partial and distorted reflection of reality through a mirror, 'in enigma' (1 *Corinthians* 13:12).

From a theological-political viewpoint, it is crucial to note that the Greek word *dóxa*, which encrypts 'true knowledge' in Platonic philosophy, was employed in the *Septuagint* – the Greek translation of the *Hebrew Bible* by the legendary seventy Jewish sages – to translate the Hebrew word *kabhod* (כָּבוֹד), meaning 'glory'. According to the rigorous philosophical archaeology that Agamben presents in the eighth chapter of *The Kingdom and the Glory*, glory corresponds exactly to the theological-economic-political apparatus that serves, with all its ceremonial and liturgical machinery, to remove power from Earth and redirect it to Heaven. In this way, we definitively transition from the Greek epistemic-ontological encryption to the true encryption of power. With the advent of glory, politics (kingdom) is reduced to mere 'economy' (ὀιχονομία), that is, administration (government), thereby paving the way for capitalism's ascent to a religious status, a topic explored further in section 3.1. As Agamben argues, the theological-economic apparatus of glorification conceals – or, to use a more precise term, encrypts – the void that underlies all power. Its *an-archic* dimension – God's 'without beginning' nature – manifests in the worldly sphere through processes of acclaim and spectacularization orchestrated by media and public opinion. These contemporary forms of glory encrypt the Nothing upon which power is founded.

Agamben's extensive discussion of glory is not merely an academic exercise or a display of his erudition. Rather, it highlights the apparatus through which we transition from Greek cryptophilosophy to contemporary political-economic theology. In this context, returning to the discussion already mentioned in section 1.2, Agamben contends that there is little distinction between a political theology like Schmitt's and a theological politics like Assmann's. He claims that the pivotal task is not to prioritize one dimension (political or theological) over the other, but to demonstrate their interconnectedness as poles within a non-univocal network of tensions that run in both directions: from theology to politics and from politics to theology. The threshold of this polar machine is precisely glory, the nexus between theology and politics that enables their communication, articulation, alternation and reciprocal influence (Agamben 2011: 193–4). To grasp the radical implications of Agamben's position, it is essential to understand that glory extends far beyond mere songs of praise directed toward God. It is not confined to that 'uncertain zone in which acclamations, ceremonies, liturgies, and insignia operate' (2011: 188); rather, it encompasses a much deeper significance. Glory – or more precisely, the process of glorification – 'creates' God and the theological-political power that flows from Him, which is rooted in a void, an *an-archic* Nothingness that must be encrypted at any cost, as illustrated in detail in section 2.2.

Among the various meanings of glory in the biblical tradition, a particularly significant one portrays it as something that hides God. A notable example is the passage in *Exodus* (33:18) where Yahweh refrains from directly revealing Himself to Moses, as such an absolute vision would be fatal. Maimonides, in his interpretation, identifies God's glory (*kabhod YHWH*), manifested as a powerful blinding light, as the very veil that prevents Moses from beholding the divine face (2003 [1, 64]). However, glory is much more than a veiling illumination, also appearing as a process of self-knowledge (*autosophia*) of God, so that the Father can only know Himself through glorification in the Son. In this sense, God's glorious self-knowledge, an operation in which the Son and the Father glorify each other, is fundamental for God to be known (and also glorified) on Earth. According to Origene, 'no one knows the Father unless the Son reveals him, and the Son was about to reveal the Father with an economy; therefore, God was also glorified in Him' (1992 [32, 29, 359]: 341–2).

Based on these and many other theological materials that cannot be reproduced and commented on here, Agamben rejects the orthodox (and absurd) thesis that God does not need glory, since, in His completeness, he could not depend on the adoration of his human and angelic creatures. On the contrary, philosophical archaeology demonstrates that the centre of all power is a void that needs to be encrypted. Glory assumes this role, giving rise to both political and theological power. These two forms of power are inextricably linked, mutually reinforcing each other. In effect, there is no priority of the political over the religious and vice versa, given that one circulates within the other: 'Just as liturgical doxologies produce and strengthen God's glory, so the profane acclamations are not an ornament of political power but found and justify it' (Agamben 2011: 230). Thus, the process of glorification is not merely an addition to power, as if it were only a dynamic that makes something already existing visible; rather, it is constitutive of power, functioning as a performative act that, through words and gestures, creates a certain reality (Agamben 2011: 181). In this case, it pertains to the creation of God and the political-legal power that He represents, which, as powerful beings made of words, encrypt the radical void – the *an-archy* without depth or foundation – that must be continuously transformed into glory.

In this sense, glory not only survives but thrives in contemporary times, as Kantorowicz astutely observed long before Agamben in the last chapter of his work on *laudes regiae*, the songs of praise sung to both popes and medieval sovereigns. With a touch of irony, Kantorowicz noted that contemporary forms of *laudes regiae* more closely resemble a parody of ancient traditions than a genuine revival (1946: 180–6). He ultimately identified the totalitarian and dictatorial regimes of the first half of the twentieth century as fertile ground for the resurgence of glory in the form of political acclamation. In fact, Kantorowicz revisited and provided a contemporary interpretation of a thesis originally conceived by Erik Peterson in his 1926 work, *One God: Epigraphic, Form-Historical, and Historical-Religious Studies*, which Schmitt deemed 'fundamental' (1927: 34). Peterson examined the development of monotheism in early Christianity, focusing on the formula 'One God' ('*Héis Theós*', 'Εἷς Θεός'), a concept central to the operation of glory in the medieval Christian world. According to Peterson, acclamations are not mere professions of faith; rather, they represent a distinctly political expression of the consensus of the publicly gathered people. In fact, it is through the process of acclamation that a disorganized crowd ceases to be merely a multitude and transforms into a cohesive people (Peterson 2012: 177–9). In this context, although Schmitt did not explicitly emphasize the theological-political dimension of acclamation as Peterson did, in his 1927 text titled *Referendum and Popular Initiative*, the German jurist asserts that acclamation is an eternal phenomenon of every political community, with no State existing without a people and no people without acclamation. This highlights the performative dimension of acclamation, which not only embellishes power but is also essential for its constitution, functioning in a manner akin to glory. In this context, it is important to remember that Schmitt was opposed to political liberalism and its 'debating' parliamentarians, and as such, acclamation, being a political form devoid of discussion, was bound to captivate him. A year later, in his *Theory of the Constitution*, Schmitt completes the argument by asserting that the modern equivalent of acclamation is public opinion:

> *Public opinion is the modern type of acclamation*. It is perhaps a diffuse type, and its problem is resolved neither sociologically nor in terms of public law. However,

> its essence and political significance lie in the fact that it can be understood as an acclamation. There is no democracy and no state without public opinion, as there is no state without acclamation. (2008a: 275)

The terrible novelty that Agamben introduces to this picture lies in his observation that contemporary glory, in the acclamatory form of public opinion, is no longer exceptional, tied to a specific religious or political authority and a particular moment. Instead, it has become an intense and pervasive process of mediatization that, independent of any specific authority or event, *normalizes the exception* by conflating itself with the totality of social time, thereby becoming umbilically linked to political power in general. This represents yet another moment in which the exception becomes the rule, in line with the overarching thesis that informs Agamben's *Homo Sacer* project. Whereas acclamation was once exceptional, celebrated during special occasions and by specific individuals, it has now become the norm for the entirety of social dynamics. Without requiring individualization, acclamatory glory permeates society, transforming it into a self-celebrating spectacle that encrypts the emptiness upon which it rests.

Currently, there is a dual articulation of glory: on one hand, the real and immediate acclamatory people, which, descending from the dictatorships of the first half of the twentieth century referred to by Kantorowicz, seemed destined for extinction but has surprisingly re-emerged in recent times within the context of the far right. This people can be exemplified in the United States by those who stormed the Capitol in 2021, and in Brazil by the masses that attempted the Bolsonaro-led coup in 2023, processes that, had they been successful, would have amounted to the acclamation of Trump and Bolsonaro as sovereigns who, according to Schmitt's formula, would have 'decided on the state of exception'. Alongside this acclamatory state people, there is a much broader dimension: the communicational people mediated by spectacle, which, being non-state, does not translate into a classic political subject, but rather reveals itself in the uninterrupted processes of self-glorification sustained by social and communicational networks. Thus, from the 'One God' of early Christianity studied by Peterson, we move to the glorification of 'One Society', which, detached from history and critique, sees and celebrates only itself, either immediately with the acclamatory people, or mediately through the communicational people.

Therefore, only by tracing the millennia-long evolution of glorification apparatuses (as detailed in Byttebier, Dale and Figurski, 2022) can we finally glimpse the underlying reality that traditional political theology encrypts through glorification: Nothingness, *an-archy*, the intrinsic potential of the human being, a 'sabbatical' animal that has no destiny, essence or purpose.[15] According to Agamben, there is no archaic principle that determines the human being, a creature without any work of his own, inoperative, placed in the centre of an *an-archic* void that, however, needs to be encrypted so that the separate power typical of law and the State can emerge. This theological-political function belongs to glory, which is translated both in the liturgical songs of the Church and in the political acclamations today transformed into a spectacular flow of (dis)information:

> The indescribable mystery that glory, with its blinding light, must hide from the gaze of the *scrutatores maiestatis* is that of divine inoperativity, of what God does before creating the world and after the providential government of the world is complete. It is not the *kabhod*, which cannot be thought or looked upon, but the inoperative majesty that it veils with its clouds and the splendor of its insignia. Glory, both in theology and in politics, is precisely what takes the place of that unthinkable emptiness that amounts to the inoperativity of power. And yet, precisely this unsayable vacuity is what nourishes and feeds power (or, rather, what the machine of power transforms into nourishment). That means that the center of the governmental apparatus, the threshold at which Kingdom and Government ceaselessly communicate and ceaselessly distinguish themselves from one another is, in reality, empty. (Agamben 2011: 242)

In light of these ideas, Claude Lefort's celebrated thesis, while seemingly sympathetic and libertarian to self-proclaimed 'progressive' constitutionalists and political scientists, can be critiqued as an important theological-political apparatus. Lefort characterizes the great democratic transformation of Western societies as the establishment of a void where once solid laws, powers and knowledge existed.

According to Lefort, throughout history, humans have organized themselves around theopolitical authorities that represented them. This paradigm shifted with the advent of democracy, which emptied the political centre of society. Consequently, all laws became precarious and subject to question, and the notion of a centralized authority underpinning political legitimacy disappeared. Thus, democracy has given rise to a sense of societal incomprehensibility and uncontrollability. The Sovereign People, though proclaimed as a unified entity, remain permanently fragmented, latent and disputed, a thesis that, in the theory of the encryption of power, will be taken to its radical dimension – something Lefort does not do – through the idea of *hidden people* discussed in the next section. In any case, what characterizes the democratic revolution, Lefort concludes, is a dual negation: the rejection of a power tied to a particular body and the rejection of a fixed, transcendent and immutable law (1981: 180–3).

Lefort's theory of the democratic void exemplifies very well how it is impossible to escape the gravitational pull of political theology through simple denial, a point I have emphasized throughout this work. In attempting to eliminate political theology, Lefort inadvertently legitimizes the most powerful theological-political apparatus ever devised: glory, *dóxa*, worship. Indeed, the empty centre that underpins representative democracy praised by Lefort is precisely the space occupied by glory, which fills and encrypts this void through institutions and *potestas*. From this perspective, it is significant that Lefort reduces democracy to its representative dimension, focusing on constituted power (*potestas*) and neglecting the possibility of a radical democracy (*potentia*). In doing so, he aligns with the contemporary celebration of liberal representative democracy as the sole legitimate political regime. This form of democracy, glorified by media and society, serves as a contemporary manifestation of glory, encrypting the underlying void of foundational power. The spectacular glory that constitutes representative democracy is the empty throne (*hetoimasía toû thrónou*) that articulates religion and politics to capture inoperativeness and *an-archy* through an idolatrous action that has no precedent in human history. If before glory was restricted to the liturgical and ceremonial dimensions of acclamation – whether of God, the *Führer* or the *Duce* – it now spreads throughout the communicational and spectacular network in which we live.[16]

In this regard, it seems important to emphasize that public opinion is not something secondary or merely 'curious' in the fabric of the theopolitical power that governs our societies. As demonstrated by Francis García Collado (2024), public opinion today embodies a new form of governmentality, no longer grounded in the classical biopolitics, but in what the Spanish author refers to as *phobiopolitics*, a form of governance of both bodies and souls that is simultaneously totalizing and individualizing (*omnes et singulatim*), based on a socially constructed fear that is disseminated, signified, maximized and made sovereign. Drawing on a series of analyses that intertwine philosophical, historical, sociological, psychological and neuroscientific elements, García Collado indicates that the power of contemporary public opinion does not solely reside in 'positive' activities, such as celebrations and acclamations, but is also present in the ritualization of suffering which, considering human brain plasticity, instils fear, anguish and uncertainty in social subjects through constant narratives that persistently explore real or imagined harms and threats. This creates a climate of social paranoia and diffuse fear that prevents the development of any critical stance against the power structures that, benevolently, would be protecting us from the horrors lurking around every corner in the form of diseases, terrorists, natural catastrophes, communists, wars, poverty, anticonformism, and so on. As can be seen, this is a celebration of the glory of the God *Phobos*.

Finally, it is a bitter irony that glory today manifests itself as public opinion, that is, as an epochal development of the original figure of Platonic thought (*dóxa*) that forms a system with *epistéme*. However, in our times, there exists a pervasive and all-encompassing public opinion that no longer feels the need to structurally oppose the *epistéme*. This is evidenced by the proliferation of fake news, which is not only uncontrolled but also desired. The democratic-representative order perpetuates a self-glorifying spectacle, closing off paths for difference in a characteristically theological-political manner. In Guy Debord's exact terms: 'By means of the spectacle the ruling order discourses endlessly upon itself in an uninterrupted monologue of self-praise' (2006 [§ 24]: 19). In this context, difference emerges as a challenging path, one that radical-democratic political theologies, as discussed in section 2.4, seek to open. Ultimately, it can be argued that every encrypted politics is a politics of glory and, as such, a sovereign political theology.

Notwithstanding, from this critical-archaeological perspective, we can envision a radical political theology centred on the concept of *an-archy*, no longer veiled by glory but understood as *ayin* (אין). According to the oldest Kabbalistic traditions, *ayin* is the primordial Nothingness that precedes God and serves as the foundation of all creation.[17] This creation can be understood as something emerging from nothing (*yesh me-ayin*) or nothing emerging from something (*ayin-me-Yesh*). This apparent contradiction between the two formulations is of utmost importance, as it serves to illustrate the truly radical and undecidable character of *an-archic* thought, of which *ayin* is one of the most powerful expressions. Indeed, one might criticize *an-archy* conceived as the *nothing of foundation*, arguing that in such a conception, Nothingness is being taken as a principle, that is, that in the beginning there was nothing, which would then serve as an *arkhē*. From this perspective, original Greek thought would seem more radical in proposing that things have always existed, such that it would be impossible to isolate a primordial moment of Nothingness from which Being was generated. Nonetheless, to reason in this way would be to misunderstand the radicality of Nothingness, which cannot be taken as a concept or a principle without falling into performative contradiction. The word *Nothingness* is merely a linguistic crutch – here emerges, in full force, its *an-archic* use – employed to indicate, to point toward a dimension in which it no longer makes sense to think in terms of beginning and end, language and silence, work and unworking, act and potency, and so on. It is not the substratum from which Being is conceived and posited, but the insubstratum that renders possible its de-thinking and de-position. The movement between substratum and insubstratum is what we call reality, and, as Kabbalah teaches, it translates as something that comes from nothing (*yesh me-ayin*) or nothing that comes from something (*ayin me-yesh*), indecidably so. This is because, according the thirteenth-century French Kabbalist David ben Abraham ha-Laban, Nothingness possesses an ontological status superior to all existing things. Its simplicity, when confronted with itself, generates complexity, thereby misleading the wise. In this vein, with a gesture that is surprisingly cabalistic, the young Hegel (1770–1831) – who, it seems, was not easily misled – asserts in his essay *The Difference Between Fichte's and Schelling's Systems of Philosophy* that Nothingness is the principle of all principles: 'The Absolute is night, and light is younger than night. [. . .] Nothingness is the first, from which all being and the entire multiplicity of the finite emerged' (Hegel, 1967: 24–5).

Consequently, as Gershom Scholem (1897–1982) observes in his *Ten Unhistorical Aphorisms on Kabbalah*, this kind of mystical knowledge is inherently paradoxical, as its object is, by definition, unknowable, existing in a perpetual tension between knowability and hiddenness. Unlike historical mysteries, which arise from incomplete or misinterpreted sources, Kabbalah's secrets stem from the fundamentally transcendent nature of God (Biale 1985: 72) and, ultimately, the universe itself, which emerges from divine Nothingness. While Scholem might reject this pantheistic interpretation, the fundamental point remains, since Kabbalah's object is fundamentally beyond human comprehension: 'the essential plenitude of the hidden God, which remains transcendent with respect to all knowledge (even intuitive knowledge), becomes Nothingness in the primal act of emanation, an act which is above all the pure turning toward creation' (*in* Biale 1985: 79).

Nothingness is the origin of the Without-End (*Ayin Sof*, אין סוף), a Hebrew expression often translated as 'God', but which literally means 'the unlimited', 'the boundless' or more precisely, 'the Infinitely so', since, according to Agamben, the expression carries an adverbial value (2014b, 211). This idea differentiates the Jewish tradition from the Western one, considering, for example, that the *ápeiron* (ἄπειρον) of Anaximander's fragment, despite not being identified with a determined matter such as Thales' water or Anaximenes' air, is still a material element (even if, literally, indeterminate). In contrast to Greek philosophy, Kabbalah does not posit a primordial matter, whether determined or indeterminate. In it, Nothingness corresponds to the *non-ek-sistence* (the non-exit toward Being) of God before creation, alone in the world and without form or likeness (*Zohar*, 2003: 217). In more radical interpretations, *Ayin Sof* is reduced to *Ayin* (the Without, the Non-Existent), the pure non-Being that transcends all human comprehension and is accessible only through intuition, never rational thought (*Zohar*, 2003: 288b).

Thus, there is an original void, a meaninglessness, an *an-arkhé* constantly resignified by the work of divine creation. Yet, this creation is ultimately contingent and insubstantial, emerging from this very Nothingness. This suggests that all human creations do not express any essence or first foundation, as they too emerge from Nothingness. Even God himself derives from Nothing and, in the end, on His Sabbath, in His Nothingness, He rests. Our *ek-sistence*, our leap – *ex-* is a prefix that indicates a movement from the inside out – toward Being, just like God's, is woven with the infinite and fragile matter of Nothingness. This is what Kabbalah seems to teach, self-limited by the intrinsic inexpressibility of its 'truths' (Biale 1985: 85), which are merely conventional and metaphorical, never archic. According to Scholem, 'the "true" language cannot be spoken, just as the absolutely concrete cannot be realized. [. . .] [the name of God is] absolute, meaning-bestowing, but itself meaningless' (*in* Biale 1985: 87). Therefore, there is no fixed reality that cannot be transformed. No ultimate foundation justifies political power, which always remains subject to the process of reduction to Nothingness, the very source from which it emerged and which glory seeks to encrypt.

1.4.2. Theory of the encryption of power

Considering that one of the main objectives of this book is to read the political theology from the perspective of the theory of the encryption of power, it seems essential to know some of its characteristics and vector lines.

Encryption is one of the most crucial functions of political theology, which inherited this task from Greek cryptophilosophy. However, when adopting this perspective, two preliminary observations should be made. First, while the previous section briefly alluded to classical Greek philosophers, their focus was on the general epistemological encryption of immanence, rather than the specific political encryption of power, which, as we have seen, reaches its critical mass only with the political theology of glory. Second, philosophy cannot be taken as an amorphous set of theories and thinkers but rather as a field of polar and tensioned forces. If there is a cryptophilosophical tradition dedicated to encrypting *an-archy* through transcendent (medieval theology) and transcendental (Kant, Habermas, constitutionalists in general, etc.) structures, on the other hand, there is a *minor tradition* whose tendency flows in the opposite direction, only recognizing as legitimately philosophical a thought focused on the decryption of being (Deleuze), language (Wittgenstein) and power (Agamben). These tasks, to a certain extent, must be considered together because they are different aspects of the same radical plane of immanence. This second tradition aligns with the theory of encryption of power developed by Ricardo Sanín-Restrepo and others, although it maintains distinct perspectives and critiques certain 'minor' philosophers, particularly European thinkers who may not fully grasp the more perverse manifestations of power encryption. Sanín-Restrepo (2018: xiv–xv), for instance, criticizes Deleuze and Negri for drawing immense distances between identity/difference and power/politics, thus rendering their theories somewhat innocuous.[18]

The concept of encryption was originally introduced by Ricardo Sanín-Restrepo and Gabriel Méndez-Hincapié in 2012 within a critical analysis of sovereignty and the Constitution,[19] and was later expanded upon by several other authors. Encryption can be defined as a process that suppresses politics understood as difference and immanence by imposing a closed and universalizing discourse centred on power as *potestas*. This process is closely related to the dictionarization of politics, a topic explored in the next section. In this sense, encryption impedes communication, since communicating means, above all, communicating difference (Sanín-Restrepo 2018: xiv), that is, *potentia*.

At this point, it is necessary to make a succinct reference to the categories of act and potency as understood by the theory of the encryption of power.[20] One of its innovations lies in the understanding that potency and act are inseparable. Thus, the entire discussion already present in Aristotle (*Metaphysics*, 1049b, 10–15) – and taken up, in opposition to the Stagirite, by Agamben – about the superiority or priority of one over the other makes no sense. Agamben asserts that '[. . .] potency precedes the act and exceeds it' (2023a: 87), an idea that was already present in his discourse long before the *Homo Sacer* project, marking much of his more 'ontological' writings (e.g. Agamben; Deleuze 2011). Apparently, this preponderance of potency over act in Agamben's thought directly derives from Heidegger's reading of book Theta of Aristotle's *Metaphysics*, the subject of his 1931 course later published in 1981(a) under the title *On the Essence and Reality of Potency*. In any case, it is curious how Agamben, despite recognizing the failure of Western ontology, does not resign himself to relinquishing one of its central dichotomies, which is precisely the one separating act and potency.[21] An attempt in this direction emerges in *The Use of Bodies* – the final volume of the *Homo Sacer* project – through the notion of use, as it is liberated from consumption and production and brought closer to a type of self-affection. From this perspective, Agamben asserts that the being-in-use is a potency that is never separated from the act because it does not need to operate, as it is constantly using itself (2014b: 88). Nevertheless, the Italian philosopher soon returns to the priority of potency by stating that use, being constitutively inoperative, occurs only when the Aristotelian apparatus potency/act is deactivated, which, however, depends on potency itself, as use is an internal principle of potency that prevents it from being exhausted in the act, leading it to turn back upon itself, 'making itself the potency of potency, potentiating its own potency (and, then, its own impotence)' (2014b: 130). Therefore, the dichotomy of act/potency remains, albeit radically modified, with the predominance of the latter reaffirmed both positively and negatively (potency-of-not).

On the other hand, now within the context of the theory of the encryption of power, the categories of act and potency can only be thought of separately if one disregards the dimension of time, artificially viewing them as static snapshots of a process that is, in reality, constantly evolving. Potency is not opposed to act, considering that substance must be understood within time to truly comprehend its nature: something immersed in the incessant and immanent production of itself. Everything exists as a constant *actualization of an inexhaustible potency*. Moreover, this potency is inexhaustible because it reveals itself only *through* time, or rather, *as* time itself. As we can note, it is a virtuous cycle where act and potency are eternally intertwined (Sanín-Restrepo 2016: 83–9).

If, as we will see in section 2.2.1, authors such as Heidegger and Agamben are right in criticizing Western philosophy, viewing it as a kind of forgetfulness of the truly important issues, it is necessary to take this accusation in a radical sense and abandon the conceptual and categorical apparatus that shapes traditional philosophical thinking, as Heidegger attempted, albeit without great success, in his *Contributions to Philosophy*. Well then, act and potency are central categories in Western philosophy and, as such, should be abandoned by the theory of the encryption of power. Nonetheless, there is a more creative and genuine alternative, which consists of giving a new use to these categories, understanding, in line with Sanín-Restrepo's reasoning, that they can only be thought of concomitantly, thereby decrypting the core of power that appears as *entelechy* (ἐντελέχεια) in Aristotelian metaphysics. This is a complex concept that indicates the full and total realization of a potency in the form of an act, with which Being would fulfil the purpose (*télos*, τέλος) it possesses (*ékhein*, ἔχειν) within itself (*en*, ἐν-). In this sense, entelechy encompasses the three main mechanisms of encryption of power, namely totality, finality and immunization (Sanín-Restrepo and Machado-Araujo 2025a: 21), so that contemporary encryption machines such as the State, the Constitution and capital are direct descendants of the ancient and now almost forgotten – but still powerfully operative – entelechy of Aristotle. This indicates the fixation of substance (*ousía*, οὐσία), which previously appeared as something mobile in the thought of the Stagirite, at least while he referred to the interplay between act and potency that would constitute it.

Against this powerful substantialist apparatus, it is necessary to reaffirm that potency only potentiates itself – that is, exists – in an act. Even the potency-of-not – which, for Agamben, would reveal the superiority of potency over act because it does not need to be actualized – works in this way, for there is only a potency-of-not in the face of an act that does not actualize it, as when the pianist does not play the piano. His passivity, which is an omissive act, reveals the potency-of-not. Similarly, as I will discuss below, all act is an acted potency. Potency is not originary in relation to act, nor act in relation to potency. Neither can be the *arkhé* of the other, as they are co-originated and infinite.

By thinking of act and potency in this way, one can reveal not only movement, which occurs through the continuous passage from act to potency and from potency to act, but also contingency, meaning the *necessity of possibility* (Meillassoux 2012), which indicates the inexistence of destiny, finality and, ultimately, Being itself – an ontological concept that has been translated over the past 200 years into political terms through the representative idea of Sovereign People, just as, in theological terms, it corresponds to God. Thus, the Sovereign People is the *Deus absconditus* of the theologians, the mysterious entelechy of Aristotle, which, however, when decrypted, allows us to perceive that there is nothing substantial in the universe, only movement, possibility, difference, play and dance between *dýnamis* and *enérgeia*. To this end, it seems essential to shatter the empty shell of power in order to find, within it, where the *arcana imperii* should rest, a festive Nothing. This, however, is not a simple void, but the possibility of being, rhythm, vibration, as in the quantum theory of superstrings.

Nevertheless, if potency and act are inseparable moments within a more complex ontological-temporal process, one might legitimately question why potency appears to hold a certain prominence in the theory of encryption of power. After all, both the hidden people and the *an-archy* to be decrypted are ultimately identified with *potentia*. First, I emphasize that in the theory of encryption of power, potency is never presented in an abstract or universal form as a mere concept. When this theory refers to potency, it always refers to an actualization of potency, that is, to an *acted potency*. Actuality is always actuality in motion, an actuality 'at work' and historically situated. From this perspective, it is important to remember that the Greek word for 'actuality', *enérgeia* (ενέργεια), derives from the adjective *energós* (ἐνεργός), which means 'at work, active'. *Energós* is a combination of *en-* (ἐν-, 'in') and *érgon* (ἔργον, 'work', 'activity'), literally meaning 'in activity', 'working'. In turn, potency serves as the ontological operator of change, difference, novelty and resistance to the solidification of power as *potestas*. This occurs in a very concrete and not merely theoretical way, since potency acts as the constant resistance of the people against the unifying movement of *potestas*, which seeks to incorporate it into the state of exception through its exclusion. As Sanín-Restrepo argues: 'It is a striving to keep difference from being absorbed by unity and identity, and it is what inhibits *potestas* from taking it over, thus converting living labour into exchange value' (Sanín-Restrepo 2016: 110).

As discussed earlier, potency is equivalent to Parmenides' non-Being and is responsible for creating the space, the void, the gap necessary for any movement and change (Aristotle, *Metaphysics*, 1046a). If there were only actuality and presence, neither movement nor change would be possible. This would result in a Being of absolute extension, centred on itself, occupying all the space of the Real, similar to Parmenides' sphere, as described in his impressive verses:

Αὐτὰρ ἐπεὶ πεῖρας πύματον, τετελεσμένον
ἐστί πάντοθεν, εὐκύκλου σφαίρης
ἐναλίγκιον ὄγκῳ, μεσσόθεν ἰσοπαλὲς
πάντῃ· τὸ γὰρ οὔτε τι μεῖζον

οὔτε τι βαιότερον πελέναι χρεόν ἐστι
τῇ ἢ τῇ. Οὔτε γὰρ οὐκ ἐὸν ἔστι, τό κεν
παύοι μιν ἱκνεῖσθαι εἰς ὁμόν, οὔτ᾽ ἐὸν
ἔστιν ὅπως εἴη κεν ἐόντος τῇ μᾶλλον τῇ
δ᾽ ἧσσον, ἐπεὶ πᾶν ἐστιν ἄσυλον· οἷ γὰρ
πάντοθεν ἶσον, ὁμῶς ἐν πείρασι κύρει.
(DK 28, VIII)

Where, then, it has its farthest boundary,
it is complete on every side, equally
poised from the centre in every
direction, like the mass of a rounded
sphere; for it cannot be greater or

smaller in one place than in
another. For there is nothing which is
not that could keep it from reaching
out equally, nor is it possible that
there should be more of what is in
this place and less in that, since it is
all inviolable. For, since it is equal in
all directions, it is equally confined
within limits. (Burnet, 1892)

However, contrary to Parmenides' belief, it is the non-Being that enables the empty space necessary for movement and differentiation of Being. In this regard, Hegel, with his peculiar language, speaks of the 'immense potency of the negative', understanding that negativity, lack and emptiness keep the machine of dialectics running, which, for him, is identified with the total and totalizing logic of the world.[22] Therefore, it seems clear that potency emerges as a possibility to change the reality, and for this reason it is privileged in the theory of encryption of power, as long as we remember that it is always centred in a potency in action. Through potency, the possibility of transitioning from a state X to a state Y becomes possible.

Thus, we can understand why the encounter between ontology and politics occurs within potency. Its dimension of absence does not signify a lack but rather the opening of an *an-archic* dimension, serving as an ontological operator in which absence does not merely mean privation or inferiority but the immanent (un)foundation of the flow of power, which I call 'democracy'. Potency is flux, reflux, journey, change, play of forces, self-decryption: 'A potency is an idiosyncrasy of forces in which the dominant force is transformed by passing to the dominated, and the dominated by passing to the dominant: center of metamorphoses' (Deleuze 1993: 167). In contrast, *potestas*, which should not be read simply as a synonym for actuality, indicates a dimension of solidity of power, of insurmountability and fossilization. In this sense, it refers to an encrypted, falsified reality, since power is not an entity, a static object or a tangible possession but a dynamic process (Sanín-Restrepo 2016: 110–11). Consequently, *potestas* corresponds to the concealment, encryption and corruption that constitute an ontological falsification of *potentia*.

To comprehend the concept of encryption of power, it is crucial to recognize two dimensions of power: power as command (*potestas*) and power as collective capacity for self-institution (*potentia*) (Kalyvas 2018). In the former, power manifests as *potestas*, a power-dominance that blocks difference (Sanín-Restrepo 2016: 71). This is the predominant model in our tradition, as exemplified by authors such as Bodin, Hobbes and Schmitt, who conceive of power as a 'thing', a metaphysical entity that, being in the beginning, is also the ruler, thus enabling a vision of power as *arkhé*. In his seminal 1576 treatise, *The Six Books of the Commonwealth*, Jean Bodin (1530–96) famously defined sovereignty as the absolute and perpetual power to command entrusted to the ruler (1993: 74). *Potestas* corresponds to the negation of *potentia* through the stratification and monopolization of power's conditions of exercise, solidifying it within closed, violent and self-sufficient structures.[23]

Despite this, as previously discussed, another tradition exists that does not conceive of power as an experience of command. Instead, assuming the literal meaning of this word in the Latin tradition not as a noun ('il *potere*', 'o *poder*', the *power*) but as a verb ('cosa noi *possiamo*', 'o que nós *podemos*', what we *can*), understands it as the capacity to act, to perform, that is, *potentia*. In this context, in a brief but influential article, Josiah Ober (2008) argues that the original meaning of the word 'democracy' does not refer to a rule imposed by the majority but rather to a collective capacity to do things.

But the reality is more complex. The distinction between *potestas* and *potentia* is not merely a matter of perspective, with some individuals perceiving power as *potestas* and others as *potentia*. We are not dealing with a mere linguistic problem. Instead, this perception lies at the heart of the theory of encryption of power. Fundamentally, it is an ontological question (Sanín-Restrepo 2018: x), as power-*potestas* is only an encrypted form of power-*potentia*. Here, we must again ask what encryption encrypts, what it hides and, in doing so, what it distorts. The answer can only be: the *an-archic* and collective experience of constructing social meaning, which occurs immanently and is conditioned by *difference*. Yet, this experience ultimately becomes encrypted and codified in the form of universal apparatuses – sovereignty, Constitution, representation, and so on – that solidify power

Potency does not denote an original experience in a substantialist sense but rather the fundamental condition of all human action. Consequently, the task of decryption is not equivalent to seeking a more original origin or a more real reality, as there is nothing beyond *potentia*. It is a type of constant flux that circulates within Being, not tied to any chronological past but rather manifesting as contemporaneity, such as the embryo's continued influence on the formed organism and the child's enduring presence in the adult psyche (Agamben 2023b: 97). Traditionally, potency has been perceived as an entity rather than a process largely due to its linguistic conversion into *arkhé*. Derived from the Greek verb *arkhó*, *arkhé* simultaneously connotes 'to command, to order' and 'to be prior to something'. Thus, in archic terms, 'to begin' also means 'to be the leader' and 'to command'. Conversely, the theory of encryption of power is profoundly *an-archic*, as demonstrated in section 2.2, given that it denies at the same time the command and the beginning inherent to *potestas*. Therefore, '[. . .] we are wrong to state that anarchy is simply the lack of power. Anarchy literally means the lack of principle, the lack of a transcendent model that directs action' (Sanín-Restrepo 2018: xvi).

The *potentia* decrypted by the theory of encryption of power has no origin and has always existed as an instituting process. Nevertheless, it is continually encrypted as *potestas* so that the constituent appears in the form of the constituted, whose most perfect expression is the Constitution. Indeed, 'Constitution' is a concept of theological-political lineage that presupposes the idea of creation *ex nihilo*, wherein constituent subjects – whether God in the Middle Ages or 'The People' in contemporary times – preexist the constitutive process and remain external to it. In contrast, within instituting processes, the singularities who enable them are internal, arising from the very dynamics that seek to shape life for its protection and promotion (Esposito 2023).

In this sense, encryption does not entail denying access to a more authentic reality, as a Platonic perspective might suggest. Instead, it involves capturing the differences that continually constitute and deconstitute Being, which, once liberated, can manifest as language and social practices. Power becomes encrypted by presupposing an *arkhé* that operates under a meta-representative logic, serving as a mandatory model for all political experiences (Sanín-Restrepo 2018: xxii). What encryption conceals is the fact that all power emerges from language games and cannot be 'possessed' (Sanín-Restrepo 2018: xvi) as it is not a tangible entity but rather a collective relationship, a process that is always contingent, immanent and differential.

Similarly, encryption, such as the dictionarization of politics explored in the subsequent section, suppresses the recognition of the variability, difference and immanence of language that exists outside of institutional norms, namely those labelled as 'solid', 'serious', 'objective' or 'scientific'. Evidently, by suppressing alternative languages, it precludes the development of other forms-of-life, given that Being, language and politics are intertwined and can only be separated through the violent transformation of *potentia* into *potestas*. As Eduardo Viveiros de Castro (2014: 118) asserts, this transformation is not merely illusory but a real process enacted by an implacable abstract machine of overcoding, which finds its empirical concretions in imperialism, colonialism, *machismo*, racism, war and, as we shall see, in political theology. Therefore, if encryption involves employing an archic language to depotentiate, limit, constrain and determine the experience of the immanent and contingent self-institution of Being, decryption entails the liberation of Being *with* and *in* language, without presupposing any universalizing framework.

At this point, the transition from ontology to politics occurs. Indeed, if the interplay between act and potency can only generate *difference within contingency*, something like a single, unchanging and substantial Sovereign People seems impossible, because in the continuous movement between potency and act, multiple and plural peoples always emerge. In order to make them appear as a single Sovereign People and founding entity – without transforming them into such, since ontologically peoples are and always will be multiple and different – the difference is encrypted through devices such as the Constitution. Thus, the dimension of a hidden people arises, which in reality are many peoples, countless concrete expressions of difference that become overcoded in the form of Nation, Homeland, Race, State, and so on. To decrypt these new and terrible entelechies, it seems indispensable a radical-democratic political theology that functions as a threshold and articulator between ontology and politics to reveal the truly spiritual element of the theory of the encryption of power: the hidden people, an antagonistic formation generated within sovereignty – and not ontologically independent from it, as Hardt and Negri's multitude – and therefore capable of, by occupying the place of the *Deus absconditus* of constitutionalists, bringing it to light of the critique, so that, like a vampire, it dissolves in the overwhelming clarity of difference and contingency, made concrete through collective life projects that do not depend on the conditions imposed by God, the Constitution or capital.

The hidden people – or the hidden peoples, in the plural – constitutes the only ontological reality, since it corresponds to the real that becomes encrypted in order to assert the Sovereign People, which, however, is nothing more than a depotentialized and simulated version of the hidden people. In this way, as Sanín-Restrepo and Machado-Araujo note, the theological-political machine must negatively assert the hidden people, who function as the secret foundation of the Sovereign People:

> The people are legalized as an impossible totality where they are both subject and agency, zenith and bottom, chosen and disposable. However, this totality is necessarily split at its core. The key lies in how constitutions transformed the concept of 'the people' into a *pars pro toto synecdoche*. Here, an arbitrary part – such as the white population within a nation-state, the debtor, the citizen – defines an unattainable infinity, the people. Nevertheless, it nominally needs to incorporate the marginalized, including forced migrants, homeless, racialized people. The interplay is not accidental or merely operative, it is constitutive. The hidden people are not just an excess, or a surplus of the concept of the people

> as a synecdoche, on the contrary, they are the foundational sustenance of the totality of the people. Without the hidden people, the concept of the people would not exist or function. Nevertheless, at the same time they are what is missing in the totality, for it to declare itself a true totality. It is thus a crack, an opening that seals the system and at the same time makes it function through an absence. (2025a: 19)

It is this dimension of the Sovereign People's dependence on the hidden people that needs to be brought to light and explored, no longer as an exception – that is, an inclusive exclusion – which secretly underpins the rule, but rather with regard to the ontological truth that the hidden people do not need the Sovereign People, in the same way that, in Marx's thought, labour does not need capital. On the contrary, the Sovereign People is inconceivable without the hidden people, just as capital does not exist without labour. It is then a matter of understanding the hidden people not as a structure that enables sovereignty, but rather as a *rest*.

Rest is a potent theological-messianic operator that indicates, as Agamben (2000) perceives when reading Paul's letters, a type of ontotemporal structure that is inexhaustible, a figure of time that, not corresponding either to history or to eternity, remains existing when everything has already been spent and fulfilled, pointing not to the end of times, but to the time of the end that, literally, never stops passing, having no proper finality or destiny. According to Agamben's reading in another of his books – the controversial *What Remains of Auschwitz* – the idea of rest in the Old Testament indicates that what is saved in the messianic event is not the whole people of Israel, but a rest, a remainder (*še'ar Jisra'el*): 'Remainder is the consistency that Israel assumes at the point where it is put in immediate relation with the *éskhaton*, with the messianic event or with the election. In its relation to salvation, the whole (the people) necessarily positions itself as remainder' (2018a: 875). To understand this idea, it is necessary to comprehend that the rest has no numerical meaning, as if it were a portion of the totality. Similarly, the hidden people do not correspond to a part of the total, unified and Sovereign People. And this is because there is no totality, only multiplicity, contingency and infinitude, so that all peoples are, structurally, rests of a totality that only exists in the simulated dimension of encryption. Recognizing this ontological truth is, in theological-political terms, participating in the always-present messianic event of salvation, which is neither destiny nor purpose, but that which is properly indestructible not only in the human but also in the infinite dance of act and potency. It is in this sense that the hidden peoples, being indestructible because they always correspond to what remains, open up to the infinitude with which closed and totalizing models such as the State and capital can only deal through encryption. Indeed,

> Totality refers to a state of being complete, final, and closed. It also implies finality, as it announces perfection (nothing else can be added). [. . .] When we inquire about the world, the answer is already predetermined. [. . .] Totality opposes infinity and infinity is the sign of contingency. Infinity means that the potential relations among beings are incalculable and immanent to the relations themselves. (Sanín-Restrepo and Machado-Araujo 2025a: 23)

The hidden people – the rest – emerges as the indestructibility of the real, that is, the infinitude of contingency that lives, dies and resurrects in the movement of self-affection between act and potency, ontological processes that are politically translated in the concrete struggles that immigrants, women, Black, indigenous and many other hidden peoples wage against the overcoding machines that aim to block the flow of being by transforming it into a model of fixed Being. In this sense, the hidden people is the authentic people of God, as the young Agamben intuited when reflecting on the Heideggerian concept of *Dasein*: '*Dasein* means: each person is in god, each person risks, loses, or guards his being-in-god. Simplicity: the ability to be effortlessly in god. In the past, this mode of being was called "people"' (2024b: 57).

At this stage, a delicate question arises: in its struggle against the Sovereign People, should the hidden people take the lead and cease to remain hidden? In other words, must the hidden people always remain hidden? This is a dramatic dilemma, for if the hidden people cease to be hidden, they end up transforming into a single, visible, total People. However, we have already seen that this is an ontological impossibility, since the real is always the 'hidden', not in the sense of something that is concealed and needs to be discovered. 'Hidden' here equates to difference, contingency and infinitude, attributes that the Sovereign People denies by concealing the multiple and plural peoples. Thus, it is not for the hidden people to 'cease to remain hidden', as if that depended on them, as if they were an obscure Heideggerian *Seyn*[24] that could only reveal itself at the appropriate epochal moment. The hidden people are concealed by the Sovereign People, meaning that the latter imposes identity and totality where there is only difference and infinitude. So the task is not so much to find ways to cease being hidden or come to light, but to combat the discourses and conditions (material, ideological, theoretical, linguistic, historical, etc.) that make possible the concealment – that is, the encryption – of the infinite and contingent flow of difference.

In this perspective, decrypting the hidden people is equivalent, in political terms, to living a non-fascist life. As I will discuss in section 3.2, fascism does not simply equate to a specific far-right political orientation that emerged in Italy, but rather to a *figure of thought* that evokes the attempt to block the course of immanence, revealing itself as an always-renewed and violent effort to reconstruct the old, deny the flow and prevent change. In this sense, fascist are the self-narratives that the seemingly triumphant capitalism makes of itself, claiming to be the end of history, after which nothing new could emerge and only the repetition of the same would domain. As I understand it, fascism corresponds to a contradictory movement of the real that denies movement itself and aims to block transformation and variation, thereby closing off access to the indefinable and contingent reconfigurations between act and potency. In this context, the non-fascist form-of-life is one that confers truth to politics, revealing a non-principled principle, an *an-archic* principle that rejects any and all tendencies of immobilizing immanence, a paralysis which, moreover, seems impossible to me.

1.4.3. Dictionarization of politics and democracy

In the Western philosophical tradition, to be is to exercise power.[25] Deconstructing this relationship requires a critical and decrypting process that challenges the monopolization and depotentiation of the political lexicon by *potestas*. In Linguistics, the lexicon constitutes the ensemble of words and expressions that speakers of a given language utilize to articulate their thoughts. Analogously, the concept of a political lexicon refers to the set of forms through which individuals conceive and experience the *pólis*, or more precisely, power. Saying, acting and being are intrinsically connected. This fact explains why the prolonged crisis afflicting Western politics is not merely a symptom of decadence or the progressive inadequacy of pre-modern mechanisms applied to postmodern times. Instead, it stems from what I call *dictionarization of politics*, which is nothing more than a device for encrypting power.

The dictionary constitutes an apparatus that seeks to capture the inherent multiplicity of language within a closed system. When applied to politics, this scheme attempts to definitively circumscribe its nature and procedures. Consequently, anything outside this circumscribed definition is perceived as either anti-political or utopian. The lexicographers of politics, committed to the closure of their field, are those instances that personalize power, not only exercising it but also imposing it upon others as a burden. They control and determine permissible choices, all of which are fixed and labelled within the institutional lexicon.

The dictionarization of politics is a practice of encrypting power that is especially useful in current times, when absolute novelty is always read in catastrophic terms, since everything that is not included in the dictionary is automatically wrong, false, impossible – in other words, terrorist. This is why the so-called crisis of politics should be understood as the perception, still very confused and negative, that there is something outside the dictionary, that the language of politics cannot be limited and domesticated, as the evidence of power's unfoundability is far more real than any institutional design or model. From this *an-archic* viewpoint, revisited in section 2.2, political thought involves a foundation that is perpetually absent, rejecting the grandiloquent gesture of the dictionary and, at most, preparing an introduction to one that will never materialize, thus affirming the inexhaustibility, immanence and contingency of power. Mustapha Khayati, a Tunisian member of the Situationist International, exemplified this approach in March 1966 when he wrote a preface to a *Situationist Dictionary* that, of course, never existed. His words are worthy of consideration:

> Every revolutionary theory has had to invent its own terms, to destroy the dominant sense of other terms and establish new meanings in the 'world of meanings' corresponding to the new embryonic reality needing to be liberated from the dominant trash heap. The same reasons that prevent our adversaries (the masters of the Dictionary) from definitively fixing language enable us to assert alternative positions that negate existing meanings. But we already know that these same reasons also prevent us from proclaiming any definitive certitudes. A definition is always open, never definitive. Ours have a historical value, they are applicable during a specific period, linked to a specific historical practice. It is impossible to get rid of a world without getting rid of the language that conceals and protects it, without laying bare its true nature. As the 'social truth' of power is permanent falsification, language is its permanent guarantee and the Dictionary its universal reference. Every revolutionary praxis has felt the need for a new semantic field and for expressing a new truth; from the *Encyclopédistes* to the Polish intellectuals' critique of Stalinist 'wooden language' in 1956, this demand has continually been asserted. Because *language is the house of power,*

> the refuge of its police violence. Any dialogue with power is violence, whether passively suffered or actively provoked. When power wants to avoid resorting to its material arms, it relies on language to guard the oppressive order. This collaboration is in fact the most natural expression of all power. (2009: 2)

In a few strokes, Khayati highlights the often overlooked yet fundamental link between language and power. Like an image too close to our eyes, this connection, though obvious, is frequently imperceptible. Khayati developed an entire revolutionary programme by realizing that the critique of the dominant language must become the permanent practice of revolutionary theory, which is responsible for imposing continuous *détournements* on the dominant language. With this term – translated into English as 'detour' – the situationists indicated their main method, which consisted of appropriating periods, sentences and ideas from other thinkers and, by altering some of their elements or simply changing their context or place in the sentence, building powerful critical weapons directed against the misery of the contemplative daily life into which they saw the world sinking. Today, however, simple detours from the dominant political language are insufficient to resist dictionarization, since the integration of lies into politics has imposed an epochal change, creating a seemingly unprofanable horizon.

The dictionary defends itself against all attempts to think outside of it by reaffirming the true as merely a moment of the false[26] and reducing the options available to speakers to the bare minimum, a scenario presciently foreseen by George Orwell. In *Nineteen Eighty-Four*, Orwell depicts busy lexicographers whose duty and pride consists of producing ever smaller editions of the Newspeak dictionary, highlighting not only the narrowing of the field of thought but also the very articulation of power, increasingly identified with its impoverished institutional practices. In this context, a new political lexicon is not a mere fad but an urgent strategic imperative. It must acknowledge the non-fundamental nature of power, which does not occur as something natural, but historical; which does not necessarily identify with the ideas of hierarchy, command and separation; and does not develop in a linear or progressive manner, but to a large extent randomly. However, it does not mean to say that this experience is not directed by certain powerful interests that capture it, encrypt it, depotentiate it. In this regard, Heidegger's (1993c) critique becomes fully understandable, as he argues that the history of metaphysics is nothing but a history of bad translations, which, for instance, results in the loss of the possibility of understanding the radicality of the experiences of original Greek thought rooted in *phýsis* (φύσις) and *lógos* (λόγος), which are then redefined through prosaic terms like 'nature' and 'reason'. The same, as we will see, applies to *arkhé* and *anarkhé*.

For those who perceive power as potency, that is, an inexhaustible field of collective action capable of altering the world order, the initial and most formidable challenge consists of being forced to use the lexicon of the current political dictionary to express new forms, structures and realities. To experience the problematic nature of this situation, one should attempt to construct a critical thesis today without resorting to words such as 'person', 'individual', 'law', 'revolution', 'sovereignty', 'people', 'identity' and 'left', which were created precisely to solidify certain experiences of subjectivation and to encrypt power.

These word-realities enable communication while simultaneously constraining it, functioning as insurmountable boundaries that relegate any other possibility to the messianic ineffability of the unsaid, of a silence that only beckons and evokes, as Walter Benjamin did with desperate insistence. It is exactly this difficulty that, working as a *continuous electrical tension*, runs through this book, as I intend to transcend the confines of traditional political theology while still utilizing its lexicon, albeit critically. The paradox is exquisitely cruel: to think and say something new in politics, we are constrained by old instruments that inherently deny the possibility of novelty.

Indeed, the linguistic models of tradition paradoxically enable their own deposition, much like an English speaker relies on the often limiting structures and forms of English to initiate the learning of a radically different language, such as Chinese. In this sense, as Franco Volpi noted in his reading of the strenuous engagement with the German language contained in *Contributions to Philosophy: From the Event*, a work in which Heidegger sought to create a non-metaphysical language, 'every will to overcome must inevitably presuppose that which it overcomes, remaining conditioned' (2011: 292). Perhaps for this reason, linguists recognize that true language acquisition involves abandoning the linguistic instruments of one's native tongue and beginning to think and feel in the foreign language, ceasing to refer to the language with which we grew up and until then seemed completely glued to things. The tragedy lies in the absence of alternative access to the political world beyond the confines of the current dictionary, creating a paradox wherein thinking an outside necessitates affirming an absolute inside.

Benjamin's much-discussed and controversial concept of pure violence, explored in section 2.1.2, attempts to radically transcend this paradox. As a pure medium, devoid of purpose and distinct from political-legal violence, it opens space for what is to come. This theoretical-critical earthwork, by dismantling the old, acknowledges that the deconstructors cannot construct the new without repeating the same traditional gestures that claim to be universal and insurmountable.

Giorgio Agamben, in a beautiful early text originally published in 1970 and immediately sent to Hannah Arendt, was one of the first to recognize the truly dramatic and fascinating nature of Benjamin's proposal. Like a fearsome *mana*, it haunts the so-called 'revolutionary tradition', an expression that is an undeniable oxymoron. According to Agamben (2009), the revolutionary vanguard class, which violently inaugurates the new by denying the old, is ultimately compelled to suppress itself. This is because, if this vanguard takes its mission seriously, it recognizes its intrinsic complicity with the old. Indeed, the Marxist working class, conceived as the universally exploited class, is tasked with ending universal exploitation, a contradiction inherent to its position within the class-based social structure. The contradiction lies in the fact that the working class, as a historical and hierarchical social formation, can only fulfil its destiny of a classless society by perpetuating its existence as a class. The problem of the new theological-political lexicon is isomorphic to that of the revolutionary class, since only with the old lexicon, which constitutes our political language, can we think and construct something new, which is thus born infected by the old. The only solution then seems to be a suicide, the revolutionary self-suppression of oneself that Agamben foresees as the task of the revolutionary class. Transposed to the dimension of language, it evokes the sepulchral silence of a world that, destituted, falls silent when it becomes inoperative.

Nevertheless, I believe that alternative and less tragic approaches are possible. To visualize them, we must heed Khayati's suggestion and magnify it, imposing potent detours on traditional theological-linguistic ideas, which inevitably result in theological-political practices. We must learn to play with words and assume a ludic dimension that, lucidly and joyfully, favours the desubjugation of language. One way to do this is through philosophy, a serious game that, in these purportedly post-historical times, teaches us with Kafka (and perhaps with Marx) that history has not even begun, since 'the decisive moment of human evolution is permanent. That is why revolutionary spiritual movements are right to declare everything that happened before null and void, since nothing has happened yet' (Kafka 2006: n. 6).

Thus, the words of the official political dictionary can be rendered pre-historical, pointing to something that surpasses them, that plays with them, and for this reason, can deactivate them at the very moment they are uttered, considering that the process of encryption of power conceals the abundance of the world and the possibility of existing in different ways. At this juncture, the Pauline strategy – already referenced by Agamben on more than one occasion and which I will revisit in the conclusion – reveals itself in all its potency: *acting as if not acting*, which only makes sense if one understands that there are no certainties in the world of politics, except the certainty that everything that exists not only deserves to perish, as Goethe's Mephistopheles said, but that it will perish; because everything is a human arrangement, everything is an act of a potency that is never exhausted; everything is provisional and precarious and as a result it can – and in this 'can' lies the whole meaning of *potentia* and politics – be different.

From this perspective, thinking *an-archically* means, for example, not conceiving the notions of superiority or inferiority in politics. Such a dyad constitutes an unthinkable dimension in a radical democracy. This is not a moral evaluation, which could indicate whether this fact is good or not. It is a linguistic and, at the same time, an ontological question. All languages limit our perception of reality, and thus reality itself. *An-archic* thinking involves not only the opening of a new lexicon but also the closing of another, so that certain political experiences are unthinkable in an *an-archic* context. In this sense, a truly radical political dictionary would exclude entries like 'superiority' and 'inferiority'. By the way, in its most radical configuration, this dictionary would have a single entry, namely, 'Dictionary: 1. The only impossible word. 2. A non-democratic artifact that reveals the impossibility of necessity. 3. An attempt to encrypt contingency'.

A simple and powerful example of a new use of language that can open up political spaces for *an-archic* libertarian practices is the meaning that the Zapatist Army of National Liberation (EZLN) gives to the notion of leadership, as its 'leader' is called subcommander. The word 'subcommander' would apparently be an oxymoron, as it indicates someone who commands but who is below (sub) another, in other words, he is commanded. However, it is a common category in traditional military lexicon, where it does not seem paradoxical. This is because the term 'subcommander' is understood in relation to a 'commander', a hierarchically superior position. But in Zapatism there is no commander. The subcommander represents the highest level of named authority, creating a beautiful and paradoxical democratic structure in which authority is both above and below, commanding by obeying and obeying by commanding, as stated in the EZLN motto that inspires the seven principles of the Good Government Juntas (*Juntas de Buen Gobierno*) operating in various autonomous Zapatist communities: 'to serve others, not serve oneself; to represent, not supplant; to construct, not destroy; to obey, not command; to propose, not impose; to convince, not defeat; to work from below, not seek to rise' (Galeano and Moisés 2016). Therefore, the Zapatist subcommander is not subordinate to any individual authority but rather to a collective, anonymous and contingent instance that is always in motion. In this way, the Zapatists not only challenge the Greek dichotomy between governing (*árkhein*) and being governed (*árkhestai*) but also the very concept of hierarchy. The literally sacred (*hierós*) order/power (*arkhé*), rooted in medieval theological thought to describe the rigidly stratified angelic society (Coccia 2024), has become an indispensable component of today's disempowered representative 'democracies'. By having a subcommander without a commander, the Zapatists divest power as a title with the same gesture that they name it; neutralizing it, they transforms it into potency.

Therefore, as the Zapatists demonstrate, opposing the dictionarization of political language is akin to seeking the *unspeakable* of contemporary politics. Because it challenges all existing political models, this unspeakable remains outside the realm of any dictionary. This permanent absence, however, is partially filled by certain words in our potential dictionary of radical politics: democracy, *an-archy* and disobedience. When isolated and translated into so-called 'real-world' structures and events, these three words appear contradictory and mutually exclusive. For instance, democracy seems to be the antithesis of *an-archy*, while disobedience suggests a limit situation that could transform the former into the latter. But from a critical-radical perspective, these words converge towards a similar meaning. While not synonymous, these terms point to the unspeakability of politics. Their radicality becomes apparent when they mutually reference and subvert each other, indicating, for instance, that political theology is not limited to a doctrine of foundation of power and can also reveal its radical and constitutive lack of foundation.

This *an-archic* configuration is evident in the Greek formation of the word 'democracy'. As Luciano Canfora (2012) rightly noted, it could not evoke anything good in the minds of those who invented it and put it into circulation, that is, the Athenian aristocrats. The word 'democracy' inherently carries a connotation of forceful power, stemming from the root *krátos* (κράτος). This root signifies a power imposed by force, unlike other political terms derived from more 'noble' roots such as *arkhé* (ἀρχή), from which the terms 'monarchy' and 'oligarchy' are generated, evoking well-established, ancient and traditional forms of governance.[27] What distinguishes the violent *krátos* from the ancient *arkhé* is a keen awareness of power's inherent absence of foundation. The Athenian ruling classes, reliant on tradition, blood, religion or wealth, perceived this unfoundability as a threat to their established order. Therefore, they could not name the new political organization with the root *arkhé*, which was reserved for traditional forms of government, realizing that democratic power imposed itself beyond any and all titles and, for this very reason, has no foundation. Moreover, its sole and radical foundation, self-sufficient and requiring no other, lies in its very lack of foundation. Notwithstanding, remains the supposed contradiction that lies in the word 'aristocracy', which indicated the form of government preferred by detractors of democracy. However, the fact that 'aristocracy' is also rooted in *krátos* does not reveal a contradiction. Instead, it highlights the aristocrats' understanding of the inherently violent nature of their own power, despite its traditional and supposedly legitimate foundations. Even though this power, like democratic power, has a violent basis, it is nonetheless grounded, that is, 'archaic', which is confirmed by the use of the term *áristos* (ἄριστος), referring to the 'best', against whom the nascent democracy imposed the artificial construct of the *démoi* (δῆμοι), reconfigured by Cleisthenes' reforms in 508 BC.

Thus, in an evanescent dictionary of radical politics that will never exist, the most accurate translation of 'democracy' would not be 'government of the people' – a horrible oxymoron whose mere enunciation already reveals its impossibility – but rather 'power without foundation'. This unfounded character sets democracy apart from other forms of government. It is not merely a specific governmental structure or a quantitative method for decision-making or elite selection. As Jacques Rancière (2005) rightly concluded, democracy will never be forgiven because it exposes the radical lack of foundation of power, embodying in itself the (un)foundation of the power. All forms of government, from ancient aristocracies and monarchies to modern technocracies and mediocracies, require justification, self-glorification and a legitimizing title to persuade the vast majority to be governed. Whether ruled by the wisest or the richest, the noblest or the son (or representative) of God, all forms of government need legitimation because, deep down, they are unjustified when contrasted with the evident equality of all members of the *démos*.

Only democracy, since it has no foundation, justifies itself, thus being the (un)foundation par excellence. Rather than addressing the age-old question – why should one human being obey another? – democracy negates it by affirming that any human community is non-original, non-transcendent and non-traditional. Such a community is always one of potentiality, an *an-archic* community. Now, if democracy is *an-archic*, lacking both *arkhé* and foundation, being ever-potential and never fully realized, disobedience emerges as its defining experience. It is the central passion that potentiates democracy because only free beings can disobey, and they do so collectively. Indeed, a constitutive link exists between community and potency, as potency is never self-sufficient and must always be directed toward others.

As Rafaelle Laudani (2011) has shown, the tradition of Western political-legal thought reveals its conservative nature by its inability to conceive of a specific experience of *potentia* that it mistakenly terms 'disobedience'. In fact, disobedience is only conceivable through a word that, with the prefix 'dis-', evokes an authority. In Judeo-Christian and patriarchal theological-political culture, obedience is a central and original category, representing the duty of the creature to the creator, the child to the father, the governed to the ruler, the woman to the man and the primitive to the civilized. To obey, in this sense, is to produce glory (*dóxa*). According to the traditional political dictionary, disobedience can only be conceived negatively, as a lack of something fundamental and necessary. From this perspective, the great works of traditional theological-political thought revolve around obedience, with disobedience appearing only marginally and secondarily, always linked, even linguistically, to the experience of successful command. In the traditional political dictionary, obedience is merely a euphemism to indicate that separation has occurred, that hierarchy has imposed itself, that order has been accepted, that the foundation has been founded. Conversely, when separation and hierarchy are rejected in favour of the common, the established order is disrupted and the foundation loses its grounding power. We then experience what is inaccurately termed 'disobedience', which should be urgently renamed to signify not insubordination to transcendent authorities but a shared responsibility, a common *munus* that unites us as precarious beings. This shift opens the door to new political and theological-political practices.

The American activist Howard Zinn (1970) observed that the problem lies not in civil disobedience but in civil obedience. He is absolutely right. His diatribe invites us to envision a political theology centred on disobedience rather than obedience. In such a world, atrocities like Auschwitz would be not only impossible but also inconceivable, and all the main metaphysical categories that constitute the afflictive body of current politics – duty, property, guilt, right, citizen, Constitution, representation, and so on – would lose their centrality and operationality, making room for something that, if we still want to call it politics, would be very different from the experience of servitude and aristocratization that today is known by that fearsome name.

Democracy can be understood as a space of disobedience because it is an *an-archy*. However, it is important to clarify that this does not refer to any historical anarchist movement. *An-archy*, with its root *archy* emphasized through its concomitant separation and conjunction with the negation prefix *an-*, is not a political doctrine or ideology, nor is it inherently socialist or left-wing. It transcends these labels that, perpetually spinning in the void, always require their polar opposites – capitalism and the right – in a kind of hostile fraternity that keeps the theological-political machine running. *An-archy* is far more demanding than classical anarchism, as it aims to bring power to the surface as *potentia*, rather than separating, hierarchizing and glorifying it as a natural and given entity. *An-archy* is the name of decrypted democracy; it is the entry that replaces obedience in the non-existent dictionary of radical political theology, revealing the secret void that precedes the machine, that is, the radical absence of foundation that makes power democratic.

From this perspective, *an-archy* opposes the principle of *nómos* identified by Carl Schmitt (1997), this localizing ordering – or ordering location – that seeks to reproduce the earth's fixity and legitimize the sovereign's authority, who delimits and assigns it. If the *nómos* is of the order of the frontier and the military line, *an-archy* indicates the immanence of a common experience of living beings that refuses to be confined by legal codes. It strives for an absence of limits and an experience of the entirety of reality, thus antagonizing the mediation of glorified sovereignty and deified commands. For this very reason, *an-archy* is intertwined with democracy, always disobedient to those who flaunt their titles of dominion, their papal bulls, their diplomas and notarial certificates. Faced with the *uti possidetis* that the masters of this world intend to assert as a permanent title to the right to govern, *an-archy* operates on a microphysical scale to make all property and all guilt *terra nullius*, that is, no man's land, land of use, land that is sea, and therefore, unappropriable.

Living an *an-archic* (without foundation) and disobedient (without hierarchy, division or command) life means understanding that there is no vocation to be fulfilled, no historical destiny to be realized, no natural ethics to be satisfied, no divine duty to be accomplished; there is only a life of *potentia*, where possibilities open up before beings who are not obligated to execute any of them. It is in this *structural non-duty* that the specific dignity of humanity resides, not in deterministic and exceptive constructions like human rights and representative democracy. These constructs trace a predetermined path to be fully followed, even if the price of this 'progress' is almost always the negation of the rhetorical principles that apparently underpin such ideas.

A proof of this lies in the fact that, in the land of human rights and representative democracy – central entries in the current political dictionary – the crudest denial of these supposed values has occurred, whether through centuries-old colonialism or, domestically, through concentration and extermination camps. As Aimé Césaire (1950) perceptively noted, these atrocities are unforgivable and criminal to European sensibilities precisely because they brought to the old continent, especially to its most developed and 'humanist' part, a technobiopolitics – in fact, a necropolitics – already practised for a long time with 'success' in the Americas, Africa and Asia.

It is not more human rights – which always require, as structures of the State, more institutional violence, more police, more judgement, in a word: more law – or a renewal of representative democracy – always operationalized to violently separate the living from politics, that is, life from its form-of-life – that can make alternative spaces possible today. As many of their defenders do not admit it, what these and other apparatuses continually accomplish is only to reaffirm, with ever clearer virulence, the unshakeable rule of a closed theological-political dictionary in which the dangerous word 'progress' shines on every page.

It is time to awaken from the dreams – and the slumber – of reason and understand that the wealth of a community, the wealth of a species, lies not in what it has done but in what *it has not yet done*, in what it *can* do, in the fact that no path is blocked by God or nature, but rather by our own prejudices, fears and complacencies in the face of a collapsing world. To achieve this, we must decrypt the glorious centre of power that resides in political theology, and not to abandon and ridicule it as if it were a curious medieval relic. We must take seriously Heidegger's last *boutade*, for whom only one God can save us.[28] Yes, only one God can save us. But today this God is multiple, contingent and immanent. He is Black and feminine; He is Latin American, African and Asian; He is the very process of self-institution of the *an-archic* potency of the real: *Deus sive demokratia*.

2

Tendencies

When [. . .] the male and the female shall be no longer male nor female, then will you enter the Kingdom.

(*Gospel of Thomas*, 22)

2.1. The classical debate

2.1.1. The creation of a legend: Carl Schmitt's *Political Theology*

One can only speak of political theology when religion no longer dominates politics. Yes, this idea by the controversial German jurist Carl Schmitt (1888–1985) not only seems paradoxical, *it is* paradoxical. Schmitt elaborates it in a baroque manner in a booklet of enormous influence entitled *Political Theology: Four Chapters on the Theory of Sovereignty*,[1] which, for the Italian scholar Carlo Galli, is equivalent to the irruption *avant la lettre* of Heideggerian *Dasein* – understood as being-toward-death – into Public Law.[2]

According to Schmitt, political theology comprises a set of modern apparatuses designed to justify political and legal authority in an era in which such legitimacy can no longer be established in a singular and axiomatic manner (2017: xxxiii). This contrasts sharply with the European Middle Ages, when the social roles of individuals were defined unambiguously by the overarching metanarrative of the Catholic Church. The religious wars of the sixteenth and seventeenth centuries shattered the consensus that had previously existed within the *Res Publica Christiana* and led to the proliferation of diverse social micronarratives, initially with the rise of Protestantism and subsequently with the emergence of science, public opinion and various ideologies. This shift resulted in the recognition that the political order is neither natural nor predetermined; rather, it is artificial and indeterminate, essentially unfounded. This idea is exemplified in the prominent self-narrative of Modernity articulated in Thomas Hobbes' *Leviathan*.

Unlike classical and medieval political ontology, which viewed society as a natural fact, often compared to an organism, Hobbes (1588–1679) introduced the modern notion that human beings are not inherently sociable. Consequently, the State does not emerge from natural impulses. Rather, it is the artificial product of an agreement among individual wills that, while not necessarily good, just or ethical, are nonetheless rational and calculating, that is, technical (1965 [I, 17]: 132). Thus emerges the State-mechanism, which, in the absence of God, imperfectly assumes the role of a 'mortal God'. In the lack of a transcendent authority, it is the State's responsibility to manage the chaos and contingency that have become structural in the modern world. To fulfil this function, the State monopolizes violence, independent of any metaphysical justification. As Hobbes succinctly asserts, it is authority – that is, effective political-legal power – and not truth that creates law: '*sed Authoritas non Veritas facit Legem*'.[3]

It was in this context that modern political theology emerged, with Schmitt asserting that its central thesis lies in the understanding that each era is intricately linked to a particular metaphysical image of the world (1996: 50–1). Thus, the key modern political and legal notions are secularized theological concepts, meaning they have been transferred from the religious sphere to the secular realm (2009: 10). The following passage from Schmitt's *Political Theology* of 1922 is justifiably renowned:

> All significant concepts of modern State theory are secularized theological concepts. Not only in their historical development, because they were transferred from theology to State theory, insofar as, for example, the all-powerful God became an omnipotent legislator, but also in their systematic structure. Such knowledge is necessary for a sociological consideration of these concepts. (1996: 43)

To briefly illustrate this idea, one can say that theism – the belief in a personal God who actively engages in the world – legitimizes the absolute State. In contrast, deism, defined as the belief in a God who created the world and then withdrew, leaving it governed by natural laws, aligns with the Liberal State and its faith in the supposed laws of the market and in impersonal subjective rights. The Democratic Rule of Law, characterized by a proliferation of identities, social narratives and specific regulations, evokes a sense of polytheism. Finally, the culmination of this theological-political fresco is found in the Socialist State, which obviously corresponds to atheism.[4]

In addition to its impressionistic tone, characteristic of both the period and the author, Schmitt's book is situated within a broader debate regarding the legitimacy of Modernity, particularly centred on the so-called 'secularization thesis' (Marramao 1994; Vallauri 1981). Originally part of the legal lexicon, the term 'secularization' referred to the transfer of domains from the Church to the secular realm. Philosophically reinterpreted, this concept shaped the discourse on Modernity throughout the twentieth century.

To some extent, the debate on secularization was influenced by the renowned theory of German sociologist Max Weber (1864–1920), who contended that capitalism – and, by extension, Modernity – arose from what he called inner-worldly asceticism, a hallmark of Protestantism, as will be explored in subsection 3.1. According to Agamben's interpretation, this debate was not about a hidden conceptualization or a theological framework of Modernity – as its participants might have believed – but rather about the strategic function of the idea of secularization. This idea serves as a *signature* – an archaeological paradigm – that, by marking the modern conceptual system, refers it back to medieval theology. In this manner, secularization 'signs' modern concepts – similar to how a painter alters the value and meaning of a painting with a simple signature – by marking and transcending them to link back to their theological origins, all without creating entirely new concepts (2008: 77–8).

Having stated that – and before delving into the significance of the debate on Modernity and secularization – it is essential to emphasize that the term 'modern' is fundamentally empty, signifying nothing substantial. It is merely a contraction of the Latin expression *modus hodiernus* (with *hodiernus* deriving from *hodie*, meaning 'today'), which refers to 'the time of today', encompassing any time without specific characteristics that distinguish it from others. This emptiness of the term 'modern' has been acknowledged by many intellectuals, particularly those who, critical of the scientific-rationalist paradigms of Modernity, perceive this era as a thinly veiled continuity with other historical periods.

From this perspective, Weber argues that Modernity does not correspond to a specific time (as in Hegel's notion of immanentization or Marx's concept of capitalism) or to a critical stance (as suggested by Foucault). Instead, it represents an ongoing process of rationalization that originated with the secularization of Protestantism. Following Weber's assertion, intellectuals divided into two camps. The first group, including thinkers like Hans Blumenberg in his 1966 work *The Legitimacy of the Modern Age*, argued that Modernity is a distinct historical period that does not directly derive from its predecessors. In contrast, authors such as Karl Löwith, Eric Voegelin and Carl Schmitt, each in their own unique way, contended that Modernity represents a continuation of the medieval Christian era, with its transcendent structures still at work today, albeit under new immanent forms.

The debate regarding the legitimacy – or perhaps more accurately, the 'novelty' or 'specificity' – of Modernity is extraordinarily complex and cannot be fully detailed here. In the same way, I cannot present here the rich discussions related to the colonial dimension of Modernity, as the focus of this section pertains to the theological matrix of the modern State as conceived within the intellectual environment in which the classic political theology with a Schmittian profile was formed. In any case, I will briefly discuss the thesis of Modernity as a specific creation of the European colonial system in the section where I address decolonial political theologies. For now, it is worth pointing to the work of Ecuadorian philosopher Bolívar Echeverría (1941–2010), *The Modernity of the Baroque* (2000), in which he argues that among the various 'available' modernities – realist, romantic, classical and baroque – Latin America developed – or rather: 'was developed' as an object and not a subject – based on the latter version, which has undeniable theological foundations, especially in light of the Jesuit enterprise. In this perspective, Walter Mignolo's book *The Darker Side of Western Modernity* (2011) is also important, since the Argentine semiologist demonstrates that coloniality, which emerged during the modern era, is not merely a historical process but a pervasive and continuous structure of domination that sustains Western *potestas*. In fact, coloniality emerged during the Renaissance and the Enlightenment as Europeans colonized the Americas, building on the theological-political idea that Western civilization and Modernity represent the highest point of human history, an ideology propelled by Christian theology and now embraced by neoliberalism.

According to Agamben, the debate about the legitimacy of Modernity began with the publication of Karl Löwith's *World History and Salvation: the Theological Presuppositions of the Philosophy of History* in 1953. Löwith argues that both the philosophy of history in German idealism and the Enlightenment concept of progress are secularizations of Christian theological history and eschatology (Agamben 2011: 4–5). However, I contend that this 'debate' can be understood in a broader context, without explicitly referencing Löwith's work and the critical responses it elicited. My perspective encompasses authors and ideas that predate 1953, emerging from the Weimar cultural milieu, and adopting a critical stance toward Weber's and Schmitt's interpretations of secularization discussed in this section. Both of these interpretations have proven to be far more influential and pivotal in the history of thought than Löwith's arguments presented in 1953.

For the German philosopher and historian Hans Blumenberg (1920–96), Modernity represents a *novum* because it is an autonomous era, that is, a historical period characterized by its own metaphor, rooted in the Copernican revolution, which led to the self-affirmation of humans as *homo artifex*. In this way, individuals are seen as having emancipated themselves from religious perspectives, thereby gaining the ability to dominate reality and create their own scientific-rational world. This position was also shared by other significant figures, such as the Austrian jurist Hans Kelsen (1881–1973). In his later years, Kelsen wrote *Secular Religion*[5] to argue against the notion that Western science, philosophy and politics are merely heirs and continuators of earlier metaphysical thought, a thesis fervently defended by his former disciple, the conservative German philosopher Eric Voegelin (1901–85).

In his 1939 work *Political Religions*, Voegelin argues that totalitarian regimes are essentially political religions – though this does not imply they are political theologies – since both phenomena share the same ideal structure. He goes further to assert that secular religions – a term coined by the French sociologist Raymond Aron (1905–83)[6] – are false religions akin to Gnosticism, a medieval Christian heresy characterized by an absolute dualism between Good and Evil, as well as spirit and matter. Voegelin posits that the task of the intellectual committed to a 'new' science of politics is to unmask and dismantle these false religions, allowing the only true religion – that is, Christianity inspired by Platonic ideas – to reclaim its 'natural' role in guiding the West. However, it is important to note that Gnostic dualism stems not only from a radical interpretation of Christianity but also from Neoplatonic theories. Thus, Voegelin's grand 'mission' appears contradictory. Nonetheless, the focus here should not be on the reactionary or illogical aspects of Voegelin's theories – as Kelsen (2004) effectively points out when he states that there is nothing 'new' about them – but rather on the underlying perception that legitimizes them, according to which Modernity is a distorted version of the Middle Ages (and Antiquity) rather than a distinct new era.

In a more measured tone, the German philosopher and former disciple of Heidegger, Karl Löwith (1897–1973), afirms in his 1949 book *Meaning in History* that every philosophy of history rooted in the idea of progress – including the theories of Hegel and Marx – represents a secularization of the Judeo-Christian salvific message. He explains that the Heaven-Earth dyad, which encompasses immanence and transcendence, was secularized in Modernity into the present-future dyad. Notwithstanding, Modernity fails to acknowledge its theological-Christian foundation, leading to a repression of this heritage and resulting in a contradiction that is further exacerbated by Marxism. In this context, Löwith asserts that Marx's thought corresponds to the pinnacle of the paradoxical and futurocentric tendency of Modernity, as it proposes, through the idea of communism, a form of kingdom of God without God, or, if one prefers, an atheistic Christianity. In a very obscure manner, Marx (1968) identifies this concept in the third book of *The Capital* with communism, that is, the 'kingdom of freedom' ('*Reich der Freiheit*').

Löwith comments that this notion seems to evoke the ideas of the millenarian mystic Joachim of Fiore (1135–1202), who is considered the first philosopher of history. Joachim of Fiore perceived the course of events not as the cyclical recurrence of paganism, which characterized various Greek histories, but as the unfolding of a single history that culminates messianically in the Kingdom of God. It is through constructions like these that Marxists were able to displace theological categories such as salvation and redemption – rooted in the transcendent universe of the Middle Ages – into a temporal dimension associated with future communism. It is interesting to note that the heterodox Marxist philosopher Ernst Bloch (1885–1977) shares Karl Löwith's interpretation but, unlike Löwith, he views the Christian character of Marx's thought as a positive aspect. For Bloch, Marxism represents a form of Hegelian sublation (*Aufhebung*) – a movement that elevates while simultaneously preserving and cancelling an idea – rooted in original Christianity and its primitive communism. Without this Christian foundation, Bloch (1921, 1954–9) contends, Modernity risks descending into nihilism, thereby rendering the transformation of the world impossible.

According to Löwith, the passion for the future is a decisive factor characterizing modern secularization, influencing even those philosophers who critique this process, such as Nietzsche, with his obsession with the time to come, the 'Overman' (*Übermensch*), and so on. In fact, very few authors in the Western canon manage to escape this mechanism. One notable exception is Walter Benjamin. As we will explore, Benjamin views the future as nothing more than a pile of debris that the Messiah must suppress rather than continue to accumulate. Consequently, the messianic salvation envisioned by Benjamin does not occur in an indefinite future; it takes place in the present, in each insignificant and even trivial moment of the 'nowtime' (*Jetztzeit*), which serves as a small door through which the Messiah can enter (Benjamin 1991 [I]: 704).

At this point, it is important to note that it is not only Marxists who unconsciously employ a 'sacred' notion of history. Radicalizing Löwith's thesis, Agamben asserts that the Western concept of history is rooted in medieval theology. According to the Italian philosopher, the idea of history serves as a Trojan horse through which theology infiltrated the citadel of reason, unifying the notion of simple narration – the *historíai* (ἵστορῖαι) of the Greeks, exemplified by Herodotus' foundational work – with a substance that imbues it with a salvific meaning progressively revealed over time. It is no coincidence that the great historian Marc Bloch stated in his beautiful *Apology for History* that Christianity is a religion of historians (1993: 38).[7] In this view, the *Bible* is the history book *par excellence*, as it extends beyond the past to encompass the present and future, the latter ultimately culminating in the apocalypse. This final event signifies the end of history, marking the completion of the biblical narrative as time itself ceases and eternity begins.

In this manner, Christianity has led to the merging of history in both subjective and objective senses, meaning that history as a scientific discipline or historiography (*historia rerum gestarum*) and history as a collection of factual events (*res gestae*) are no longer differentiated (Agamben 2024a: 4–5). Evidence of this merging can be seen in the seemingly neutral concept of 'century', originally understood as a period of 100 years, which was gradually developed by Christian theologians and later adopted by 'secular' historians from the seventeenth century onward (Agamben 2024a: 9–18). Key figures in this evolution included Sextus Julius Africanus (third century), who used the six days of creation in *Genesis* to calculate a timeline of approximately six thousand years for the world; Dionysius Exiguus (470–544), who introduced the division of time into periods before and after the birth of Christ; and Matthias Flacius Illyricus (1520–75), who first employed the notion of 'century' (*centuriae*) in his *Ecclesiastica Historia, Integram Ecclesiae Christi Ideam Secundum Singulas Centurias*, a work written between 1559 and 1574 that presented the history of the Church according to distinct centuries.

It is essential to note the extreme arbitrariness of the concept of 'century', which presupposes a fixed number – 100, but it could be 60, 200, 1,001 or any other – to indicate a unit of epochal meaning. This assumption, which uncritically conflates notions of quantity and quality, clearly lacks a scientific or material basis. Nevertheless, historical science has adopted this concept, which should remain purely numerical, imbuing it with an almost metaphysical significance to the extent that specific disciplines have emerged to study particular centuries, each characterized by distinct traits, such as the 'baroque' seventeenth century and the 'positivist/scientific' nineteenth century. Evidently, other cultures established milestones and periods to mark time, such as the Olympics in ancient Greece; however, they maintained an awareness that these were merely arbitrary measurements. In contrast, driven by the desire to divide time based not only on the birth and the second coming of Christ but also to imbue it with meaning, Christian theologians developed the concept of 'century', which feels so familiar and 'rational' to us today. As a result, secular history is, constitutively and unconsciously, sacred history, since it is organized not only functionally but also meaningfully, understanding that a given portion of time signifies much more than mere duration, configuring itself as a unit of meaning. This represents a typically political-theological presupposition and, as such, was never problematized by the Greeks. Aristotle, in his *Poetics*, asserts that history is inferior to poetry because it creates nothing, being merely a narration (*diégese*, διήγησις) of what happened. History, concludes the severe Stagirite, serves only to recount what Alcibiades did, without evaluating whether those actions are good, bad, convenient, correct, unjust and so forth (*Poetics*, IX, 50).

From this standpoint, it is interesting to note, as Umberto Galimberti (2023) points out, that Christianity and science – this later, seemingly secular and free from religious irrationalism – share the same conception of time: the past is evil (original sin and pre-scientific ignorance), the present is hope (redemption and research), and the future is the realization of this hope (salvation and progress). Marx, as a good son of the secularized Christian tradition in the form of science, sees in the past social injustice, in the present the struggle against capital and in the future the communist society. Even Freud, despite his critique of all religions, unconsciously repeats the Christian temporal framework: the past is repression, the present is therapy and the future is healing. Everything is Christian in the West, Galimberti concludes, especially those dimensions that, unaware of the salvific historical process and the linearity they are immersed in, fail (or refuse) to comprehend this obviousness.

Returning to the discussion on the secularization debate – which now takes on new significance after clarifying the origins of the concept of 'century' – it is crucial to present Blumenberg's position in some detail. His views diverge significantly from those of Schmitt, Voegelin and Löwith, whose theses he considers mere historical substantialisms, presupposing a kind of immutability over time. Notwithstanding, Blumenberg's ideas are not simply a negation of political theology, nor is he merely an antipode of Schmitt, as many scholars suggest. In reality, Blumenberg's philosophy of history engages with both continuity and discontinuity across all historical epochs, dimensions that cannot be fully understood if we restrict ourselves to their own epochal self-interpretations. In this sense, the conception of Christianity as both a successor and continuator of Antiquity is simultaneously true and false. Likewise, the self-perception of Modernity as an era of total rupture with the medieval world contains elements of truth and falsehood. To grasp Blumenberg's sophisticated – and at times hermetic – position, we must explore his notion of reoccupation (*Umbesetzung*), which describes how various historical epochs seek to address the same fundamental questions. This can occur through providing new answers, adopting traditional responses, or, ultimately, by eliminating the questions altogether.[8] From this perspective, Modernity perceives itself as a period in which new answers are offered to longstanding questions with an intensity and novelty previously unseen. This dynamic would ensure the 'legitimacy' of Modernity and the relative autonomy of the political sphere in relation to the religious realm in our contemporary world.[9]

On the other hand, Blumenberg acknowledges that Modernity is unthinkable without medieval Christianity (1971: 27). However, he chooses to concentrate on the new structures that modern times established to address the central questions – political, ontological, metaphysical, religious, and so on – that emerge in all epochs, thus presenting itself as an unprecedented era that breaks away from the old and often disparaged Middle Ages. Blumenberg argues that the Middle Ages attempted to obscure its novelty in relation to Antiquity, viewing itself as a pure continuity, which he deems misleading. Inversely (but isomorphically), Modernity represses its connections to the Middle Ages, portraying itself as an absolute novelty, which is also inaccurate. Thus, much more than a denier of political theology, Blumenberg seems to defend a 'weak' version of this thesis, relativizing and complexifying Schmitt's unappealable and explosive sentence according to which all the key concepts of modern State theory are secularized theological constructs.

In fact, Carl Schmitt intervened early in the debate on Modernity through his concept of political theology, which posits that the medieval understanding of a creator God has been replaced by the modern conception of sovereignty. Similarly, the notion of miracle, representing a suspension of the laws of nature, finds its contemporary counterpart in the state of exception, which entails the suspension of legal statutes. However, this does not imply that the modern State is inherently religious.[10] On the contrary, Schmitt argues that, in its essence, the State can no longer be religious; thus, it must develop a political theology.

Notably, theological-political apparatuses do not possess religious content. Their significance lies in their ordering function – akin to that of ancient medieval theology – whereby they organize chaotic and conflicting social scenarios, creating islands of order amid a sea of disorder.

Considering that theological-political structures such as sovereignty, Constitution and state of exception can only create order in a provisional manner because it is constantly overcome by the entropy of a godless reality disintegrating into multiple and agonistic micronarratives, Schmitt recognizes that the role of political theology in Modernity is limited to the precarious legitimation of authority. This legitimacy functions more as a fragile form than as substantive content, necessitating continuous reaffirmation and reconstruction in a world that, since the emergence of the irreconcilable modern dissent exemplified by the religious wars of the sixteenth and seventeenth centuries, is inevitably stripped of an ultimate foundation and thus moves toward its own dissolution. Schmitt concludes by invoking Juan Donoso Cortés (1809–53), a nineteenth-century Spanish counter-revolutionary politician, suggesting that the choice lies between the violence of the dagger or that of the sword. Faced with the threat that the revolutionary and irreligious masses pose to order, it becomes essential to reinforce and sustain the sovereignty of the State.

As can be seen, Schmitt's political theology – arguably the most recognized and influential of the twentieth century – constitutes a discourse that encrypts *an-archy* while legitimizing sovereignty, the State and authority. These entities, although not divine, serve to perform God's ordering function, albeit imperfectly, thereby preventing society from descending into total violence and self-destruction, even through dictatorship and exceptional decisions. Indeed, as medieval theologians who distinguished between the kingdom and the government – that is, the Being (Father) and the praxis (Son) of God – recognized, the will manifest in decision-making is the apparatus that enables action and governance in the world, despite lacking any ontological foundation in Being. As Agamben articulates, '[the] will [*volontà*] can only entail the groundlessness of the praxis, that is, the fact that there is no foundation of acting in being' (2011: 55). Thus, it is significant that Schmitt grounded his functional political theology specifically in sovereign decision – that is, a dimension of the will – which lacks any ontological foundation and relies, in Schmitt's terms, on Nothingness (1996: 38).

The Schmittian model gained wide acceptance from the 1920s onward, even attracting Protestant and Catholic theologians such as Friedrich Gogarten (1934) and Karl Eschweiler (1931–2) to the Nazi orbit – a context in which

Schmitt himself was active from 1933 to 1938 – under the banner of 'theological-political studies'. Even today, while the Schmittian interpretation can no longer be regarded as the sole dominant perspective, it remains a significant entry point for political theologies focused on sovereignty, such as that of Paul W. Kahn (2011). According to Galli, the success of the political theology conceived by Carl Schmitt can be explained by the fact that it is more than a simplistic analogic device that aims to establish a substantial analogy between politics and religion. Instead, it is a theory of secularization – or, more precisely, a theory addressing the impossibility of total secularization upon which modern politics purports to rest. In this light, Schmitt's political theology allows for a radical critique of the modern project that naively assumes political-legal power to be a self-founded reality. On the contrary, Schmitt argues that it is Nothingness (*Nichts*) that lies at the origin of modern power, which is incapable of grounding itself in the divine order.

In summary, it can be concluded that Schmitt's political philosophy derives from the ontological premises he adopts, which, according to Michael Marder (2010), are based on a rejection of traditional metaphysics – it is not, in fact, a matter of asserting a simple continuity between the Middle Ages (and its constructs) and Modernity – and on the assumption of an existential and phenomenological stance that relates to a sharp perception of the lack of foundation, from which, for example, the completely empty concept of decision arises. The German jurist comes close to the notion of *an-archy* developed in this book, although he views it not as an opening of Being, but rather as an immanent risk of dissolution to be controlled, albeit very imperfectly, by the State. In this sense, Carlo Galli teaches:

> This is political theology in its proper sense: not the deduction of politics from theology, but the theory according to which modern politics – its concepts and institutions – preserves something of religion, emptying religion of its theological concepts without also overcoming those concepts (especially when it comes to the unity of order and its sovereign creation). It follows from this that the relationship between modern politics and theological tradition is twofold. On the one hand, modern politics is structured by the absence of foundational divine substance, and is therefore contrary to theology. On the other hand, modern politics reproduces theology's monistic ordering function, even if only in a formal-rational way. [. . .] Political theology, consequently, is not a theory of the theological foundation of politics, but of the historical and categorical context of the origin of the Modern and of the compulsions that dominate it. It

> is the horizon of the absence of transcendence in which modernity is given; and to the extent that it's able to allow for the emergence of the foundation of absence – the Void-of-Order – that is the unsaid and unthought of the Modern, it is a figure, or even the main figure, of 'concreteness' and of genealogy. (2015: 45–6)

In 1970, Schmitt published a sequel to his most famous work, titled *Political Theology II: The Legend of the Liquidation of All Political Theology*. This text serves as a polemical response to both Blumenberg and Erik Peterson, a German Protestant theologian who converted to Catholicism and was both a friend and rival of Schmitt. In his 1935 work *Monotheism as a Political Problem*, Peterson argued that a political theology akin to Schmitt's 1922 proposal was impossible. He contended that Christianity is not a true monotheism; rather, due to the dogma of the Trinity, it resembles a form of polytheism. Thus, Schmitt's functional analogy between the one sovereign power of the State and the one Christian God is called into question (1994c: 58–9). In another 1935 book, this time focused on angelology, Peterson asserts that the song of praise to God sung by angels and echoed by humans embodies the public and political essence of liturgy. This is evident in the terms *maiestas* and *rex* found in the *Te Deum* (1994a: 206–43). As noted in section 1.4.1, Peterson contends that only glory is political and bears no relation to the concept of sovereignty or to the correspondence – however functional – that Schmitt obstinately proposes between the authorities of Heaven and Earth.

Schmitt's response, which took thirty-five years to develop, is extremely confusing, characterized by sibylline theological arguments and ironies that resemble 'inside jokes', sometimes rendering it incomprehensible. Many scholars attribute this style to the German jurist's advanced age. Notwithstanding, from this challenging work emerges one final concept that is crucial for understanding the conclusion of Schmitt's theological-political theorizing: the *katéchon*. It originally refers to an eschatological figure that appears in the *Second Epistle to the Thessalonians*,[11] a dense messianic text in which Paul presents the *mysterium iniquitatis*, that is, the historical drama – this is the sense of the Greek *mystérion* (μυστήριον) for Paul – in which Evil must necessarily reveal itself in order to be defeated by Good at the end of times.

The term *katéchon* (κατέχον) is a neutral Greek participle meaning 'the one who delays' or 'the one who holds back'. In theological terms, the *katéchon* functions as a decelerator of the Messiah's coming, preventing the arrival of the Antichrist. In fact, Christ can only return – this time as judge rather than as victim – after the appearance and defeat of the Antichrist (Cacciari 2013; Monateri 2023). Therefore, without the Antichrist, there can be no second coming. It is the *katéchon* that directly blocks the Antichrist and, indirectly, the judging and apocalyptic Christ. In interpreting this obscure Pauline passage within a theological-political context, Schmitt claims that the *katéchon* is embodied in the figure of the State – historically represented by the Empire of the medieval Germanic kings – which slows the progression toward the end of times and the final judgement. This configuration ensures the continuity of the Christian Republic while postponing the arrival of the Antichrist, whom Paul literally calls 'the lawless one', the *ánomos* (ὁ ἄνομος). Therefore, the *katéchon* represents yet another manifestation of the (fragile) order that Schmitt believed should be established in the chaotic modern world, perfectly aligning with his conservative political theology (Meuter 1994: 212).

In turn, the anti-Semitic Catholic Erik Peterson interpreted the *katéchon* – defined as the 'restrainer' that prevents the arrival of the judging Christ – as the refusal of the chosen people, the Jews, to accept Jesus as the Messiah (1994c: 247). Thus, Peterson – who, unlike Schmitt, was a genuine theologian – argues that a cultic rationale, rather than a strictly political one, is what delays the second coming of Christ. Indeed, the Jews' denial of the Messiah, and consequently their rejection to glorify and encrypt power, effectively delays the final judgement. This interpretation can be understood, as we will see in subsection 2.1.3, in a theological-political key close to the thought of Jacob Taubes. In this context, the obstinate refusal of the Jews to recognize Jesus-Messiah and celebrate his glory is framed as evidence of the revolutionary character of the Jewish non-people, who obstruct the complete glorification and, consequently, the total encryption of the *an-archy* that is God.

However, there is an even more drastic and serious interpretation. As Agamben (2011: 16) notes, the seemingly hermetic ideas articulated by Peterson in the late 1920s took on a horrifying significance during the years of the extermination of the Jews by the Nazis, who, in their actions, may have unconsciously prepared the way for the coming of Christ by destroying the *katéchon* embodied in an entire people. Finally, there is a fourth possibility for understanding the mysterious Pauline passage, which can be interpreted in radical theological-political terms reminiscent of Benjamin as representing a final, decisive and bloody world revolution. Schmitt, of course, approaches this Benjaminian reading from a conservative and authoritarian perspective, viewing it as synonymous with disorder and apocalyptic-political chaos.

In summary, Schmittian political theology represents a desperate attempt to confront the entropy, indeterminacy and instability characteristic of the contemporary world, in which Schmitt sees a harmful manifestation of a planetary technique, echoing criticisms of Modernity similar to those of Martin Heidegger and Ernst Jünger. In this sense, Schmitt seeks to oppose the absurd desire for self-representation inherent in modern technique. He does so either by highlighting the structural analogies between religion and politics, without which establishing an order seems impossible, as articulated in his 1922 text; or, in a more resigned manner, by asserting that the State itself must function as a decelerator, a *katéchon* capable of moderating the inevitable, all-encompassing process of technical domination, as proposed in his 1970 text. Both attempts ultimately failed, and with them the possibility of a Schmittian political theology in our time, which is so thoroughly dominated by the automatisms of technique that it no longer requires any foundational justification.

In this context, technique is no longer just a tool; it has become an entire world. Yet, it is a mute world, devoid of meaning. When a quantitative reality develops intensely, it inevitably brings about qualitative changes. For instance, a five-degree rise in global temperature would be enough to completely alter the Earth's landscape. This is precisely what has happened with technique, as it was initially a means (like money) to achieve specific goals, but today it has freed itself from any purpose other than its own expansion, turning everything into tools or available resources (*Bestand*). Technique does not make decisions, think, save or condemn. Technique simply technicizes. When asked what technique is, Heidegger (1981b) provided no definition, only stating: technique works. In fact, technique itself is incapable of grasping the significance of the archaeological problem concerning the origin of order, which Schmitt previously framed in terms of exceptional decision-making but which is now eclipsed by the pure contingency of a world in which, as Agamben (1995) notes, the exception has become the paradigm of government. Indeed, according to Galli, it is not indeterminacy but contingency that prevails in contemporary times, rendering Schmittian political theology increasingly irrelevant:

> Thus it is that Schmitt's final published words on political theology amount to a death certificate. Neither as decision, nor as a modern *katechon* of modern dynamics, is political theology able to overcome technics and its mobilizing power – a power that destroys the concrete stability of the State and every possible value and sense that once accrued to the concepts of authority,

> legitimacy, transcendence, form, relationship with tradition (and also, it would seem, to the concepts of 'political' and of 'politics'). The triumph of the logics of modernity, uncontrolled in their automatism, signals the end of political theology and of the very possibility of political thinking, as Schmitt understands it. He admits that his categories do not give him the power to understand the age of technics, that is to say, the age of automatism and, at the same time, of disorder. (2015: 56–7)

Carl Schmitt himself appears to agree with this stark assessment. In a letter to Galli dated 7 November 1979, Schmitt asserts that, as a theological-political epoch, Modernity is over: 'this epoch has come to an end' ('*diese Epoche zu Ende* [*ist*]') (Galli 1996: 912). He seems to have recognized that his political theology, although merely functional, was no longer equipped to address the senselessness of technique, which tends to reduce every qualitative problem to a quantitative one, ultimately leading to the replacement of politics with economics. Agamben, as discussed in section 3.1, adopts this thesis, contending that the world we inhabit is no longer governed by a political theology – whether material or functional – but rather by an economic theology that, far from embodying any political rationality demanding sovereignty, instead produces glory to encrypt the Nothing, the *an-archy* of God. While this conception may appear apolitical, I argue that it remains a political stance, albeit one distinct from Schmitt's conception of sovereign politics. It aligns more closely with Peterson's understanding of power as rooted in rituals of acclamation and glorification once directed toward God and now aimed at the idols prescribed by the spectacular society. Such an idea has nothing to do with the outdated structural isomorphism between the earthly sovereign and the celestial one. Thus, political theology is far from extinct. Only its Schmittian version has reached exhaustion; on the other hand, the empty and self-justifying political-economic theology of glory perfectly reflects the epochal poverty of our world.

By way of conclusion, we can cite Heinrich Meier's reading, according to which the analogy between political and theological concepts put forward by Schmitt is nothing but a legend (2006: 78). It is true that Schmitt did not develop a comprehensive theory of political theology in Modernity; he merely presented his explosive thesis in 1922 and illustrated it with only two significant examples related to the structural correspondence between sovereignty/God and exception/miracle. As mentioned, he revisited the theme in 1970 to explore the concept of the *katéchon* with even greater hermeticism. However, it seems excessive to characterize this as a 'legend', considering that Schmitt's work, despite its difficult and limited nature, has significantly influenced twentieth-century political philosophy.

Indeed, one cannot deny the significance of Schmitt's political theology, which was so profound that, for many scholars it seemed to be the only possible political theology, influencing a wide array of disciplines beyond political philosophy. A notable example is found in Ernst Kantorowicz's seminal 1957 work, *The King's Two Bodies: A Study in Medieval Political Theology*. Through a comprehensive analysis of numerous historical documents, Kantorowicz posits that the absolute monarchs of sixteenth-century England possessed two bodies: one carnal and one mystical. The latter, deemed immortal, serves as a precursor to the modern concept of the nation-State. Earlier, in 1951, Kantorowicz had already acknowledged the sacred and religious dimensions of the State, without which the traditional notion of sacrificing life for one's country (*pro patria mori*) would be untenable. This notion was one he had uncritically embraced while serving alongside the nationalist *Freikorps* against the communist revolution in Germany in 1919. Later, Kantorowicz had the opportunity to reevaluate this position when he became a target of the Nazi regime due to his Jewish heritage, which prompted him to emigrate to the United States. There, he would establish the most significant phase of his academic career.

2.1.2. Political theology, messianism and violence in Walter Benjamin

With Schmitt and his followers, the theological-political discourse became closely linked to a conservative and authoritarian defence of sovereignty, characteristic of right-wing and, at times, extreme right-wing political positions. However, even during Schmitt's era, revolutionary and libertarian political theologies emerged, notably those suggested – I say 'suggested' rather than 'developed' because they are even more cryptic than Schmitt's – by Walter Benjamin (1892–1940) and Jacob Taubes (1923–79), two Jewish philosophers who were complex figures, both in their personal lives and in their intellectual contributions.

Benjamin is recognized as one of the most intriguing and unconventional thinkers of the twentieth century, navigating seamlessly through politics, aesthetics, literature, history, philosophy and other disciplines, while never completely departing from his theological roots.[12] This 'non-specialist' approach enabled him to engage, in a radically new and powerful manner, with several themes that have become central today, such as violence and the critique of bourgeois historiography. Nonetheless, Benjamin himself acknowledged that his thought is fully immersed in theology, comparing it to blotting paper soaked with ink. He added, however, that if he were to simply follow the blotting paper, nothing would remain of what he has written (1991 [I–3]: 1235). This suggests that his work cannot be solely equated with theology; instead, it utilizes theological concepts in an innovative – and decidedly heterodox – way. Indeed, since his early writings, Benjamin showed a great interest in religions in general and in the Kabbalah – an intellectual tradition of Jewish mysticism – in particular, which intensified over time and surfaced in works that, while often unfinished, were remarkably insightful. These works presented alternative possibilities for interpreting political theology, exemplified by *Capitalism as Religion* (1921), which I analyse in section 3.1, and by the *Theological-Political Fragment*, a concise yet exceptionally complex sketch from the early 1920s, possibly even originating in 1919.

In the *Fragment*, Benjamin asserts that theocracy has nothing to do with politics, thereby separating the sacred from the profane order. The latter is paradoxically presented as both decadent and a potential site of happiness, as true happiness can only arise with the dissolution of the profane through the advent of the messianic kingdom. The immanence and contingency of profane life suggest that as history approaches its end, the possibility of salvation emerges. Benjamin contends that the mundane and the profane must be considered together – in this synthesis, he perceives a form of *restitutio in integrum* – but not in the way that Christians do, who derive from this union the unacceptable idea of individual immortality. For Benjamin, the mundane and the profane converge in an eternity of decay, a time of the end that never truly concludes. Only this eternally decaying mundane dimension aligns with the essence of messianic happiness, representing a struggle against the linear progression of time in favour of a more authentic temporal experience, a theme that will be further elaborated in his 1940 theses.

In his youthful fragment from the 1920s, Benjamin already critiques historicist and social-democratic attempts – but also, in a certain way, the Schmittian ones – to reconcile history, continuity and immortality, thereby venerating the self-justifying mediation that Schmitt, in his nihilistic Catholicism, referred to as Modernity. In contrast, Benjamin proposes that salvation resides in the complete lack of justification of the profane, in the contingency and innocence of a world that transcends Good and Evil, rendering it beyond judgement and, consequently, devoid of guilt. Benjamin suggests that salvation consists of neither wanting it nor conceptualizing it, advocating for the abandonment of finite self-justification so that happiness merges with the absolute immediacy where the mundane and the messianic intersect. In Benjamin's words, not always – or almost never – comprehensible:

> Only the Messiah himself completes all history, in the sense that he alone redeems, completes, creates its relation to the messianic. For this reason, nothing that is historical can relate itself, from its own ground, to anything messianic. Therefore, the Kingdom of God is not the telos of the historical dynamic; it cannot be established as a goal. From the standpoint of history, it is not the goal but the terminus [*Ende*]. Therefore, the secular order cannot be built on the idea of the Divine Kingdom, and theocracy has no political but only a religious meaning. To have repudiated with utmost vehemence the political significance of theocracy is the cardinal merit of Bloch's *Spirit of Utopia*. The secular order should be erected on the idea of happiness. The relation of this order to the messianic is one of the essential teachings of the philosophy of history. [. . .] The secular, therefore, though not itself a category of this kingdom, is a decisive category of its most unobtrusive approach. For in happiness all that is earthly seeks its downfall, and only in happiness is its downfall destined to find it. (2006: 305)

According to Agamben, the messianic in Benjamin corresponds to the annihilation of profane time at each present moment, rather than in a historical-chronological sense. As such, no politics can be grounded in the messianic (2024a: 35), an idea that stands in stark contrast to Schmitt's views. Therefore, theocracy and politics are unrelated, since theocracy pertains to an experience that is, quite literally, otherworldly, indicating a direct governance by God, devoid of human powers, institutions and intermediary agents. Nonetheless, throughout his work, Benjamin emphasizes the connection between theology – and not theocracy – and politics, invoking the extraordinarily complex figure of the Messiah, who serves as an allegory for the revolution that could lead to communism. This suggests a distinctive and paradoxical type of political theology that flirts with theocracy understood as *an-archy*, that is, an absence of human governance powerful enough to bring an end to all political theology, at least in the Schmittian sense. Thus, only political theology has the potential to destroy political theology itself.

Unlike orthodox Marxists, Benjamin argues that the socialist revolution does not depend solely on objective factors, elaborate plans or an enlightened vanguard to lead it. In his 1940 theses *On the Concept of History*, he criticizes these prerequisites as stemming from a bourgeois methodology that interprets history as continuous progress, where each stage logically follows from the previous one. However, if we approach history from the perspective of the tradition of the oppressed, we do not observe progress but rather an accumulation of horrors. This is vividly illustrated in the much-cited ninth thesis, in which the angel of history appears. Turning his gaze to the past, the angel perceives in the place where others see progress as a chain of events, 'one single catastrophe which keeps piling wreckage upon wreckage and hurls it in front of his feet' (1968: 257). It is no coincidence that Benjamin selected Paul Klee's unsettling and, for some, ugly *Angelus Novus* to symbolize his angel of history, as it is a painting devoid of perspective – hence, lacking in progress. According to Georges Didi-Huberman (2018: 175), Benjamin's angel of history might also have been inspired by a relief by Andrea Pisano representing hope. Benjamin describes it in *One-Way Street* as follows: '*Florence, Baptistry.* – On the portal the "Spes" by Andrea de Pisano. Sitting, she helplessly stretches her arms for a fruit that remains beyond her reach. And yet she is winged. Nothing is more true' (1979: 83).

Against the progressive historiographical perspective (*historia rerum gestarum*) that prevents even Marxists from recognizing history (*res gestae*) as an open field of disputes where nothing is settled definitively, and where there are no historical 'laws' of progress, Benjamin invokes the allegory of the Messiah. In this context, the messianic event conceives time not as a homogeneous and empty dimension but as an experimental terrain accessible to human revolutionary action. At any moment, the Messiah can enter the world through the narrow gate of revolution, as articulated in appendix B of thesis 18, which concludes Benjamin's final text (1991 [I]: 704). In this way, it is the historicist bourgeois conception of time that hinders revolutionaries from enacting genuine revolutions, as they perceive time as a linear progression from the past to the future, passing through the present and resulting in a form of chronological evolution. In contrast, Benjamin argues that history does not exhibit development; rather, it consists of a series of opportune moments (*kairós*) in which everything is perpetually at stake. As Hebrew eschatology suggests, these moments always represent opportunities for the new – specifically, for the emergence of the Messiah – who stands in opposition to *Chrónos*, the time of progress that ultimately only repeats itself.

Building on this reflection, the concept of *Jetztzeit* (nowtime) in Walter Benjamin emerges, which resonates with the idea of *hô nýn kairós* (ὁ νῦν καιρός), central to the messianic argument in Paul's *Letter to the Romans*. Although these ideas arise from distinct contexts, they share an understanding of time not as linear or continuous, indicating the possibility of an interruption in the flow of history. Benjamin's *Jetztzeit* marks a moment of crisis and potential revelation, when the present is no longer seen as a continuation of the past, but rather as a temporality capable of radically reconfiguring history. According to Benjamin, the nowtime can rescue an oppressed past by projecting itself toward a future of liberation. It thus represents a theological-political chrono-logic that is neither linear nor teleological, but disruptive. Similarly, Paul's conception of *hô nýn kairós* (literally, 'the instant of now') refers to the opportune moment for a divine intervention that does not follow the laws of chronological time, but is, on the contrary, unforeseen and decisive, opening up the possibility of salvation within the continuum of human time. *Kairós* is a type of divine window within historical time, a moment of messianic revelation that interrupts the course of history with the coming of Christ. Thus, both Benjamin's *Jetztzeit* and Paul's *hô nýn kairós* share an understanding of time that goes beyond the simple succession of moments. Both point to a time lived in an absolute present, one that carries the potential for a break with the past and a radical transformation of the future, whether in the sense of redeeming an oppressive past, as in Benjamin, or in establishing a new regime of salvation, as in Paul's thought. These frameworks emphasize the urgency of a moment of intervention that, by subverting the continuity of history, points to a new beginning, a new 'now'.

In addition to the angel of history and the Messiah, another notable theological-political figure invoked by Benjamin is the hunchbacked dwarf mentioned in the first of his theses. This figure remains concealed within a supposed automaton that consistently wins chess games in the name of 'scientific' historical materialism. Thus, what appears to be a secular Marxist thought is, in reality, merely a more palatable manifestation of the small and grotesque theology embodied by the hunchback:

> The story is told of an automaton constructed in such a way that it could play a winning game of chess, answering each move of an opponent with a countermove. A puppet in Turkish attire and with a hookah in its mouth sat before a chessboard placed on a large table. A system of mirrors created the illusion that this table was transparent from all sides. Actually, a little hunchback who was an expert chess player sat inside and guided the puppet's hand by means of strings. One can imagine a philosophical counterpart to this device. The puppet called 'historical materialism' is to win all the time. It can easily be a match for anyone if it enlists the services of theology, which today, as we know, is wizened and has to keep out of sight. (Benjamin 1968: 253)

Through this disturbing and evocative allegory, Benjamin alludes to the construction (left unfinished) of a Jewish and revolutionary political theology that diverges significantly from Schmitt's Catholic and conservative perspective.[13] In fact, while Schmitt's political theology emphasizes an appeal to form, advocating for the imposition of order on a chaotic world, Benjamin's political theology, rooted in the deepest principles of Judaism, seeks to explore the formless, the 'un-mediated', a reality that can never be adequately represented, much like the God of the Hebrews, who, unlike the Christian God, lacks a corporeal form. The most significant implication of this distinction is that Benjamin's political theology does not focus on the 'kathekontic' maintenance of the existing world but instead directs attention toward its destruction through a socialist-messianic revolution. To this end, Benjamin appropriates, in a profanatory and radical manner, one of Schmitt's central theological-political concepts: the state of exception (*Ausnahmezustand*).

According to Schmitt's well-known postulate, the sovereign is the one who decides on the state of exception (1996: 13). This means that the sovereign, by positioning himself outside law and order, creates law and order from a normative void, as there is no ontological foundation for politics in Modernity, an idea elaborated in the previous subsection. This situation gives rise to the paradox extensively examined by Agamben, whereby the sovereign, existing outside the law, determines what the law includes and excludes, thus constructing a dialectic between order and exception, law and violence, norm and anomie. Contemporary societies, in this view, are condemned to this dialectic, lacking the transcendence characteristic of earlier eras. Benjamin's perspective is quite different. As he states in his eighth thesis, the political-legal exception – crucial for Schmitt because it manifests as the sovereign decision capable of functioning as a *katéchon* – does not constitute a true exception. Instead, it merely reveals and reinforces a historical constant: the rule according to which oppressors always triumph over the oppressed, a situation in which even the dead are not safe, as Benjamin adds in the second thesis.[14] To overcome this historical constant, it is essential to establish an effective state of exception (*wirklicher Ausnahmezustand*)[15] capable of achieving something unprecedented, that is, dethroning the masters of this world who have institutional politics and law on their side. The eighth thesis articulates this idea as follows:

> The tradition of the oppressed teaches us that the 'state of emergency' in which we live is not the exception but the rule. We must attain to a conception of

> history that is in keeping with this insight. Then we shall clearly realize that it is our task to bring about a real state of emergency, and this will improve our position in the struggle against Fascism. (1968: 257)

As noted, the effective state of exception that Benjamin refers to in the aforementioned thesis can only be realized through the coming of the Messiah, a figure that Benjamin associates with the socialist revolution. In a dense and fascinating youthful text published in 1921, *On the Critique of Violence*, Benjamin articulates an even more radical position, emphasizing the necessity of a pure, non-state and non-legal violence capable of creating space for new forms of sociability. This type of violence is purposeless and unjustified, in stark contrast to the political-legal violence of the oppressors embodied in Schmitt's sovereign exception. While some scholars argue that Benjamin's stance leans toward nihilism and anarchism, I find it to be distinctly Jewish-apocalyptic and, consequently, theological-political.

Benjamin begins his essay by asserting that violence – which is both 'authority' and 'power', according to the polysemic German word *Gewalt*, derived from the verb *walten*, meaning 'to be worth', 'to have strength'' – serves as the absolute means of law, appearing both in its dominant and so-called 'progressive' forms. Law is not defined by any value-based content – such as justice, equality, inequality or freedom – but rather by its means, that is, violence, which it monopolizes and does not share with any other social order, such as religion or ethics. In this context, the various 'philosophies of law', whether positivist or grounded in natural law, converge in their justification of law through its violent nature. This violence reveals itself in two distinct moments: the violence that establishes law (arbitrary violence, *schaltende Gewalt*) and the violence that maintains law (administered violence, *verwaltete Gewalt*) (Benjamin 1991 [II]: 189). Together, these comprise the category of mythical violence, which Benjamin contrasts with the concept of pure violence (*reine Gewalt*).

Much has been debated regarding why Benjamin intertwines the dimensions of myth, law and violence, a question, truth be told, which he does not clarify in his intricate 1921 essay. Nevertheless, this connection appears relatively simple (and brilliant) in its obscured obviousness. Legal violence, whether it serves to establish or maintain order, is mythical not only because it imposes guilt upon the living, echoing the Greek conception of myth, but also because it unfolds in a narrative form. Mythical violence is, therefore, a self-narrating force that justifies and legitimizes itself, ultimately degrading the originally divine and creative essence of language. As a result, it manifests as idolatrous violence, namely, a violence that seeks to usurp the role of God. In this sense, Agamben is correct in explaining that the foundation of violence is the violence of the foundation (1982: 132–3), that is, violence flows from the *arkhé* that imprints its iron law on Western metaphysics and, as will be seen with Heidegger, finds its highest point and simultaneously its epochal fulfilment in nihilistic technique.

The law employs its idolatrous and argumentative violence to the extent that it constructs complex narratives to justify itself, a dirty job that all legal practitioners do, from judges in their rulings to professors in their writings, from lawyers in their petitions to police officers in their reports. The only escape from this fatal logic is to employ a violence that does not narrate, one that is neither justified nor legitimized. In Benjamin's words, this is a violence that simply destroys and, being deadly without being bloody, exceeds legal violence, always 'rational', that is, argumentative and mythical. In contrast, pure violence is non-legal, non-institutional and non-argumentative. As Benjamin says, using the theological-political lexicon that is essential to him, we then have *divine* violence, which is a synonym for pure violence. It is neither a means to any end nor does it seek to justify or legitimize any reality or value, as it simply strikes without bloodshed (Benjamin 1991 [II]: 200). In contrast to the idolatrous violence of myth, pure violence opens up a new time and a new kingdom devoid of law. As will be discussed in section 3.1, the theme of idolatry recurs in Benjamin's thought, as he perceives capitalism as an idolatrous religion akin to the idolatrous violence that shapes law. Both capitalism and law aspire to usurp the role of God, who, in Benjamin's framework, is not the Christian God of love but a God of vengeance and the sword, a potent allegory for the revolution to be led by the oppressed classes.

Benjamin's characterization of pure violence has always been contentious, leading to numerous interpretations,[16] some of which are utterly unacceptable. A notable example is the reading offered by Derrida (1989–90), who posits that the concept of pure violence articulated by Benjamin in 1921 anticipates the violence of the Nazi concentration camps in the 1940s, which killed without shedding blood. Despite the excessive hermeticism of Benjamin's text, there is no justification for Derrida's grotesque interpretation, which is constructed entirely outside the temporal and social contexts that shaped Benjamin's work. To grasp this, it is crucial to remember that the 1921 essay was written in the aftermath of the failed German communist revolution of 1919, during which its leaders, Rosa Luxemburg and Karl Liebknecht, were brutally murdered by the *Freikorps* supported by the social-democratic government.

The context of Benjamin's text is shaped by the social tragedy that followed Germany's defeat in the First World War, during which one of his close friends – the poet Fritz Heinle (1894–1914) – took his own life, leaving a profound impact on the young Berliner. At this time, Benjamin found himself intellectually aligned with anarchism and radical thinkers like Georges Sorel (1847–1922). Thus, his article can be seen as both a dialogue with and a deepening of Sorel's radical theses, particularly those fervently expressed in his 1908 work, *Reflections on Violence*. In this environment of pervasive and total violence, it was inconceivable for Benjamin to envision an escape from the law that was not itself violent, even though, and this seems to be his most significant innovation, it takes the form of non-juridical violence, i.e., an immediate, non-medial and non-instrumental form of violence.

As I have argued elsewhere (Matos 2016; Matos and Matos 2023), Benjamin's concept of pure violence becomes significantly clearer when considered in light of two other key works. The first is *On Language as Such and on the Language of Man*, of 1916 (1991 [II]: 140–57). In this dense early essay, Benjamin outlines his understanding of language, asserting that, in its pure form, language cannot be viewed as a mere instrument or means to an end, given that the spiritual essence communicates *as* language and not *through* language. Roberto Esposito has aptly noted that Benjamin conceives of language not as a neutral instrument that conveys meaning in a neat, symmetrical and horizontal manner as, for instance, Jürgen Habermas' theory of communicative action would suggest (Esposito 2012: 200–1). For Benjamin, all human language – unlike divine language, where naming and being coincide – is inherently imperfect and carries within it an incommunicable rest. He challenges the assumption that everything is fully sayable within an unlimited horizon of communication, asserting that there are things that are literally unspeakable, and perhaps these unspeakable things are the most decisive. Nonetheless, in the 1916 essay at least, Benjamin does not fall into the opposite extreme of a mystical nihilism of silence and total unspeakability. On the contrary, it is the unspeakability itself – an ever-present rest within language – that, when communicating, communicates itself. Language does not communicate by establishing an intermediary relationship between subjects but rather in itself, communicating not a specific content but a *pure communicability*. This communicability is an opening of its pure linguistic being, which is both unspeakable and undecidable, something that is far beyond the rationalizing games typical of modern thought founded by Descartes.

In its pure (*reine*) sense, language communicates *in itself*, being the means (*Medium*) of communication. This stands in stark contrast to the bourgeois conception, which views the intermediary (*Mittel*) of communication as the word, a sign that points toward an object (the thing) and a recipient (the human being). According to Benjamin's allegory, the lost pure language known to Adam and Eve was non-separating, existing as a pure immediacy in which there was no distance between words and things, naming and being. Building on these ideas, the concept of pure violence becomes more comprehensible: it is pure because, like pure language, it has no instrumental purpose. Indeed, pure violence does not aim to achieve any specific end; it is, in fact, an expression of the immediate – that is, unmediated, non-medial – force that interrupts the catastrophe reigning in the existing order. Both pure language and violence are *means without end*;[17] they are more akin to an atmosphere, an 'environment' (*Medium*), rather than a 'through' (*Mittel*). In other words, it is not *through* pure violence that current law can be deposed. Pure violence is already, *in itself*, the deposition of law. Therefore, we can see that Benjamin does not seek to deny violence per se, but rather the law that monopolizes and encrypts it through state forms that present themselves as civilized and rational. For Benjamin, pure violence operates outside the constraints of institutionalized norms, revealing the iniquity inherent in law's very structure and, in doing so, enacting a rupture with the legal order.

The second decisive text for understanding the theological-political proposal presented in the 1921 essay and further radicalized in the 1940 theses is a brief – but profoundly impactful – essay titled *The Destructive Character* (1991 [IV]: 396–8), written in 1931. This text marks a moment when Benjamin contemplated suicide, an idea he later abandoned, though it continued to haunt him.[18] In *The Destructive Character*, Benjamin explores a form of violence that does not aim to construct, legitimize or justify anything, but rather seeks to open up space. This violence is not driven by vengeance or any negative emotion; it destroys not out of hatred but by anticipating the new paths that will emerge through destruction. This indifference – or rather, this impersonality – is what is truly divine about the destructive character. Benjamin seems acutely aware of the paradox inherent in the messianic revolution he proposes: those who carry it out and seek to create a new world cannot fully partake in it. In effect, revolutionaries are subjectively shaped by the corrupt world they wish to overcome; they are its inevitable fruits and products. The very hatred and violence that fuel their revolutionary efforts are born out of their intimate relationship with the world they seek to dismantle.

In this perspective, as indicated in section 1.4.3, a comparison with language can be instructive. When we begin to learn a completely new language, it is inevitable that we will initially try to understand it through the lens of our native tongue or other we are already familiar with. However, just as to truly master a new language we must reach a point where we abandon the model of our native language and begin to think – and even dream – in the language that was once foreign, in the realm of revolutions it becomes necessary, at a certain stage, to renounce all the references, habits, institutions and forms of subjectivation that belong to the regime we seek to overcome. As I have already mentioned, the young Agamben (2009) identifies in this circumstance – the need to completely discard the old in order to establish the new – the solution to the enigma of pure violence, which then appears as an act of self-suppression: pure is the violence that, to make room for what is coming, suppresses itself, because it recognizes that it is itself a product of the old world. There is an undecidable paradox in this idea because 'the new is in the new, precisely because it is indescribable, which means that the new in the new is precisely the absurdity of wanting to explain it' (Flusser 2010: 165). Nevertheless, the act of self-suppression suggested by Agamben is not necessarily synonymous with suicide – as Benjamin may have considered when writing *The Destructive Character*, which at that time may have served as his philosophical 'testament' – but rather with a sacrifice of the old so that the new may be born, which points to a theological-political reading that is at once messianic and apocalyptic— and this, in fact, constitutes Benjamin's true testament, materialized in 1940 in the theses *On the Concept of History*.

2.1.3. Political theology and apocalyptics in Jacob Taubes

The field of apocalyptic thought is central to the work of the Austrian Jewish philosopher Jacob Taubes (1923–87), a fascinating and enigmatic figure who, despite writing little, left behind a legacy of profound ideas. He passed away dictating his final, complex and brilliant seminar titled *The Political Theology of Paul*.[19] Taubes contends that the political theology of sovereignty cannot be simply denied. Rather, it must be brought to light as a critique of power, a position that clearly extends far beyond Schmitt's own project. In this context, and not without a touch of irony, Taubes asserts that he is neither a theologian nor a moralist but, rather, a historian concerned with the political potential embedded in theological metaphors. Schmitt, on the other hand, he argues, is preoccupied with uncovering the theological potential inherent in legal concepts (Taubes 2007: 84).

According to Taubes, the secret core that links theology and politics is rooted in power, such that only by inverting its universal principle – which separates rulers from the ruled – can Schmitt's political theology, centred on the concept of sovereignty, be overcome. This inversion, which Taubes interprets as the advent of *parousía* (παρουσία) and the fulfilment of the law through its deactivation, can be understood as a *sui generis* form of the decryption of power. Prior to this inversion, Taubes states, the critique of the theological element embedded in politics is not only legitimate but also necessary (1996: 258).

At the end of a letter in which Taubes ambiguously praises Schmitt – a letter that, incidentally, was copied and distributed by a vain Schmitt to his admirers – he suggests the existence of human relationships that transcend and surpass the law, thus fulfilling it in a certain sense. These relationships involve love, mercy and forgiveness, understood in a 'real' and not 'sentimental' manner (Taubes 2007: 178). From this perspective, Taubes' works serve not only as a potent antidote to Schmitt's counter-revolutionary political theology but also as a demonstration that there are alternative ways of engaging with theology and politics. In doing so, they offer valuable insights for constructing a messianic thought dedicated to overcoming the separations, hierarchies and encrypted forms of power encapsulated in *potestas*.

To structure his particular political theology, Taubes reconstructs the figure of Paul of Tarsus not in the classical terms of authors such as Alain Badiou (1998), who sees him as an apostle of Christian universalism battling against Jewish exclusivism. On the contrary, the Paul presented by Taubes is a vehement critic of the universalism characteristic of the Roman Empire, denouncing the emptiness of all human power. According to Paul interpreted by Taubes, power resides solely in God, and any attempts to ground secular politics in the theocratic realm are illegitimate, as the latter bears no connection to the mundane world. For Taubes, Paul's critique of secular power is not a negation of the world itself but a rejection of any human power that seeks to stand in for divine authority, especially when it attempts to encrypt itself in law or institutionalized forms of sovereignty.

In this same horizon, in his 1947 doctoral thesis entitled *Western Eschatology*, the only major work published by Taubes during his lifetime, he presents the Jewish people, as spoken of by Paul, as a 'non-people' who evoke a dimension devoid of sovereignty and territory. For this very reason, the Jewish 'non-people' is a symbol of a different kind of universal. The Jews, in Taubes' view, represent a radically different type of people, one that transcends traditional conceptions of national or religious identity. Rather than being a primitive or exclusivist sect bound by a covenant with Yahweh, the Judaism embody a self-negating figure that challenges all forms of heteronomous or externally imposed power. For Taubes, this position is not a rejection of identity per se, but a critique of sovereignty, territory and the structures that define they.

In other words, the Jewish people, as Paul presents them, symbolize a movement that rejects institutional politics and religious hierarchies, pointing instead to a form-of-life that exists beyond the conventional structures of power and authority. This interpretation emphasizes a radical discontinuity with traditional models of political and religious organization, highlighting a community that exists in tension with the structures of sovereignty, law and domination. For Taubes, this radical form-of-life embodies a messianic potential, wherein the true fulfilment of the promise to Israel lies not in the establishment of a sovereign State or in territorial power but in the transformation of time itself, opening the way for a new order that transcends the current world of mundane power.

At this point, a reading of messianic time as a zone of indistinction between the 'time of the end' and the 'end of time' is essential, as presented by Agamben in his important book *The Time That Remains* (2000). In Agamben's analysis, messianic time does not simply refer to a linear, future event but rather to a disruption of the temporal order itself. It is a moment where the boundaries between history and eternity, temporal and timeless, become blurred, creating a dimension of a *rest* where the 'end' is not a final conclusion but a potential for a radical transformation. This concept of messianic time challenges the conventional understanding of temporality as a continuous progression towards a predetermined end, instead opening up the possibility for new modes of existence and a different kind of political organization. Agamben's interpretation of messianic time emphasizes the tension between the end of a historical epoch and the arrival of something radically new, making his contribution a crucial resource for understanding the theological-political implications of messianism, a theme of great significance to Taubes.

In fact, Taubes (1991) concludes, Israel represents the restless, disruptive force within universal history. Unlike other civilizations, which are anchored in space and territory, Israel, as a people without State and territory – at least during the period Taubes addresses – is fundamentally connected to time. The promise nurtured by the Jews will, therefore, be fulfilled only with the arrival of the messianic event, a turning point capable of inaugurating a new way of experiencing temporality. For Taubes, the messianic rupture is not merely a theological concept but a profound political gesture that defies the structures of territorial sovereignty, pointing toward a radical transformation of human history.

Taubes' concept of 'non-people' bears a striking resemblance to the notion of *multitude* articulated by philosophers Michael Hardt and Antonio Negri (2004), as both formations involve a political index of revolt against the sovereign One. Despite the significant differences in their intellectual traditions, these concepts share a common commitment to a radical rejection of the transcendent bond that encrypts, grounds and makes mundane political power possible. In this respect, Taubes, in conversation with Herbert Marcuse (1898–1979) and other scholars, emphasized that the possibility of a free society is increasingly manifest in ways that are: (1) characterized more by rupture than continuity; (2) defined more by negation than affirmation or reformism; and (3) expressed more through difference than progress (Taubes 1980: 87–8). As can be seen, these three characteristics refer directly to what the theory of the encryption of power calls the hidden people, which can be understood as the current form of the non-people conceived by Taubes based on the historical experience of the Jewish people before they were overcoded as a Sovereign People in the context of Israeli Zionism. Since the emergence of the State of Israel and, especially today, thanks to the deepening of its genocidal tendencies translated into the will to exterminate the hidden Palestinian people, the exceptional and sovereign element of the land erases the contingent and infinite dimension of time that previously characterized the Jew as a hidden people. In this way, the hidden Jewish people itself is simulated and reconfigured in the form of a grotesque racist and sovereign version that massacres not only its Palestinian 'enemy', but also and mainly itself, given that, by becoming Zionist, the Jew destroys himself, as Max Horkheimer had already lucidly noted long ago.[20]

Contrary to the Schmittian tradition, and pushing some of Benjamin's intuitions to their extreme, Taubes argues for the need to conceive of a political theology that emerges from the bottom up. For Taubes, it is the community – originally the Jewish one and, after Paul, all humanity – that serves as the true custodian of the covenant with God, not the sovereign ruler. In this regard, Wolf-Daniel Hartwich, Aleida Assmann and Jan Assmann (2007: 151) suggest that Taubes, unlike Schmitt, concludes that no political order is inherently legitimate – only the transcendent order of God can be – thus making possible a 'negative political theology'. By emphasizing a horizontal conception of power, Taubes' political theology directly counters Schmitt's, which, rather than focusing on society, seeks to understand power from a vertical perspective. In this way, Taubes' approach is 'sociological' in its orientation, whereas Schmitt's is 'kratological'.

Schmitt clings to the representative model to justify the powers of this world, viewing the sovereign as a functional representative of divine power, which, in itself, is self-justifying. This highlights the true function of political representation, which Schmitt only criticizes when it is reduced to a mere technique in the liberal politics of debate of modern democracies. As discussed in section 1.2, Schmitt believes that 'true' representation, rooted in medieval origins, serves as a key element for justifying political authority. The most prominent example of this, according to Schmitt, is the Catholic Church (2002), and perhaps the head of the Executive elected by acclamation, as he argues in his controversial *Theory of the Constitution* of 1928. In this context, Taubes is entirely consistent in rejecting political representation and, with it, the possibility of legitimizing mundane governance, a task that is unacceptable from the standpoint of a negative theological-political perspective. Reflecting on the ancestral experience of the Jewish people, who, since 586 BC, have not had a State, Taubes conceives of the community of God in a horizontal way, free from all forms of government, given that no human institution can represent the Messiah and, therefore, cannot be legitimized by him.

Constructions similar to those of Taubes – and of Spinoza, who defends a remarkably similar position in his *Theological-Political Treatise* – conceive of political power in its irreducible immanence, merging human society with the kingdom of God in a nowtime in which democracy is absolute. For this reason, in a post-secular era such as the present – when the death of God has been incorporated into theological argumentation, yet religiosity continues to be invoked to justify or condemn capitalism – it seems urgent to develop what Jeffrey Robbins calls a radical-democratic political theology (2014: 6–12). This will be the focus of section 2.3. Before that, however, it is necessary to examine how, at both the linguistic and ontological levels, the decryption of Schmittian political theology can occur. This task, initiated by Benjamin and Taubes, remains far from complete. To conclude the decryption work typical of both Jewish thinkers, it is essential to reveal, in all its radicality, the *an-archy* of power, that is, the ontological potency encrypted by *potestas*.

2.2. Political theology and *an-archy*

2.2.1. With Heidegger (Schürmann)

As briefly discussed in subsection 2.1.1, recognizing that a legitimate and lasting ordering of the modern world was no longer possible, Schmitt, at the conclusion of *Political Theology*, aligns himself with the need for a state dictatorship. In doing so, he embraces the alternative proposed by the Spanish counter-revolutionary politician Donoso Cortés in a speech to Congress on 4 January 1849. According to Cortés, society was faced with a tragic choice between the governmental dictatorship of the sabre and the revolutionary dictatorship of the dagger.[21] At the beginning of the same work, Schmitt recognized that the legal system is something 'born from Nothing' ('*aus einem Nichts geboren*') (1996: 38), a statement that, curiously, brings him closer to his *inimicus* Kelsen. In the definitive edition of 1960 of his *Pure Theory of Law*, Kelsen caused great scandal among his contemporaries by asserting that 'law can have any content' ('*kann jeder beliebige Inhalt Recht sein*') (1992: 201), thus indicating that the legal system lacks a substantial foundation and is defined solely in formal, that is, functional terms, much like Schmitt's own political theology.

Schmitt argued that since the religious wars that inaugurated Modernity, a material legitimation of power had become impossible, meaning that political theology now serves merely as a functional substitute for the true theology that had once governed the European world for nearly a millennium. Moreover, precisely because modern political theology is inherently formal, its current role in legitimizing power tends to devolve into an empty legality that, over time, will inevitably be questioned and overturned, leading to a scenario of perpetual instability. In a similar perspective, Agamben (2013) asserts that today legitimacy and legality have entered a zone of indeterminacy, where the latter tends to encompass the former, reflecting, in a theological dimension, the reduction of every kingdom to governance, as well as the Church's decision to abandon its eschatological vocation in order to focus on the economic-mundane management of the world. This inevitably leads, with the advent of a legality that recognizes no legitimacy, to the total domination of illegality in the State and in the Church, both of which governed by *oikonomía*. The more the Church immerses itself in the affairs of the world, that is, the more it becomes economic, the further it moves away from its original eschatological vocation, typical of early Christianity. As it distances itself from the *an-archic* Kingdom of the Father

– without beginning or end, without foundation – it becomes increasingly focused on managing this world, necessitating ever more glory, acclamation and spectacle to encrypt the Nothingness that is God.

For Schmitt, who adopts a somewhat different reading, there is an inversely proportional relationship between legitimacy and legality: the more accepted a social formation is, the less violence it requires. In contrast, in the contemporary world, where God is dead and only His phantasmatic actions of ordering persist – entrusted to an imperfect functional substitute called the State – the violence tends to proliferate and become generalized. This is because the deficit of legitimacy requires a continual and violent imposition of order in the form of legality (Schmitt 2012). It is within this context that Schmitt presents the stark alternative between the dictatorship of the sabre and that of the dagger, suggesting that dictatorship, whether that of the counterrevolutionaries – as in Germany, where the socialist revolution was thwarted in 1919 – or that of the plebs, as seen with the Bolsheviks, constitutes the only viable option for imposing order in a convulsive world rapidly heading toward apocalyptic self-destruction.

Although, the alternative between the sabre and the dagger proposed by Donoso Cortés and unconditionally accepted by Schmitt is ultimately false. It can only be sustained if power is understood purely as *potestas*, thus obscuring its emergent dimension of *potentia*. In this sense, a different alternative arises from the process of decrypting theological-political power that I explored in section 1.4. Consequently, we see that the theory of the encryption of power is not merely an intellectual game but a crucial theoretical tool capable of opening new perspectives that are both linguistic and ontological. That said, when discussing the decryption of any dimension of power, it is essential to ask: *What* is being encrypted? *What* is hidden by the veil of encryption, which, as I hope to have demonstrated, does not correspond to a more original or substantial truth in the Platonic sense, but rather to a dynamic, potential and – now it can be better understood – *an-archic* process, that is, a process without a first, fixed or ahistorical foundation.

Schmitt and his generation – Benjamin, Heidegger, Jünger, Spengler and others – were right to recognize the absence of substantial order in the world, but they were mistaken in interpreting this situation as an abyss of relativism, violence and nihilism. The experience that emerged with the exhaustion of metaphysics of the foundation is far more complex. According to several of these thinkers, the end of the history of metaphysics in the twentieth century led to a long technical-nihilistic drift, one that exposed the empty nature of every principle (*arkhé*), understood simultaneously as both origin and command, as Agamben points out in his analysis of the Western philosophical tradition. In this tradition, the One who stands at the origin – be it God, the Father or the State – holds the power to command what comes after.[22] Notwithstanding, the exhaustion of the metaphysics of the foundation does not simply give rise to nihilism and relativism, but also opens up the possibility of decrypting and abandoning the metaphysical apparatuses that have shaped the history of the West. This, in turn, creates the potential for constructing new forms-of-life no longer centred on the sovereign *arkhé*. Nihilism and *an-archy*, in fact, emerge from the same epochal condition, yet proceed to adopt fundamentally different stances. From this perspective, *an-archy* may be expressed through the formula 'all from nothing', suggesting that every foundation is inherently de-founded, that all originates from nothing. Nihilism, by contrast, appears to coincide with the formula 'nothing of all', that is, with the impossibility of positing a totality – such as God, reason and so forth – capable of grounding action and existence. The divergent understandings of 'nothing' in these two formulations – as (de)foundation in the former, and as sheer negation in the latter – invite us to discern the affirmative dimension – and, I dare say, the joy – embedded in the concept of *an-archic* Nothingness. The philosopher who, perhaps more than anyone else, grasped this process in its full depth was Reiner Schürmann.

Schürmann, born in 1941 to German parents in the Netherlands, was originally ordained as a Dominican priest before abandoning his ecclesiastical career in 1975 to teach philosophy at the New School for Social Research in New York, where he died of AIDS in 1993. Schürmann was a unique intellectual figure, known for his deep friendships with Hannah Arendt and Hans Jonas, as well as his extensive study of Meister Eckhart's work.[23] Although he wrote relatively little, his contributions were marked by great intellectual intensity, particularly his pioneering reflection on *an-archy* as the (un)foundational dimension of political power. His most significant work is *Le Principe d'Anarchie: Heidegger et la Question de l'Agir*, first published in French in 1982 and later translated into English in 1987 under the title *Heidegger on Being and Acting: From Principles to Anarchy*. As we will explore, the English title does not quite capture the paradox contained in the original French.

In his book, Schürmann offers a rigorous *an-archic* interpretation of Heidegger's thought, one that would go on to have a profound influence on contemporary post-anarchism. This influence is so significant that, in order to distinguish it from classical anarchism, many contemporary authors – including myself – now write the word *anarchy* as *an-archy*. This typographical choice signals that what is at stake here is not simply a political doctrine – one that might be seen as naïve or rooted in nineteenth-century figures like Bakunin or Kropotkin – but rather a deeply ontological discourse that challenges the concept of *arkhé*, the foundational principle upon which traditional power structures are built. As outlined in section 1.4.3, *an-archy* is not necessarily disorder or chaos because it is not necessarily nothing, or, what amounts to the same, it is necessarily everything; that is, simple existence without foundation, without base, without principle or order, oscillation and rhythm of Being that is always in the process of being, de-foundation, unending, *Bodenlos* – 'the absurd climate of the groundless' of Vilém Flusser (2007: 19–21) – the ground without foundation (*Ungrund*) of Meister Eckhart, an ontology that is also an aesthetics and, primarily, an ethics: contingency. Outside of this *an-archic* environment – that is, without *arkhé*, a Greek noun meaning both beginning and command, from which the adjectives *arkhaîos* (archaic, ancient) and *arkhikós* (archic, commanding) are derived – it seems to me impossible to speak of democracy, a common experience of potency.

Having laid out these ideas, it can be argued that Schürmann's theory functions as a decryptor, not only of Heidegger's thought[24] but also of the very notion of *potestas* as a foundational principle. As such, Schürmann's work is central to the decryption of theological-political power and to the liberation of the ontological reality that lies beneath its weight. This reality, which resists fixed hierarchies and the imposition of transcendent authority, can be understood in various terms – whether as *an-archy* (in post-anarchist thought), *potentia* (as explored by Spinoza, Agamben and Negri), *radical democracy* (as articulated by Castoriadis), or *plane of immanence* (as conceived by Deleuze). In all of these interpretations, Schürmann's legacy (whether consciously or unconsciously adopted) points toward a rethinking of power not as something determined by an external authority, but as a dynamic and immanent force that unfolds within the absence of any foundational *arkhé*, thereby even transcending Heidegger, whose thought will be referenced in this section insofar as it is essential to understanding Schürmann's proposals. Indeed, it is important to emphasize from the outset that, although I use certain assumptions from Heidegger – and also from Schmitt – I do not, in any way, adopt their 'systems', much less their conclusions and proposals, which are often translated into anti-political (Heidegger) or authoritarian (Schmitt) stances.

Well then, Schürmann begins his argument by asserting that it is impossible to derive a political philosophy from the work of Martin Heidegger, since there is no transition from Being to action in his philosophy. This seems to be confirmed by Heidegger himself, who, in the opening line of his *Letter on Humanism*, states that we are far from thinking, with sufficient radicality, the essence of action (1993a: 217). This would even make a Heideggerian ethics impossible, although some authors, such as Franco Volpi (2010), argue that *Being and Time* is essentially a book on ethics. However, the impossibility of moving from the realm of Being to that of action is not due to any supposed distinction between the two spheres, since Heidegger even asserts, at the end of the letter, that the thought of Being precedes the division between theory and practice. Rather, it is because, after the destruction Heidegger imposes on *metaphysical-epochal economies* through his aggressive onto-history, no principle can be said to supervene on Being. Indeed, action is not a subsequent or external addition to Being; it is always already inherent in it. Ontologically, Being is that which *comes into presence*, and as such, it is constitutively a form of action.

The concept of 'economy' that Schürmann invokes is not to be understood in the conventional sense of 'the science of scarce resources' nor in any quantitative terms. Instead, it refers to a highly specific interpretation rooted in Heidegger's philosophy. As usual in Heidegger – and sometimes abusive and irritating – the word 'economy' is recreated based on the interpretation of its Greek roots, imbuing it with a particular philosophical significance. Thus, the word 'eco-', derived from the Greek *óikos* (οἶκος), meaning 'house', is associated with the idea of permanence, while '-nomia', stemming from *nómos* (νόμος), meaning 'norm', is understood as a form of requirement or demand. Together, these elements suggest that 'economy' refers to 'that which situates us', a kind of worldview (*Weltanschauung*) enriched by both phenomenological and ontological dimensions (Schürmann 1987: 9). Each epochal 'economy' under which the West has lived is grounded in specific 'principles': the Greek economy, with its notions of idea (Plato) and category (Aristotle); the medieval economy, with its intricate theological structures; and the modern economy, which begins with the Cartesian subject and culminates in Nietzsche's nihilistic thought, paving the way for the total dominance of technique. These principles not only carry a chronological significance, designating them as 'primordial', but also a political dimension. In this perspective, they are linked to terms such as 'principal', 'prime', and 'prince' (from the Latin *princeps*), indicating authority and command, the very essence of political power (Schürmann 1987: 25).

For Schürmann, being and acting – life and politics – form a single, undetermined dimension without foundation, reflecting the radical absence of origin or fundamental command. This theme is explored in Heidegger's work across two phases. In the first Heidegger, *an-archy* manifests itself through the idea of *There* (the *Da* of *Dasein*), which refers to the human being's original constitution as *being-in-the-world* (1927: 87). This *There* is not a fixed, determined or stable point of reference; rather, it is characterized by its lack of a secure foundation. This opens up the possibility for the experience of anguish, as the human is a *thrown-being* (*Geworfenheit*), and its *There*, while necessarily situated within history, provides no clear indication of where it originates or where it is heading (1927: 231). It is this radical and obscure experience concerning provenance and destination that can lead to singularization, as far as the anguished human *Dasein* is capable of abandoning the inauthenticity of the world of 'the one' (*das Man*) – where an impersonal, anonymous 'one' thinks, speaks and even dies automatically and unreflectively – and instead experiences the awareness of its own finitude. Through this process, *Dasein* becomes attuned to itself as *being-toward-death* (*Sein-zum-Tode*).

In the later Heidegger (1959) – who is far from being entirely disconnected from his earlier thought, as some interpreters suggest – *an-archy* takes the form of abandonment (*Gelassenheit*), understood as a structural, unfounded and non-principled condition of all reality, not just that of the human being. Heidegger's famous *Kehre* indicates the 'turn' in the German philosopher's thought, which, starting in the 1930s, brought his *an-archic* reflections to their zenith. In this phase, Heidegger recognized the impossibility of completing the existential analytic of *Dasein* begun in *Being and Time*, and thus adopted a position that not only deactivated the classical ontological difference, understanding that the essence of Being *is* its existence – as, moreover, is already foreshadowed in §9 of *Being and Time* – but also redirected his inquiry toward another domain: the truth of Being, which simply *appears* as *event* (*Ereignis*), having no cognitive meaning, as discussed in *Contributions to Philosophy: From the Event*,[25] the most important work of Heidegger's second phase, written between 1936 and 1938. Heidegger then radicalizes his questioning of Being. In *Being and Time*, he did not fall into the metaphysical trap of asking *what Being is*, since this question, by involving the verb 'to be', already indicates its vicious and contradictory nature. But now he starts to question not the *meaning* of Being as in *Being and Time*, but its *truth*. This opens up a topology of Being that is no longer solely related to temporality, but also to space, to the dwelling of Being, that is, to language.

To understand the later Heidegger and his *an-archic* articulation, it is crucial to keep in mind that he aims to think of Being (*Sein*) itself, rather than the being/

entity (*Seiendes*) translated into human *Dasein*, God, nature, and so on. This seems only possible through negation, for the Nothing, corresponding to the negation of the being (entity) – the *ni-ente*, as one might playfully say in Italian – is necessarily placed beyond the being, shaping the horizon in which it can emerge. Now, this horizon, this *an-archic* (un)ground of the being, is Being. One of the determinations of Being is the Nothing[26] as the space that opens to the being as clearing (*Lichtung*). Herein, truth is not a matter of correctness in view of the model of a pure idea (Plato) or as the adequation of saying in relation to a discourse (Aristotle). The clearing is the primordial opening, the locus where concealment and unconcealment contend, that is, the originary condition that renders truth possible (Heidegger 1988: 177–8). This clarifies the concept of the topology of Being, which appears as a blank space (clearing, opening) in which the beings can freely become. It is in this sense that Being is Nothing, corresponding to the space that opens up for the beings, the condition for the beings to not only be, but to be in movement. As the space that enables becoming – namely, the being of beings – Being is potency. At this juncture, the issue is no longer one of essence or existence, but of truth, since it is Being that, by illuminating the being through the Nothing, negation, subtraction and withdrawal, enables something like an appearing, a truth, to emerge. This truth, however, must be thought with radicality, i.e., from the perspective of Being and not from the being of the *Dasein*, as the first Heidegger had planned. The truth of Being, much more important than its essence or existence – which, after all, are objectifying categories – is also Nothing, is also negation: *alétheia* (ἀλήθεια), non-forgetting, that is, truth as a continuous and permanent process of veiling and unveiling.

In this nearly hallucinatory horizon, Heidegger begins to view the history of metaphysics as the history of the concealment of Being, which, however, is not due to human beings, but to Being itself, for it was Being that 'consented' to being concealed. All that remains for us is to wait for Being to rearticulate itself through another kind of openness different from its own forgetting (*Seinsvergessenheit*). Hence, the destruction (*Destruktion*) of metaphysics as envisioned by the first Heidegger – who even intended to replace it with a more radical discourse – is succeeded in the second Heidegger by the idea of abandonment and overcoming (*Verwindung*) of metaphysics, which, as it will inevitably exhaust itself, must simply be set aside, a position that, as it seems to me, is reflected in Agamben's obsession with inoperativity.

Today, with the dominance of technique – the final figure of humanistic and subjectivist metaphysics – it is impossible to speak of Being within the context of philosophy, which would have reached its end, as it now apprehends Being only in its negative and subtractive declension as technique. Understood in its negativity as *a-létheia* (un-concealment), Being is also and constitutively concealment, subtraction and this is how it manifests itself in certain epochs, independently of any human action or will. Ours is one of those epochs in which Being predominantly reveals itself through its withdrawal, its non-manifestation (*Abwesenheit*), which is, paradoxically, a form (absent) of come to presence (*Anwesen*), opening space for future and more positive epochal configurations. Indeed, for Heidegger, absence is not to be confused with the lack of something in the vulgar sense of the term. For him, absence is the withdrawal or distancing of Being, the concealment of its deeper meaning, since Being does not reveal itself continuously and directly, but also conceals and hides itself. One can thus perceive Heidegger's work as the culmination of the entire cryptophilosophy of the West, which begins with Heraclitus' enigmatic statement that 'nature loves to hide itself'. Therefore, the era of total technical domination appears as the fulfilment of metaphysics, which, in an isomorphic way, represented in Greek philosophy – at least from Plato onward – a kind of prehistory of modern technique. This is why, Heidegger asserts, in the contemporary world, Being can only be experienced in the form of its withdrawal. Thus, as mentioned, it seems that human beings are left with no choice but to await the next epochal configuration of Being, limiting themselves, in this final era of metaphysics, to turning toward the entities in a non-appropriative mode, which Heidegger refers to as *letting-be* (*sein-lassen*), an existential stance translated into a type of wanting not to want that, predictably, opposes the will to will of Nietzsche's 'technique'. A poor consolation, indeed.

Nevertheless, Heidegger appears to anticipate other possibilities, insofar as they are not articulated through philosophy, but with the help of poetry, as it does not objectify or humanize Being in the manner that philosophy does. Indeed, already in *Contributions to Philosophy: From the Event*, Heidegger attempts to establish a non-metaphysical language with a poetic and prophetic character, a radical experiment that, according to many scholars, did not reach a successful conclusion. However, beyond the success or failure of Heidegger's most radical linguistic endeavour, what is striking is his immense effort to present his thought on Being in a non-metaphysical form, which leads him to relinquish categories, predicables, transcendentals, modalities, polarities, doctrines of univocity, polysemy, act and potency, dialectics, negativity, among other traditional philosophical constructs (Volpi 2011: 292). In this context, it is understandable that poetry occupies a prominent place in the later Heidegger's thought, given that it is the only art that is constructed with language, this kind of originary opening, which is, at least for now, indispensable to human beings. But does this not lead to a revival of a certain humanism? In no way, for in Heidegger's view, language is not something employed or created by human beings; rather, it is something that shapes and creates the human. In his personal notes, Agamben appears to have understood this very well when he states that, in a certain sense, language precedes thought, given that the latter would have been invented by the former. Thus, thought occurs insofar as it produces the event of language in favour of humanity, something that never ceases to happen and properly constitutes human in-fancy, our *adventure* (2024b: 206), something which comes, that is, comes (*venire*) together (*ad*), happens (*avenire*) as event. One can conclude that, for Heidegger, once the path of metaphysics has been traversed, the only possible philosophy in the age of technique is reduced to a hermeneutics of poetic language, capable of transforming human beings into shepherds of Being, which must be served and accompanied, even in its home, which is language.

Thus, all forms of humanism, voluntarism, finalism and teleologism were abandoned, paving the way for the recognition of the lack of foundation for any being or power. As a result, Heidegger's turn represents a transition from metaphysical and hierarchical times to the current *an-archic* era, which is devoid of principles in both chronological and political senses (Schürmann 1987: 25). Curiously, Agamben sees in the later Heidegger a remnant of the theological dimension of Western philosophy, insofar as, just as God is an infinite being who must operate within a finite history, after which there will be only incessant and perpetual glory (of God) and glorification (sung by His creatures), the later Heidegger attempts to think of an infinite Being whose history – the history of metaphysics – has come to an end (Agamben 2011: 211), leaving only a restful waiting for something new, namely, the God who might save us.

This gives rise to the important idea, already highlighted earlier, of *Gelassenheit* (abandonment) or 'letting-be', this way of relating to the world (and to Being) that contrasts with the technical and instrumental dominance characteristic of Modernity. This is not to be equated with mere passivity, but with a manner of allowing Being to reveal itself without attempting to manipulate or control it. It seems to me a concept close to Agamben's *form-of-life*, as it is linked to a more receptive attitude of the human, one that, rather than imposing control over things, adopts a stance of openness and 'letting be', permitting Being to manifest itself without being shaped by technique, subjectivity and, even more importantly, by *arkhé*, i.e., by principle and command. It is something both serene and extraordinarily difficult, at least for us, sons of the technique: to allow not the useful products, but the things themselves, the beings that historically embody Being, to come into presence, thus opening the possibility of approaching a different origin that is not principial.

In this regard, Schürmann differentiates, following an original intuition of Nietzsche, the two meanings of the idea of 'origin'. The first, *Anfang*, translated as 'original', refers to the beginning or command of any historical series. It marks the start of an epoch and, as such, is vulnerable to the critique of the *arkhé* that Heidegger develops throughout his entire work. The second meaning of origin, *Ursprung*, relates to the 'originary', which concerns the ahistorical coming-into-presence of Being as discussed by the later Heidegger. This *Ursprung* is a type of origin (*Ur*) that leaps (*Spring*) upon us, a true emergence (*Entstehung*), that is, something that suddenly comes to the surface, without knowing from where or to where (*nec a quo, nec ad quem*, as the Latins would say with their peculiar grace). It is the only dimension of the *arkhé* – which is no longer understood as a beginning or command – that survives the destruction of metaphysics. In a certain way, *Ursprung* takes the place of *Dasein* proposed by the early Heidegger, de-anthropologizing and de-historicizing it, presenting it as pure presence (1987: 120–54).

However, the thought of the second Heidegger is even more complex and subtle, as revealed by the exemplary course of 1955–6 titled *On the Principle of Reason*. In this course, Heidegger begins by criticizing the famous *principium rationis* of Wolf and Leibniz, according to which nothing is without reason (*nihil est sine ratione*), arguing that it is, in fact, a thesis or a 'proposition about the ground', as evidenced by the German title of the work, *Satz vom Grund*. From this standpoint, the principle of reason is not only linked to the forgetfulness of Being, but even more profoundly to the forgetfulness of the forgetfulness of Being, as it reaches back to the metaphysical origins – namely, the fundamental and principial roots – of Western thought, arriving today to the era of technique (1991b: 188). Nevertheless, Heidegger invites us to abandon this path through a leap – this is another meaning of the German word *Satz* – which indicates that the ground is not found in any principle, but in Being itself. In order to achieve this, it is necessary to listen anew to the monotonous thesis about the ground and alter its prosody, its intonation, as Franco Volpi teaches in the introduction to his Italian translation of the course. It is a matter of moving from the common understanding that '*nothing* is *without* ground' (nothing without a ground), which simply means that every being has a ground, to the much more radical idea that 'nothing *is* without *ground*' (the ground is), emphasizing that Being co-belongs to the ground (2011: 62).

As ground, Being is ontologically distinct from being, enabling thought to follow a different course, one that diverges from the path laid out by Western metaphysics, in which beings are always grounded in another being (such as God) and never in Being itself. This process leads to the gradual forgetfulness of Being, due to the ontotheological mechanism of grounding, which posits that a being is created by another being (even if supreme) or derived from an equally entified essence. At this moment, Heidegger's wager approaches *an-anarchy*, because in order to think of Being as ground, it must be thought of as something ungrounded, since if it were or could be grounded, it would merely be another being. Thus, Being emerges as groundless (*grundlos*) and, from this perspective, cannot be thought within the traditional forms and structures of metaphysics, but only, in line with fragment 52 of Heraclitus, as a game played by the divine child: 'αἰὼν παῖς ἐστι παίζων, πεττεύων· παιδὸς ἡ βασιληίη' ('Time is a child playing draughts, the kingly power is a child's'). Heidegger then offers a completely unorthodox interpretation of Leibniz's mathematizing formula, which gains an *an-archic* translation: 'Perhaps Leibniz's phrase *cum Deus calculat, fit mundus* should be translated as: when God plays, the world is generated' (1991b: 191). Having reached this limit, Heidegger seems to realize the abyss (*Abgrund*) opening before him and does not advance further. Notwithstanding, by embracing his lesson on the need to apply different prosodies to the thesis of the ground, I propose it be read as '*nothing is* without *ground*', in the sense that nothing is the ground, or in other words, there is no ground; neither in Being nor anywhere else. The *un-founded* thus means that the foundation of nothing is the Nothingness of foundation.

2.2.2. Beyond Heidegger (Deleuze-Nietzsche)

In the interpretation I propose, *an-archy* – presupposed in early Heidegger and further elucidated in his later work, according to Schürmann's analysis – emerges as the outcome of the decryption of theological-political power. It is only on the basis of this *an-archic* foundation – I fully acknowledge the inherent paradox in this statement – that the formidable Schmittian theological-political apparatus, grounded in *potestas*, can be overcome. This opens the space for alternative political theologies – such as feminist, Black and decolonial ones – that engage with the ideas of *potentia*, *an-archy* and democracy. The latter, according to Jacques Rancière (2005), represents the *an-archic* political form *par excellence* because democracy is understood as the governance of those without titles, that is, those who lack an *arkhé* to justify their authority. Similarly, Donatella di Cesare (2024) posits that *an-archy*, understood as the absence of a foundational principle, serves as the basis for the radical, self-constituting and always precarious experience of Greek democracy.

In this way, Schmitt and Heidegger's laments about the nihilism that supposedly afflicts the contemporary world can be interpreted as expressions of a conservative and anti-democratic view of the lack of a substantial foundation characterizing the current era. However, one could also regard the present epochal moment as particularly propitious for the decryption of theological-political power, given that, according to Schürmann's theory, the dominion of principles – of all principles, and not just of one in particular – has reached its exhaustion.

In fact, Schürmann argues that the principles of Western metaphysics have operated within the modalities of *pros hên* ('toward the One') or *aph'hênos* ('from the One'), meaning they are either *directed toward* or *arise from* the One, thereby sustaining the illusion of a unified dimension that functions as a command. According to classical thought, which has been fully embraced by the Western tradition, 'the beginning is not a simple debut that would be suppressed in what follows, but, on the contrary, it never finishes beginning, that is, governing that which is always an underlying beginning' (Aubenque 1966: 193). This univocal structure results in a model designed to enslave thought, intended to transform it first into metaphysical 'truth' and, in the technical age, into 'certainty', i.e., merely quantitative knowledge (Schürmann 1987: 38–43). Nonetheless, the logic of principles – whether integrative (*pros hên*) or participatory (*aph'hênos*) – as proposed by Plato and Aristotle, reinforced by the medieval scholastics and universalized by Cartesianism, can no longer function nowadays. In our age, technique has disembodied itself and thinking has been de-anthropologized, giving way instead to an *an-archic* multiplicity of contingent non-principial principles, which are also non-original and non-modelling, all precarious and domestic, representing an alternative to the extinction that is now threatening humanity.

For Schürmann, every principle emerges, develops and decays, making way for another one, thereby shaping what we understand as history. In the interregnum between two principles – when the old has died and the new has not yet been born – all sort of aberrations occur, as Machiavelli would say. Yet today, the emergence of a new, original, all-encompassing, universal and paradigmatic principle seems impossible. This is why we perceive the present as stagnant, not moving forward but rather expanding, dissolving the past and denying the future, creating a universe of sameness that encompasses everything and everyone in a state of quiet despair.

Accordingly, the alternative is between pure and simple extinction – since humanity would have reached its end (in both senses of the word, as final point and fulfilment), beyond which it could no longer progress – or opening ourselves to the difference of the new, to the play of *potentia* liberated from its *archic* form (*potestas*), revealing itself as a continuous mutation, energization and exhaustion of *anthropo-logical* time and its dualisms, as envisioned by Nietzsche.[27]

In this perspective, the reading that Heidegger (1991a) dedicates to Nietzsche reveals its limits as a thinker of *an-archy*, a fact that Schürmann does not adequately address in his study, as it would require a profound dive into the process of decryption sponsored by heretical thinkers like, for example, Deleuze. Nevertheless, even though Schürmann is far from the radicality of Deleuze, he is not entirely convinced by Heidegger's arguments. Contrary to being merely the last of the metaphysicians, according to the biased reading of Heidegger, who saw Nietzsche as the pinnacle of the veiling of Being, manifested in the form of the blind will to power that would give rise to the equally blind planetary technique, Nietzsche, in Schürmann's interpretation, appears as the precursor of our *an-archic* age:

> There are 'only multiplicities in any case; but "unity" is nowhere present in the nature of becoming'. There are only 'complex forms of relative life-duration within the flux of becoming', only configurations of forms and forces for thought but no truth in and for itself. Truth as the correlate of knowing is itself a fiction. (1987: 49)

Heidegger asserts that the fulfilment of metaphysics in contemporary times occurs through figures such as the thought that thinks itself in Hegel or the even more radical one of the vacuous 'will to will' (*Wille zur Wille*) in Nietzsche. In this sense, to say that metaphysics has been fulfilled means that the multiple and primordial openness of Being has closed within a determined epochal figure, such as technique or its philosophical translation in the Nietzschean will to power. In this context, Heidegger argues that the metaphysics which is now closing has never been able to thematize Being as Being (*Sein*), always requiring the mediation of the being/entity (*Seiendes*). It would be necessary, according to the Heidegger of *Being and Time*, to construct a philosophy of Being as Being, without references to the entity, although for this, as a preliminary phase, the mediation of a specific entity is indispensable, namely, the human *Dasein* and its language. However, even a reflection such as the later Heidegger's, which abandoned the preliminary stage represented by the existential analysis of the *Dasein*, would not be enough, as he acknowledges in his article *The Onto-Theo-Logical Constitution of Metaphysics*, since a theory of Being as Being is inherently tied to the humanistic – and thus entified (*entifiziert*) – question of the ground:

> [. . .] the matter of thinking is beings as such, that is, Being. Being shows itself in the nature of the ground. Accordingly, the matter of thinking, Being as the ground, is thought out fully only when the ground is represented as the first ground, *πρώτη ἀρχή*. The original matter of thinking presents itself as the first cause, the *causa prima* that corresponds to the reason-giving path back to the *ultima ratio*, the final accounting. The Being of beings is represented fundamentally, in the sense of the ground, only as *causa sui*. This is the metaphysical concept of God. (1969: 59–60)

The link to political theology is evident. Realizing such a relationship, Heidegger hastens to clarify that, if we abandon the realm of theology and turn to philosophy, we will no longer be facing any personal God because 'man can neither pray nor sacrifice to this god. Before the *causa sui*, man can neither fall to his knees in awe nor can he play music and dance before this god' (1969: 72). Yet this distinction does not alter the situation: even under the impersonal and abstract form of that which founds itself (*causa sui*), the fundamentalist machinery of political theology and its apparatuses for encrypting *potentia* remain operational, generating the concept of God in theology and that of *causa sui* in philosophy. In this regard, if used correctly, the later Heidegger serves as a salutary antidote to his earlier version, insofar as he allows us to recognize the persistence of the encryption of power not only in theological thought but also and especially in what is traditionally called 'philosophy'.

In any case, unlike the later Heidegger, I contend that the failure of metaphysics in its task of thinking Being as Being does not stem from an incorrect formulation of the ontological problem or a lack of radicality in its development. On the contrary, it represents a secret victory. There is no need to create or access another origin in which the foundation of Being is revealed and exposed, as if there were an 'evolution' of thought, which, by the way, the early Heidegger was eager to 'unveil' and present as his great contribution to the history of philosophy. If metaphysics – and, with it, philosophy – failed in the task of thinking Being as Being, this seems to mean, in a much simpler way than Heidegger believed in his obsession with Being (Volpi 2011: 298), that there is no Being, no foundation and even less the famous ontological difference between Being and entity, essence and existence, and so on. There is just movement, speed, transformation, process, potency, *an-archy*. Only by grasping this can we truly speak of the end of philosophy.

This represents a very different perspective from that of Heidegger (1993b), who saw the present era – the 'night of the world' (*Weltnacht*) – as the epoch of the end of philosophy because in it metaphysics, in the form of planetary technique, has become the world. Insofar as we live in technique, we are living philosophy, already 'finished' and translated into its final epochal form. In contrast, as I understand it, the end of philosophy can only occur when we begin to live not philosophy itself, but thought in all its radicality, thereby ceasing to separate it from life and embracing a dynamic dimension of life-thought. With the end of philosophy, humanity will then be able to abandon the weighty tomes not only of Heidegger's work but of the entire tradition, opening the possibility – denied by Heidegger with affected and grumpy circumspection – of making music and dancing for the divine that is ourselves. And everything else.

Then Heidegger will appear as the 'superior man' ridiculed by Nietzsche's Zarathustra, because, despite his attempt to transcend the human, it is precisely for this reason that he condemns himself to the most simplistic humanism. The 'superior *man*' remains incapable of experiencing reality, which, in its impersonal becoming, is not only dance but also song and play. As Deleuze puts it: 'To laugh is to affirm life, even the suffering in life. To play is to affirm chance and the necessity of chance. To dance is to affirm becoming and the being of becoming' (1986: 170). Here, the transvaluation proposed by Nietzsche, understood as a new way of feeling, thinking, evaluating and existing that overcomes nihilism by leaving it behind, resonates with Molly Bloom's great 'Yes' in the intense interior monologue that concludes the polyphonic *Ulysses* by James Joyce. As a pure affirmation, the great 'Yes' undoubtedly comes through negations. Nevertheless, these negations are not autonomous or original qualities in themselves; they are preliminary movements that prepare and bring to fruition the potency of affirmation, without turning into a simple nihilistic acceptance of the world and its presumed negativity. Rather, it is an affirmation – prepared through the negation of the world as burden, guilt and duty – that assumes the potent form of the transformation of both oneself and reality: 'This is the conversion of heavy into light, of low into high, of pain into joy. This trinity of dance, play and laughter creates the transubstantiation of nothingness, the transmutation of the negative and the transvaluation or change of power [*puissance*] of negation' (Deleuze 1986: 176).

The interpretation that Deleuze offers of Nietzsche can be confronted with Heidegger's in order to further radicalize Schürmann's thesis on the 'principle of *an-archy*, which, in turn, detaches itself from any necessary reference to the Heideggerian universe. Deleuze seeks to decrypt Nietzsche's thought not only in opposition to its traditional antagonist, that is, Hegelian dialectics, which always instrumentalizes and functionalizes affirmation to reach negativity, since the positive appears only as a double negation (negation of negation), but also as a response to the burden that Heidegger placed on Nietzsche's philosophy. Heidegger, in his reading, interprets Nietzsche's 'nihilism' as the final phase of metaphysics, today manifesting as a planetary technique aligned with a blind will to power. The main target of Deleuze's interpretation appears to be the burden that the 'ass' Heidegger imposed on Nietzsche's thought, particularly through his characterization of his 'nihilism' as the final stage of metaphysics. Heidegger interprets this Nietzschean nihilism as ultimately leading to a blind will to will, which, in his view, manifests today in the form of global domination. Deleuze, however, challenges this reading, seeking to free Nietzsche from Heidegger's restrictive schema and to reframe his philosophy as something that transcends metaphysical finality and embraces a radical affirmation of becoming and difference:

> To affirm is to unburden: not to load life with the weight of higher values, but to create new values which are those of life, which make life light and active. There is creation, properly speaking, only insofar as we make use of excess in order to invent new forms of life rather than separating life from what it can do. [. . .] Nietzsche's argument can be summarized as follows: the yes which does not know how to say no (the yes of the ass) is a caricature of affirmation. This is precisely because it says yes to everything which is no, because it puts up with nihilism it continues to serve the power of denying – which is like a demon whose every burden it carries. The Dionysian yes, on the contrary, knows how to say no: it is pure affirmation, it has conquered nihilism and divested negation of all autonomous power. But it has done this because it has placed the negative at the service of the powers of affirming. To affirm is to create, not to bear, put up with or accept. (1986: 185–6)

According to Deleuze, Nietzsche rejects any essentialist or principial conception of affirmation that would reduce it to a simple function of Being or of 'what is'. In traditional metaphysical thought, insofar as affirmation is understood as a function of Being, the human becomes a 'functionary of affirmation', meaning that humans simply affirm Being, which affirms itself through them. This type of affirmation becomes an assumption, an act of taking charge that establishes a foundational relationship with Being (1986: 183). Notwithstanding, for Deleuze-Nietzsche, affirmation is not an affirmation of Being, but an affirmation of *potency*, a dynamic and transformative force, and for this very reason it seems absurd to me to see the German philosopher as a nihilist. This form of affirmation is not about accepting things as they are, nor is it about bearing a metaphysical burden, such as an *arkhé* or a foundational principle. Instead, it is about liberation: unloading what lives, breaking free from established structures and decrypting the theological-political *potestas* by transforming it in *an-archy*. In this sense, Nietzsche's affirmation is not about sustaining or assuming the world as it is, but about potentiating new possibilities, about stepping outside the constraints of metaphysical systems and embracing a kind of *an-archy*, a form of existence that is free from hierarchical structures or foundational principles.

This interpretation, in contrast to Heidegger's reading of Nietzsche as a nihilist, underscores how Nietzsche's affirmation does not concern resignation to a fixed order or the imposition of meaning from above, but rather entails a radical transformation and the unleashing of forces that have been repressed or encrypted by metaphysical and theological frameworks. Thus, Deleuze-Nietzsche is not a nihilist in the traditional sense, but a mixed and impure thinker of radical potentiality and affirmation beyond the constraints of traditional metaphysics.

2.2.3. *An-archic* politics

The underlying issue raised by Schürmann is not only ontological but also related to an *an-archic* politics, i.e., a politics that does not accept any of the traditional titles of legitimacy that have historically underpinned the thought and practice of political-theological power, including those called anarchists. Indeed, the classical anarchism of Pierre-Joseph Proudhon (1809–65), Mikhail Bakunin (1814–76) and Piotr Kropotkin (1842–1921) aligns closely with Western metaphysics, as far as it assumes a sociable human nature oriented toward mutual aid, progress and rationalism. On the other hand, as Schürmann suggests, what is at stake today is not simply a politics similar to others, characterized by familiar taxonomies and more or less reasonable arguments, but rather the extreme experience of an absence of legitimacy, consensus and reason, a true *an-archy*. This perspective, further developed by post-anarchist thinkers, represents a synthesis of anarchist practices and post-structuralist philosophy (Derrida, Foucault and Deleuze), seeking to transcend the monolithic, scientistic and progressive conception of power as *potestas* that shaped the anarchism of its 'founding fathers', thus becoming more anarchist than classical anarchism.[28]

Making explicit reference to authors such as Schürmann and Derrida, Saul Newman (2015) argues that post-anarchism has a strong ontological component capable of revealing the historicity and discursivity of thought practices and social experiences, while also distancing itself from the metanarratives typical of classical anarchism, which positioned themselves as a point of anchorage for revolution. These metanarratives today survive in the form of various positivisms, such as those present in the works of contemporary theorists like Murray Bookchin, who, while not as deterministic as Marxists, still rely on universalizing discourses in which freedom is presented as a 'natural' destiny of humanity. In turn, post-anarchists, following the path of post-structuralist thought, argue that it is no longer possible to guide politics through ahistorical truths, moral discourses or any idea of shared rationality. As Newman (2001) argues, it is impossible to clearly separate the anarchist subjects from the power structures against which they rise, given that the processes of subjectivation now occur through multiple agencements that do not solely refer to a supposed psychic entity capable of acting rationally. In this way, the post-anarchism invoked by Newman is not limited to an ontological dimension, as 'the moment of ontological anarchy is [. . .] an experience of freedom and, indeed, intense ethical reflection. Importantly, it also frees action from its telos, from the rule of ends, from the strategic rationality which always sought to determine it' (Newman 2015 e-book).

In summary, post-anarchism can be defined as follows:

> Understood in this sense, anarchistic politics today – what I call postanarchism – can be understood as starting from the nonacceptability of power, a position which opens up a space of contingency and freedom rather than following a set pattern of anarchism. Postanarchism is anarchism that starts, rather than necessarily ends, with anarchy. This means that it does not have a specific ideological shape and that it may take different forms and follow different courses of action. It might resist and contest specific relations of power at

> localized points of intensity, on the basis of their illegitimacy and violence; it might work against certain institutions and institutional practices through creating alternative practices and forms of organization. In other words, taking anarchy or non-power as its starting point, postanarchism, as a form of autonomous thinking and acting, can work on multiple fronts, in a variety of different settings, producing reversals and interruptions of existing relations of domination. (Newman 2015 e-book)

Therefore, it is clear that post-anarchism is not satisfied with the mere deposition of state authority, but also demands the deconstruction of the epistemological authority of science and the moral authority of society, adding that the eventual overcoming of the State would not, by itself, mean the end of separated power, as *arkhé* infiltrates the very constitution of the subject, as Foucault taught. This idea is further complemented by the post-anarchist perception that power is not based on anything other than its own historicity, which needs to be decrypted and not simply negated, as positivist anarchisms tend to do.

It should be clear by now that the concept of *an-archy* presented here, developed from Schürmann's theory with Deleuzian touches, must not be conflated with the nineteenth-century political and social movement known as anarchism. After all, *an-archy*, as an absence of structure, method and universal models governing action, cannot accommodate the scientism, progressivism and teleology characteristic of classical anarchist currents. That said, these classical anarchist traditions, despite their differences, deserve the utmost respect for their significant role in the history of libertarian struggles.

In classical anarchism, anarchy signifies the absence of government, and consequently, anarchists advocate for the creation of a society without the State. However, this necessary rejection of the State does not equate to a rejection of the *arkhé*. On the contrary, many classical anarchists, such as Proudhon and Kropotkin, affirm a natural *archic* order, which they see embodied in social organizations based on voluntary cooperation. In this sense, they end up confusing the envisioned space of non-power with a kind of benevolent and Rousseaunian state of nature, as anarchists maintain that if humans adhered to the natural laws of their species, they would be able to live in harmony with one another (Woodcock 1998: 18). Furthermore, as James Martel explains, even in practice, anarchism tends to articulate itself through archism, that is, 'a mode of politics that engages in hierarchy, order and taxonomization and which is, at least in its Western mode, highly concordant with the idea of encryption' (2020: 34). This is clear, for example, in the dramatic history of the anarchists in the

Spanish Civil War, who were unable to free themselves from the representative forms of the party and the union and, as a result, failed in their libertarian objectives (Martel undated manuscript).

This is why, according to Schürmann, classical anarchism is just another chapter in the history of metaphysics. In fact, it is grounded in a substantialist conception of power and does not challenge the political-metaphysical principles that have long dominated thought. Classical anarchists only sought to replace one command-principle (*arkhé*) with another, as they aimed to substitute the command of the State with a natural-rational-social-voluntary form of organization. In doing so, they ultimately produced surpluses of origin. In contrast, post-anarchist *an-archy* starts from a proposal that is more ontological than purely political in the traditional sense, although it inevitably leads to very concrete political and social consequences. As already mentioned, unlike anarchism, *an-archy* does not merely aim to deny the State or construct a libertarian political doctrine; instead, it seeks to dismantle the various *arkhái* operating within the world of Being and action, a much more radical approach than that proposed by classical anarchist critique.

It is crucial to emphasize that this ontological *an-archy* entails an *an-archic* community, since the first requirement and the primary political consequence of *an-archy* is the impossibility of appropriating the common, the *munus* which co-belongs to all. Thus, it is not simply an *an-archy*, but also an *a-nomy*, an absence of government that leads to an absence of regulatory norms for the sharing of the common. This structure does not create empty, anomic spaces; rather, it facilitates the emergence of full *a-nomic* dimensions that are non-separating and non-appropriating. Such realities remain open to everyone because the basic *nomic* principle – which divides 'mine' and 'yours' and sustains hierarchical order – no longer operates within them. In this sense, every *an-archy* is inherently political, every ontology is a form of praxis, and, from Deleuze's perspective, Being is immediately political (1990: 119). The separation between Being and politics is one of the key outcomes of the process of encrypting power. Once the Schmittian theological-political *potestas* – which denies agency and difference to Being – has been decrypted, it becomes clear that *Being* is an *an-archic potentia*, a potentiality that does not *exercise* power, but *is* power itself.

Power and Being do not institute themselves as distinct ontological realities. Rather, they are historically understood as separate dimensions due to the process of encryption. As Deleuze explains, the totality of Being requires the full vital immanentization of politics, for politics does not represent something that can merely be added to or detached from Being. Instead, politics is the most intimate and authentic dimension of Being, its constitution always de/ins/tituting of itself. For the French philosopher, politics is an *an-archic* form-of-life, not a mere attribute that later qualifies or specifies Being. Surprisingly, Deleuze's position is very close to that of Heidegger (2003) in the dense – and beautifully delirious and tormented – text *Contributions to Philosophy: From the Event*, in which he attempts to approach Being through a radically non-metaphysical path. In the end of the work, Heidegger is led to recognize that Being cannot be accessed by a theory that is neutral and indifferent to action, since every ontology implies an original ethics: '*operari sequitur esse*'. Thus, to decrypt power means to reveal this political-existential reality, making it sayable and, therefore, experienciable. In this sense, it is a matter of developing strategies for the decryption of power, in line with the Spinozian ontological thesis that Being itself is power, as Being is *potentia* (Sanín-Restrepo and Machado-Araujo 2020: 4).

Nevertheless, although Schürmann does not fully elaborate on a concept of *an-archic* politics, he identifies five characteristics that can be linked to his notion of groundless action, which closely align with the concept of *an-archic* politics presented here: the abolition of all teleological order; the rejection of the concept of responsibility; a protest against the technically administered world; a certain disinterest in the future of humanity; and the overlap between thought and action (1987: 251–81). At this juncture, Roberto Esposito highlights the inherent paradox within Schürmann's framework, as these five criteria, essential to conceiving the groundless, effectively function as principles of the non-principial (2020: 65–7).

Following Esposito's line of thought, Giorgio Agamben argues that the limitation of Schürmann's theorization becomes evident in his unsuccessful attempt to separate the two intertwined meanings of *arkhé* that Western culture has always conflated: origin and command, *principium* and *princeps*.[29] According to the economic archaeology that Agamben masterfully unravels in *The Use of Bodies*, these two meanings refer to the dual poles of the same exclusive-inclusive machine, which is always underpinned by its secret foundation – its principle, its *arkhé* – i.e., the element that is apparently negated. Thus, origin and command form one of the dyads analysed by Agamben, such as *zoé* and *bíos*, animal and human, law and anomie, constituted power and constituent power, kingdom and government, and so forth. These pairs, constituting the anthropological machine, cannot be merely inverted or destroyed; rather, they must be deactivated through the lucid exposition of their constitutively empty, *an-archic* nucleus. Agamben concludes that anarchy can never occupy the position of a principle – as is suggested by the paradoxical title of Schürmann's French book – but must instead be liberated in a contact, 'where both the *arkhé* as origin and the *arkhé* as command are exposed in their non-relation and neutralized' (2014b: 348–9). Otherwise, the dyad will reconstitute itself in new and terrible forms, capable of illustrating why one of the four fascist tetrarchs in Pasolini's unbearable *Salò* asserts that true anarchy is that of power.

In a more recent text, Agamben further develops his critique, arguing that the distinction Schürmann draws between the original (*Anfang*) and the originary (*Ursprung*) is ultimately futile. According to the Italian philosopher, both concepts are rooted in a notion of origin – whether historiographical or ontological – thereby betraying the very concept of *arkhé*, which, for Agamben, does not signify the beginning of anything, but rather the interval that arises between the empirical data of historical knowledge and its emergence (*Entstehung*) as origin. Thus, the Agambenian *arkhé* is not something originary and not original as Schürmann proposes, but the ungraspable reality that functions as a threshold between both and, by articulating them, makes possible something like an archaeophilosophical discourse (Agamben 2024a: 36–7). If this distinction is not properly understood, Agamben warns, there is a risk that anarchy, in forming a system with the government, will become part of the bipolar machine that revolves in the void, preventing the emergence of the Ungovernable (2011: 64–5). This final concept, as I understand it, occupies the place of *an-archy* in the Agambenian thought.

Schürmann seems fully aware of the problem highlighted by Esposito and Agamben, yet he tends to dismiss it by arguing that we are currently in a transitional phase between the era of metaphysics and the *an-archic* phase that is to follow. This allows him to justify his continued use of the language of the former, which is inherently principial. In this sense, Schürmann reduces the problem to a mere linguistic-epochal issue. However, what if the paradox emphasized by the Italian philosophers were taken seriously, and it were understood that *an-archy* – distinct from any rationalist anarchist politics, such as those proposed by Proudhon and Bakunin – refers to something that exceeds it, as an encrypted *potentia* that has no origin? In that case, what could function as the non-principle that posits *an-archy*? And what if, contrary to conventional thought, this non-principle was neither at the beginning nor at the end, as a form of Being, but instead corresponded to the very process of the immanence of *potentia*?

From this perspective, beyond the criticisms offered by Esposito and Agamben, what seems indisputable is the necessity of contemplating concrete strategies for decrypting theological-political power, thereby enabling *potestas* to manifest as *potentia*, that is, as *an-archy*. This can only be achieved through the decryption of transcendence, which points toward the potentiality of forms-of-life that are perpetually de/ins/tituting, non-principial principles, *an-archic* principles that resist all tendencies to immobilize immanence under the encrypted guise of transcendence. To this end, as discussed in section 1.3, it is necessary to revisit Deleuze's ideas. For Deleuze, immanence does not constitute a counterpart of transcendence upon which to ground a Schmittian political theology; rather it reveals itself as an autonomous and *an-archic* terrain of flux, change and contingency, thus opening up space for political theologies of potency. These, in turn, translate into concrete forms of conflict and difference, such as feminist, Black and decolonial political theologies. All of these are democratic-radical and *an-archic* insofar as they reject fixed centres of origin and command.

2.3. The critical revival

2.3.1. Radical theologies and radical orthodoxies

To speak of post-secularism today is to repoliticize religion without reducing politics to mere religious beliefs, thereby liberating the *potentia* that has been secularly encrypted as *potestas*. Unlike the excesses of Enlightenment secularism – which rigidly separated religion and politics, treating them as distinct (and incommunicable) spheres corresponding to the private and the public, respectively – post-secularism views religion as a vital and decisive dimension of culture and of the political processes involved in the dispute and formation of social identities.

In this post-secular context, although the ideas of philosophers such as Benjamin and Taubes are very powerful, they were unable to fully decrypt Schmittian political theology, a task that was only intensified at the end of the twentieth century, following the unusual convergence between theology and the post-structuralism of thinkers like Gilles Deleuze (1925–95), Jacques Derrida (1930–2004) and Michel Foucault (1926–84).[30] They introduced into intellectual debates the fertile concept of difference, which had previously been obscured by liberal political thought, for which difference arises from politics and its technical apparatuses, such as elections, representation and Constitution. In contrast, Deleuze, Derrida, Foucault and others argued that it is not politics that creates difference; rather, it is difference that creates politics, a central insight within the theory of the encryption of power (Sanín-Restrepo 2016: 107).

In this way, the previously unrecognized opportunity of decrypting theology from the bottom up emerged, as difference made feminist, Black and decolonial political theologies possible. Classical political theology, understood as the unity and secret centre of politics, could never accommodate difference. If this kind of political theology were taken as the primary term for the creation of meaning in social reality, one could only expect more of the same, namely, the continuous reproduction of the identical, more *potestas* and more sovereignty. Indeed, traditional political theology, centred on the outdated concept of sovereignty, is incapable of addressing the flows of capital, information, bodies, languages and ideas that shape the multiplicity of the contemporary world (De Vries 2006: 27). However, if difference is taken as an (un)foundation, other political theologies become conceivable, that is, radical-democratic theologies of difference inspired by post-structuralist ideas of multiplicity, immanence, flux, etc.

The fruitful encounter between political theology and post-structuralist thought has generated quite different reactions and was preceded by an earlier convergence, beginning in the 1960s, within the domain of pure theology. This confluence gave rise to the presuppositions of two of the main currents in contemporary theology, both described as radical because each, in its own way, is concerned with addressing the root of the theological phenomenon.

The first current is known as *radical theology*. Dominant in the United States, this movement was developed by theologians who embrace postmodern innovations and seek to reconstruct theology based on philosophical structures independent of transcendence and dogmatic truths. Radical theologians include Carl A. Raschke, Charles E. Winquist, Clayton Crockett, Don Cupitt, Dorothee Sölle, Gabriel Vahanian, Harvey Cox, Langdon Gilkey, Mark C. Taylor, Paul van Buren, Richard L. Rubenstein, Robert P. Scharlemann, Thomas J. J. Altizer and William Hamilton, among others. In Latin America and parts of Europe, this critical tendency was inspired less by post-structuralism than by the ideas of emancipation and eschatology central to liberation theology, generating variants across the globe (Scattola 2009: 239–47). The second current, prominent in the United Kingdom, is *radical orthodoxy*, which seeks to engage with post-structuralist thinkers in order to purify theology of philosophical contamination and, in turn, reconstruct the transcendence of God within a postmodern context. Key figures in radical orthodoxy include Catherine Pickstock, Frederik Christian Bauerschmidt, Graham Ward, John Milbank and Phillip Blond.

Despite their significant differences, the two currents are not entirely separate, as both remain fundamentally theological rather than philosophical. While radical theology engages more deeply with the philosophical realm than radical orthodoxy, there is no doubt that it remains, ultimately, a theology, which means that it must respect some minimum dogmatic requirements. On the other hand, radical orthodoxy, which seeks to reintroduce Christian truths grounded in faith into the contemporary world, must do so in the context of, and often in opposition to, post-structuralist critical theory, which can no longer be disregarded.

The fact is that both theological orientations engage with the same text – such as the *Bible* or its centuries-old exegeses – without fully recognizing its open character. In this regard, Petra Carlsonn Redell (2014: 18–19) compares them to what Foucault terms the tradition of commentary and the tradition of critique, an important distinction found in the first section of the fourth chapter of *The Order of Things* (1966: 92–5). The tradition of commentary treats a text as given, aiming to reveal its inherent truth to the reader without judgement, presenting itself as a sacred practice of reading. In turn, the tradition of critique evaluates the text according to various criteria, not presupposing any prior notion of truth but instead constructing it critically, thereby representing a profane approach to reading. Nevertheless, Foucault concludes that both traditions are inadequate today because they assume the text is a given entity posited in reality with inherent characteristics that can be represented. A thought capable of transcending this dichotomy – commentary and critique – must be attuned to the fissures and multiple dimensions within a text, focusing not on what it represents, but on what it *presents*, what it creates. Examples of such radical reading practices include the transgressive approaches of Bataille, the murmuring of Blanchot and the exploration of the phantom by Klossowski (Foucault 1964: 457).

This third possibility suggested by Foucault is based in the recognition that, in all reading traditions – whether sacred or profane – there is an encrypted dimension that does not come to the surface as an official option but is instead constituted in opposition to the institutional authority of the text. This dimension presents itself as something unthinkable and unspeakable, at least within traditional perspectives. By embracing this creative dimension, contemporary theologies – so far, I have focused exclusively on *theologies* in this section, rather than on *political theologies* – have the potential to become radically political, as discussed in section 2.4 through an exploration of feminist, Black and decolonial political theologies. But before delving deeper into this fascinating subject, it is crucial to examine the interplay between contemporary new theologies and post-structuralist thought, as well as to consider the implications of the 'death of God' thesis. These issues will be explored in the following two subsections.

2.3.2. Theology and post-structuralism

In the previous subsection, I presented an example of the encounter between post-structuralism – specifically Foucault's thought – and theology, focusing on the traditions of commentary and critique, as well as the possibility of moving beyond them. Here, I will discuss some additional examples. Given the very nature of post-structuralist thought, it is not feasible to construct a general theory of its relationship to theology. Instead, we can only proceed analogically, examining concrete confluences that manifest as situated and singular signatures, which engage in tension between the two fields.

According to Redell, the central issue with Christianity lies in its reliance on a representative structure that separates immanence from transcendence. To address this, she draws on a post-representative theology inspired by the works of Foucault and Deleuze. These philosophers effectively deconstruct how Christian theology legitimizes itself, particularly its tendency to equate the particular with the universal. This is evident in the way, for example, the white European man is seen as representing God, and how the part is believed to explain the whole and vice versa (Redell 2014: 3–4).

Deleuze, in turn, conceives of Being in its non-hierarchical, plural presence, which renders both representation and the idea of a unified God toward which everything is directed impossible. In his thought, there is a kind of joyful anarchy of beings within beings (1985: 79). For Deleuze, God is present in the world to the same extent as any other being, manifesting as an entity that, through its non-ideal and immanent repetition, creates and recreates multiplicity and difference, outside the confines of any representative logic based on the One and identity. This is why Deleuze ironically characterizes theology as the 'science of non-existent entities', thus freeing it from the dualisms that have historically defined it (1969: 326–7). From a Deleuzian perspective, theology enriches human language by multiplying it through disjunctions that go beyond the binary of true and false, creating a plateau that affirms its potency in the repetition of the different, the only 'Being' acceptable in a metaphysics akin to Deleuze's. Indeed, to repeat something means to make it possible again, restoring the possibility of what has been (Agamben 2001:105), thus involving the establishment of a connection with the potentiality of the real.

The thought of Derrida, like that of Deleuze, has had a profound impact on contemporary theology (Mansfield, 2010; Moreiras, 2004). A notable example of this influence can be found in the work of the American theologian John D. Caputo, who, drawing on Derrida, asks what Jesus would deconstruct today. He explores what a theological perspective, founded not on sovereign power but on divine weakness – specifically, the suffering humanity of Christ – would look like: 'The crucified body of Jesus proposes not that we keep theology out of politics but that we think theology otherwise, by way of another paradigm, another theology, requiring us to think God otherwise, as powerlessness, as opposed to the theology of omnipotence that underlies sovereignty' (2007: 88). In his 2006 book *The Weakness of God: A Theology of the Event*, Caputo argues that the image of the resurrected Christ must be taken seriously in order to construct a political theology of weakness. This theology, he contends, has the potential to reorient all thought concerning the role of political power in human societies, positioning weakness against omnipotence, gesture against verticality and the many against the One:

> Suppose God is not conceived as the rock-solid ground on which the onto-theo-political edifice of sovereignty is erected but is systematically associated with the different, the marginal, the outsider, the left out; with the naked ones, not the long robes in the sanctuary within, with the least among us, the destitute, the *anawin*, those who are plundered and ground under (Amos 8:4), and hence as a subversive and 'revolutionary' impulse? (2006b: 34)

Also drawing on Derrida's interpretation, Mark C. Taylor introduces the concept of a/theology in his 1987 book *Erring: A Postmodern A/Theology*. As he explains, the object of theology exists within a dynamic interplay of presence and absence, rendering it unrepresentable. In other words, theology presupposes a constant and problematic process of representation, one that is infinite in its perpetual opening and closing to presence: 'Always hurrying to grasp the fleeting here and now, representation can only re-present a presence/absence that never is' (1987: 48). Taylor states that theology and atheism today converge in a zone of indeterminacy that transcends both. He maintains that theology is present wherever there is a fixed centre that signifies the dominance of the One, resulting in the exclusion of the Others. For this reason, atheism is entirely theological, since it believes in the non-existence of God with absolute certainty (Caputo 2006a: 267), evoking a kind of fossilized thought that does not open itself to what seems strange or unassimilable to it. In contrast, a/theology, as proposed by Taylor, embraces the ultimate undecidability of all things, betting on flow, movement and hybridization (Matos 2022: 202).

At the end of his dense *The Kingdom and the Glory*, Agamben observes that God is more present than ever in the contemporary world, and this, paradoxically, through His absence. He claims that the concept of general providence, laboriously formulated by medieval theology, aligns with the idea, now almost universally accepted in both economics and politics, that there are overarching laws governing the functioning of human societies. In this context, God is seen as the establisher of a universal order in which His presence no longer needs to be recognized – in fact, it is crucial that it remains unacknowledged – since He has turned into the very order that governs reality. In current times God has become immanent to the world, but in a manner quite different from that envisioned by Spinoza, as far as the notion of a general order derived from God necessarily leads to His encryption, rather than His jubilant pantheistic manifestation. Indeed, encrypting God is part of God's design, part of His *oikonomía*, and to the extent that He becomes an immanent order, He negates any possibility of *an-archy*, the only ontological dimension in which the sovereign God can truly be destituted. In the words that close the already cited book by Agamben:

> In this grand image, in which the world created by God is identified with the world without God, and where contingency and necessity, freedom and slavery all merge into one another, the glorious center of the governmental machine appears clearly. Modernity, removing God from the world, has not only failed to leave theology behind, but in some ways has done nothing other than to lead the project of the providential *oikonomia* to completion. (2011: 286–7)

To confront this extreme result of encryption, which simultaneously hides and affirms God, securing His command and dominion through the assertion of an inescapable political-economic order, one must consider the teachings of the Italian philosopher Gianni Vattimo (1936–2023). For Vattimo, given the dominant pluralism of the contemporary world, it is untenable to maintain the existence of absolute foundations. This pluralism, in turn, leads to the collapse of atheism, whether encrypted or not: 'If God is dead, if philosophy has recognized that it cannot with certainty grasp the ultimate foundation, then philosophical atheism is no longer necessary. Only an absolute philosophy can feel the necessity of refuting religious experience' (2002: 5). According to Vattimo, postmodern thought inherits the Judeo-Christian tradition of salvation and creation, as these ideas allow it to conceptualize existence in terms of historicity and contingency, thus opposing the objectivist metaphysics of scientism (2002: 7). Therefore, the death of God does not imply God's non-existence, but rather the impossibility of a unified, absolute and total discourse about God. This theme merits further exploration.

2.3.3. Political theology and the death of God

In 1882, Friedrich Nietzsche (1844–1900) proclaimed the murder of God by men in the famous paragraph 125 of *The Gay Science*, where he introduces the madman who, searching for God in the marketplace with a lantern, announces this profound novelty, yet is dismissed as a lunatic and not taken seriously:

> Haven't you heard of that madman who in the bright morning lit a lantern and ran around the marketplace crying incessantly, 'I'm looking for God! I'm looking for God!' Since many of those who did not believe in God were standing around together just then, he caused great laughter. Has he been lost, then? asked one. Did he lose his way like a child? asked another. Or is he hiding? Is he afraid of us? Has he gone to sea? Emigrated? Thus they shouted and laughed, one interrupting the other. The madman jumped into their midst and pierced them with his eyes. 'Where is God?' he cried; 'I'll tell you! *We have killed* him – you and I! We are all his murderers. [. . .] Do we still hear nothing of the noise of the grave-diggers who are burying God? Do we still smell nothing of the divine decomposition? Gods, too, decompose! God is dead! God remains dead! And we have killed him! [. . .]'. Here the madman fell silent and looked again at his listeners, they too were silent and looked at him disconcertedly redly. Finally he threw his lantern on the ground so that it broke into pieces and went out. 'I come too early, he then said: my time is not yet. This tremendous event is still on its way, wandering; it has not yet reached the ears of men. Lighting and thunder need time, the light of the stars needs time, deeds need time, even after they are done, in order to be seen and heard. This deed is still more remote to them than the remotest stars – *and yet they have done it themselves*!' (2008: 119–20)

The scene is profoundly rich, echoing the figure of the cynic Diogenes, who famously wandered the streets of Athens with a lantern in broad daylight, searching for something exceedingly rare: a virtuous man, a real man. Another significant element in Nietzsche's text is that the announcement of God's death is made in the marketplace, that is, in the economic sphere. Only later does the madman turn to the churches to sing a *requiem* for the dead God, thus foreshadowing the political-economic theology discussed in section 3.1. Moreover, the irony lies in the fact that those who have killed God do not believe the madman's proclamation and continue to live as though God still exists, even mocking the madman in the process.

Contrary to popular interpretations, Nietzsche's allegory of the death of God does not simply denote contemporary atheism. Rather, it points to the ongoing functional maintenance of religious beliefs in the present day. In this sense, God ceases to be understood as a metaphysical entity and instead becomes a function, a transformation noted by Carl Schmitt in his political theology. One of the most critical aspects of Nietzsche's 'death of God' is that, while human beings may not consciously acknowledge having killed God, they effectively did so by reconfiguring Him into a God-function. This shift creates a complex interplay between divine presence and absence, offering fertile ground for the development of new theological perspectives. Indeed, the death of God is more than a mere metaphor for the supposed secularization of Western societies or the decline of the sacred. Even Heidegger was not immune to reductionist interpretations of the idea of the death of God, which he saw in his deplorable Nazi-era text on the self-assertion of the German university as an 'abandonment of contemporary man amidst the entity'. (1933: 12)

Similarly, the deicide narrated by Nietzsche should not be conflated with an amplification of Freudian theories concerning the necessary parricide for the emergence of the Overman (*Übermensch*). Nietzsche himself gestures toward this potential misinterpretation by revisiting the theme of God's death in *Thus Spoke Zarathustra*, where he declares that all gods – meaning all values – have been killed, not just the singular God associated with weak, resentful Christian values. In this context, the *Übermensch* is heralded as the figure capable of inaugurating a new era through the transvaluation of all values (1961 [I, XXII]: 3).

Beyond these superficial interpretations, the death of God emerges as a potent epochal figure of *an-archy*, indicating the absence of foundational principles for political life, regardless of whether this condition is acknowledged. If there were a God in any form, Nietzsche seems to tell us, he would necessarily be an immutable principle that would determine all that exists, including what is yet to come into existence, thus preventing Nothingness, without which there is no becoming, movement or creation. In this hypothesis, Nothingness would become, in the words of Emanuele Severino, an 'auscultator of Being' (1989: 31), structurally dependent on it. On the contrary, if we think not simply of *nothing as foundation* (vulgar nihilism), but of the *nothing of foundation* – the death of God – we liberate Being (Nothingness) and affirm the potency of creation, which, if it is a true creation, can only be creation from Nothing. This is *an-archy*.

From an *an-archic* perspective, the death of God signifies the demise of absolutes, not only within theology but also across philosophy and science. Paradoxically, this opens up the possibility of conceiving and experiencing another god, one with a lowercase initial. As Vattimo puts it:

> Nietzsche writes that God is dead because those who believe in him have killed him. In other words, the faithful, who have learned not to lie because it was God's command, have discovered in the end that God himself is a superfluous lie. However, in light of our postmodern experience, this means: since God can no longer be upheld as an ultimate foundation, as the absolute metaphysical structure of the real, it is possible, once again, to believe in God. True, it is not the God of metaphysics or of medieval scholasticism. But that is not the God of the Bible, of the Book that was dissolved and dismissed by modern rationalist and absolutist metaphysics. Furthermore, if there is no longer a philosophy (like Hegelian or Marxist historicism or like the various kinds of scientific positivism) claiming to be capable of demonstrating the nonexistence of God, we are free, again, to hear the words of Scripture. (2002: 5–6)

The death of God inevitably generates profound effects on new theologies, which must grapple with the relativization of the sacred that defines our era. A prominent example within radical theology is the work of the German theologian Dorothee Sölle (1929–2003). She rejects the notion of transcendence and endeavours to conceptualize a God without absolute presence, one who nevertheless inhabits the world of human beings and experiences suffering. In her influential 1979 work, *Representation: A Chapter of Theology After the 'Death of God'*, Sölle distinguishes between the concepts of substitution and representation in theological thought. According to traditional theology, Christ continually replaces God on Earth, thereby progressively distancing from the realm of suffering and human misery, and elevating Himself to a higher, more transcendent dimension. At the moment of the resurrection, this process of substitution culminates, with the suffering and corporeal Jesus giving way to a divine, non-human form, further separating Him from the human condition of pain and mortality. In contrast, the concept of representation – understood by Sölle in a way that diverges significantly from the classical theological tradition – appears as a structure that allows for the ongoing presence of a God who, no longer eternal or omnipotent, remains accessible within the human realm.

Sölle's idea of 'Christ, the representative' points to a scenario that having little to do with orthodoxy. In this framework, Christ is seen not as a divine figure who transcends human suffering, but as a figuration of the 'not-yet', one who, while awaiting the kingdom, suffers in human form through a continuous and powerless incarnation that is rooted in the notion of absence (1965: 190–200). Echoing the meaning of the German term *Stellvertretung*, which appears in the title of her book and signifies 'to stand in someone's place' or 'for someone', Sölle's Christ is one who constantly occupies the human position, perpetually incarnating on our behalf. In Sölle's thought, representation paradoxically becomes non-representational, subverting the traditional understanding of the term and offering a true profanation of an apparatus that originally emerged within conservative theological discourse, as discussed in section 1.2.

In turn, as a representative of radical orthodoxy, Frederick Christian Bauerschmidt (1999) seeks to reconstruct the transcendence of God through a path that is quite different from Sölle's approach, which, as we have seen, is based in the notion of a continuous, suffering and powerless incarnation of the 'representative Christ'. Interestingly, in his effort to restore the transcendence critiqued by post-structuralism, Bauerschmidt, much like many post-structuralist philosophers, challenges the very concept of representation. He argues that the Jewish roots of Christianity are fundamentally marked by a vigorous rejection of representation, a refusal historically embodied in the strict prohibitions of idolatry in Judaism. Such restrictions would have emerged from a religious sensibility that, in a sense, is postmodern *avant la lettre*, characterized by a profound suspicion of all forms of representation and the emptiness that underpins them. In this way, Christian theology, long before the advent of post-structuralism, would have recognized that representations are distinct from reality, with its theological and transcendent dimension remaining ultimately unrepresentable. However, for most post-structuralist thinkers, this thesis is untenable, as they deny any clear separation between representation and reality. In post-structuralist thought, everything is represented, and there is no need to invoke a more 'original' reality beyond representation. Nonetheless, disregarding the post-structuralist focus on the various dimensions of 'reality', Bauerschmidt contends that Christ's presence was fully realized in the event of the crucifixion, when, independent of any representation, God was present, even in His death. Bauerschmidt rejects representation in order to affirm an absolute presence. In his view, the issue is not the historical or biological life of Jesus Christ, but rather a transcendent presence-in-death that surpasses any human experience or understanding.

The American theologian Thomas J. J. Altizer (1927–2018) takes a more radical position than both Sölle and Bauerschmidt, arguing that the death of God is not merely a metaphor or symbol but a definitive proof of the satanic nature of the transcendent Christian God. While his interpretation might seem Gnostic at first glance, Altizer clarifies that the death of God represents the only viable way of thinking in the contemporary world. By denying transcendence, it makes space for a profane immanence that, he argues, is the truest consequence of the incarnation. As such, Christians should not mourn the death of God but rather rejoice in it. There is no place for resurrection, since the transcendent God must remain dead, signalling the complete fulfilment of Christianity and the realization of its *télos*, as foretold in several passages of the *Gospels* (1966: 44). Altizer interprets these texts through the lens of William Blake, producing a highly original and provocative theological work in which Jesus categorically rejects all titles, names and any desire for power (2000: 120–32). Paradoxically, Altizer's approach to theology, rooted in the repetitive and ritualized affirmation of God's absolute character (as proposed by Bauerschmidt) ends up emptying and exorcizing that very concept, transforming it into a spectral, contentless entity. This vision stands in stark contrast to Bauerschmidt's view. In line with Deleuze (1968: 145), one could argue that the repetition of the sacred in Altizer's thought, by pushing itself to the point of exhaustion and meaninglessness, ultimately generates difference.

The extremely radical theologies of authors like Thomas Altizer do not remain silent after the death of God; instead, they celebrate it as a recurring and ever-present event that makes room for the pure immanence of presence, poverty and suffering in this world. Within this setting, some contemporary theologies, by focusing on the present realities of time and space – along with the injustices and imperfections that define them – open up the possibility for political theologies that sharply diverge from the model proposed by Carl Schmitt. These will be further explored in the next section through synthetic readings of three significant 'new traditions': feminist, Black and decolonial political theologies.

2.4. Radical-democratic political theologies

2.4.1. Feminist political theologies

Feminist theologies, whatever their specific forms may be, are immediately political, as they operate within a traditional domain that has long been monopolized by the male model and controlled by patriarchal power. This reflection, in some ways, also applies to Black and decolonial theologies. I present these three strands of radical-democratic political theologies in separate subsections, not because they are autonomous or independent, but in order to address didactic needs, highlighting the main theoretical constructs in each field to facilitate research for those interested in a specific topic. There is no doubt, as will be shown in the following subsections, that feminist, Black and decolonial political theologies are deeply interconnected and intersectional. In fact, it is often difficult, if not impossible, to pinpoint where, for example, a feminist theological-political theme ends and a Black one begins.

According to many feminist theologians – such as Dorothee Sölle, who coined the term 'Christofascism', explained in subsection 3.2 – the current theological-political reflection should not treat the *Bible* as an absolute paradigm that gravitates above its vicissitudes, interpretations and historical conditioning. In fact, it is urgent to introduce a strong sense of relativity and historicity into the understanding of texts considered sacred. In this way, the patriarchal and sexist elements that emanate from them can be set aside in favour of a more authentic reading that not only recognizes Christ's inevitable references to the institutions and customs of his time but also discerns the novelty of his message and how it sounded (and still sounds) revolutionary. In this context, the work of the contemporary political theologian genuinely committed to Christian thought – which is that of the weak and the dominated, subjected to political power encoded as *potestas* – involves purging the 'sacred' texts of their historical conditioning. At the same time, this work requires moving away from treating such conditionings as ahistorical truths, subjecting them to critique and acknowledging that Jesus Christ is neither absolute nor all-mighty. His incarnation corresponds to a potential, ongoing and unfinished process realized only through the active participation of all Christians in the work of critical hermeneutics applied to the spiritual legacy that has been transmitted to the present day (Sölle 1971).

This task is fraught with difficulties, given the traditional emphasis on unity in political theology. But one-dimensional models, such as those centred on the male and white experience, are no longer universally accepted. Instead, they now compete with diverse theological perspectives in pluralistic and contested spaces. How can we seriously consider a theology based on the concept of a Father God in the wake of feminist critique? Or a theology rooted in European history after the challenges posed by decolonial thought? Moreover, how can theology embrace radical openness without slipping into abstract universalism?

Can a theology that endorses radical openness avoid becoming so inclusive that it loses its distinctiveness? Rather than offering answers to these questions, Redell poses even more unsettling ones:

> [. . .] if God actually and truly may be represented in one particular way on earth, does that not necessarily render other representations in other particular times and places untrue? The long tradition of white male representations of God causes postcolonial and feminist theologians to wonder; how is the female particularity represented by the male God generality? Was God ever in labour? Was 'he' ever raped? How is women's need for redemption mirrored in the grand history of redemption? (2014: 5)

Similar questions animate the various contemporary feminist political theologies, of which I present only a brief overview, given the limits of this book. First, it is essential to recognize that all political theologies shaped by the encounter with post-structuralism – feminist ones included – reject the universal and abstract subject typical of traditional political theologies. Instead, they welcome historicized, concrete and determined subject positions. Today, some scholars even speak of micropolitical theologies (Chen 2022), drawing on Foucault's concept of the microphysics of power. Foucault views power not as a substance or institution but as a complex network of relations that permeates, constitutes and can ultimately destitute subjects, understood in their concrete historicity and materiality. In this way, to approach feminist political theologies, I adopt a distinction between their Southern and Northern global branches, as the theological-political experiences of women differ significantly across these geopolitical spaces.

Regarding the Global South, the key issues addressed by its political theologians extend beyond the liberal themes of representation and participation in state power, which are common in Northern global feminism. In the Global South, the central concerns involve a much broader critique of society, encompassing race, class, culture and socio-environmental elements, as articulated by Filipina theologian Virginia Fabella and Ghanaian theologian Mercy Amba Oduyoye (Fabella and Oduyoye 1988: xi). However, this does not entail a return to the abstract universalism of traditional political theology. Rather, this localized approach avoids the pitfalls of abstract thought, enabling a more nuanced understanding of the specific challenges faced by women in the Global South.

In Latin America, feminist political theologies emerged from the broader liberation theology movement – a current that I address in subsection 2.4.3 – and initially adopted a Marxist framework. Notwithstanding, they soon expanded to include theological questioning of racism and sexism, recognizing that the sexual theology of colonialism is not only sexist but also heterosexist (Althaus-Reid 2001). These theologies challenge the *macho* model, which dominates the region's religious landscape, by proposing an alternative model that Cuban theologian Ana María Isasi-Díaz (1993) describes as *mujerista* theology. In Asia and Africa, by contrast, theologians focus on the role of traditional goddesses, who were persecuted and denied by colonial Christianity but are now being revalued through readings that emphasize syncretism, an important cultural trait in both Asia and Africa. Additionally, Asian and African political theologians critique the religious legitimization of female submission, an ancient phenomenon that found support and justification in the patriarchal and colonial vision of Christianity imposed in these lands. As a result, Eastern and African theologians engage in several critical tasks, such as denouncing the role of Christian missions that use the *Bible* as an instrument of oppression, deconstructing racial and gender hierarchies and defending religious practices of hybridization and resistance (Kwok 2019: 194). It is crucial to note that theologians from the Global South work within their specific historical and cultural conditions, which is why religious practices like polygamy, circumcision and female rites of passage, issues that may seem unacceptable to political theologians from the Global North, have become subjects of far more sophisticated and complex theological-political debates in the South (Oduyoye 1992).

In addition, political theologies of the Global South reinterpret certain classic biblical figures, such as Mary, whose virginity is understood not as a symbol of submission to man, but rather as a dimension of choice stemming from her autonomy (Kyung 1990: 74–84). This reappropriation of her figure is particularly significant in Latin America, where, since the sixteenth century, the white and docile Mary of the *conquistadores* has been contrasted with the mixed-race and indigenous figure of Our Lady of Guadalupe (*Nuestra Señora de Guadalupe*; in Nahuatl: *Tonantzin Coatlaxopeuh*), seen as a mother of justice and a defender of the weak (Bingemer and Gebara 1989). In a similar vein, Jesus is stripped of his divinity and masculinity. The Brazilian theologian Ivone Gebara (1999) sees in him the mark of precariousness and poverty, an encounter between humanity and nature capable of overturning the dichotomies between God/creation, masculine/feminine and mind/body, among others. Another biblical character that has been resignified by feminist theologians of the Global South is Hagar, the servant with whom Abraham had his first son and was later repudiated. According to the Mexican theologian

Elsa Tamez (1986), Hagar – a 'woman who complicated the history of salvation' – brings to the forefront issues related to reproductive and minorities rights. Hagar was an Egyptian slave among the Jews, and her story resonates especially in Latin America, where these themes remain of vital importance.

Regarding feminist theological-political movements in the Global North, it can be said that they align, to some extent, with the so-called 'waves' of feminism, with all the complexities and questions this categorization entails. Nevertheless, it is noteworthy, as the British theologian Elaine Graham (2019) points out, that even prior to the formal emergence of feminism, there existed a tradition of egalitarianism within radical dissenting Christian movements. These included groups such as the Baptists, the Levellers and various Puritan sects in both the United States and Europe during the seventeenth century. This trend further developed in the eighteenth and nineteenth centuries, spurred by the introduction of ideas advocating for social reforms. In the twentieth century, the opening of the Church following the Second Vatican Council (1962–5) and the intensification of social protest movements in the 1960s and 1970s facilitated the emergence, in the Global North, of a first generation of theologians and academics, including Valerie Saiving, Mary Daly, Margaret Brackenbury Crook, Catharina Halkes, Elisabeth Gossmann, Kari Elisabeth Børreson and Dorothee Sölle. These and many other scholars strongly criticized the androcentric and patriarchal structures of Christianity, calling for the inclusion of women in the intellectual, ecclesial and pastoral life of the Church. For centuries, the Church had failed in its purported universalist mission by excluding the experiences of women, thereby distorting the evangelical message and perpetuating female stereotypes of submission, self-sacrifice and superficiality (Miller-McLemore 2000: 239–41).

The second generation of Northern feminists took a further step, arguing that the mere inclusion of women in the Church, Christianity and religion in general was insufficient, given that these structures were built according to masculine models and therefore required critique and deconstruction (Fiorenza 1996: 167). In this regard, the Jewish theologian Judith Plaskow (1983) contends that it is not enough to overcome the religious prohibitions imposed on women in Judaism. The real issue, she asserts, is theological and concerns a fundamental critique of religious language and symbolism that, for instance, prevents women from seeing themselves in the image of God. Therefore, the task is to carry out a true *exégesis*, an interpretation that, from within traditional theological concepts, can restructure and open them up to a feminine outside perspective. This contrasts with the traditional *eségesis*, which interprets from the outside in, mechanically including women in the ancient theological-political apparatus without altering it (Woodhead 1997). Of course, it is neither possible nor desirable for feminist theologians to abandon and condemn the entire theological tradition (texts, sources, institutions, etc.), as if they were expected to attain a certain degree of purity. Rather, as the American theologian Kathryn Tanner (1997) teaches, the task is one of reappropriation and realignment, recognizing that the theological tradition itself is fluid. Moreover, interpreting it through innovative ideas means not only reading the canonical texts in new ways but also identifying the 'usable tradition' and incorporating elements and practices from both the past and the present that were previously considered heretical or marginal (Ruether 1983). Indeed, according to the American theologian Rebecca Chopp (1995, 1996), the old distinction between theoretical and practical theology is a typically patriarchal dualism, which must be overcome in favour of understanding theology as an inseparable form of thought and praxis that is inherently critical.

Finally, although several feminist theologies face challenges in engaging with contemporary feminist philosophers such as Donna Haraway and Judith Butler – who, following the third wave of feminism, critique and deconstruct the substantial notion of woman – important steps, though still timid, are being taken in this direction by understanding the feminine not as an essence but as a historical construct. From this perspective, the American theologian Sheila Briggs (1997) asserts that feminist theologies have a dual task of both critique and reconstruction, which can be broken down into three stages: destruction of the patriarchal foundations of theology, recovery of feminine traditions that have been rendered invisible by official history and transformation of actual and future religious institutions. Similarly, the Romanian theologian Elisabeth Fiorenza (1996) emphasizes the need for a feminist-theological hermeneutics of suspicion that critically examines patriarchal constructs, many of which are often subtle or imperceptible, while also drawing attention to the important contributions women have made throughout the history of theology, something that have long been overlooked by traditional political theologies. This approach seeks to transform tradition in such a way that the 'church of women' (*ekklesía gynaikón*), which has always existed, can now manifest itself concretely in the present.

2.4.2. Black political theologies

Much of what has been said about feminist political theologies also applies to Black political theologies,[31] as both emerge from the need to critique and overcome various ideas and practices centred on a subject that claims to be universal but historically presents itself as male and white. Although the underlying concerns are strikingly similar to those of feminist political theologies, it is indispensable to highlight some specific authors and theorizations within the field of Black political theologies in order to give them their own distinctive voice.

In this context, Black political theologies highlight the racial dimension of oppression, which is often overlooked in broader gender discussions. By seeking to reconcile Marxism with Black liberation theology, Cornel West (1982) shows how the experiences of slavery, segregation and systemic racism have profoundly shaped Black spirituality and theology. He also proposes a theology committed to the struggle for social and racial justice. Meanwhile, Black women theologians such as Katie Geneva Cannon (1988) and Emilie M. Townes (1989) provide vital insights into the intersection of race, gender and sexuality in theology, particularly through the concept of 'womanism'. Their work contributes to the development of a Black feminist theology that challenges both racism and patriarchy, extending beyond gender issues alone. While Cannon contends that Black women have historically appeared as 'moral guides' in the context of Black oppression, Townes seems to counterbalance this somewhat essentialist view by offering a feminist reinterpretation of Jesus, which relativizes and complexifies his masculinity and whiteness, presenting these dimensions as contingent rather than inherent.

According to Shaw Copeland (2019), Black political theologies began to take shape in the late 1960s and early 1970s in the United States, South Africa and England. The British branch of Black political theology emerged largely through the contributions of Caribbean immigrants. While important, this strand will not be the focus of my analysis, as its central ideas derive from American and South African Black theologies and are often intertwined with themes specific to decolonial political theologies. For an overview of the British perspective, the works of Beckford (1998) and Jagessar and Reddie (2014) provide valuable insights, as well as articles published in the journal *Black Theology in Britain: A Journal of Contextual Praxis*.

Nevertheless, I must briefly mention one of the most radical and compelling contributions in the field of Black political theologies in England: the work of British theologian Robert Beckford (2001). He investigates and denounces the prison conditions faced by Black people worldwide. From a theological-political perspective, he explores the rage – *rahtid*, a Jamaican term with biblical roots – that prisoners experience and how this rage can be transformed into a form of 'redemptive revenge'. Beckford's project, which includes teaching and screening films in prisons to reframe inmates' anger with political, historical and communal significance, has been met with resistance from the academic establishment. His documentaries go beyond prison issues, addressing the slave trade, colonialism, imperialism and the complicity of Protestant and Catholic churches in these historical injustices. Considering that the Christian ideal has been corrupted, Beckford asserts that his films serve as a kind of exorcism, aiming to heal theological-political wounds (2014: 192).

In the United States, Black political theologies were closely intertwined with the Black civil rights movements, with prominent theorists including Albert B. Cleage Jr., James Deotis Roberts and the influential theologian James Hal Cone (1938–2018). It is important to note that Cone's seminal works, *Black Theology and Black Power* (1969) and *A Black Theology of Liberation* (1970), precede *Liberation Theology* (1971) by Peruvian Catholic theologian Gustavo Gutiérrez (1928–2024), one of the founders of the liberation theology movement, which I will address in the next subsection. Cone developed several groundbreaking theoretical constructs, including the understanding of Blackness not merely as a racial or individual trait, but as a collective experience that places one's body and soul alongside the dispossessed, a perspective that, for its time, was remarkably advanced and which has been taken up today by thinkers like Achille Mbembe (2015). In the theological-political field, Cone argues that Jesus was the first person to be lynched, serving as a kind of negative prophecy for the Black bodies tortured in the United States. This horrific historical reality, for Cone, delegitimizes the faith of all white churches that are complacent or indifferent to the lynchings that have marked American history (2011: 158–9).

In South Africa, the odious apartheid regime sparked a significant theological-political flourishing, with key figures such as Allan Boesak, Frank Chikane, Manas Buthelezi and Simon Maimela. These theologians were deeply critical of the white churches and theologies that not only accepted but also actively justified the system of racial segregation and white domination, based, for example, on the biblical myth of Babel, which was used to 'prove' that God Himself had ordained the separation of the races (Mosala 1989). In response to this distortion, Buthelezi (1976) and Boesak (1976) argued that apartheid represented a direct violation of Christ's commandment of universal love (*agápe*, αγάπη) and, as Maimela (1981) further emphasized, was an evident sin. In addition, as Secretary-General of the Institute for Contextual Theology, Chikane led a collaborative effort between Black and white theologians which culminated in the 1985 *Kairos Document*.

This collective text, interpreting a passage from Paul's letter to the Romans (13:1-7), denounced the complicity of white churches and theologies in sustaining apartheid. It outlined three theological-political orientations in South Africa: the first, official, white and state-sanctioned, supported and defended apartheid; the second, which sought an abstract peace without critique, social transformation or restorative measures; and the third, prophetic in nature and oriented toward social transformation, emphasized Christian praxis as a pursuit of justice, particularly within the context of the deeply unjust apartheid regime.

From their inception, Black political theologies have focused on humanity as a whole, with particular attention given to Black, brown, *mestizo* and Chicano communities. In this regard, American theologian Vincent Lloyd (2012) highlights how the antiracist struggle is often obscured by the abstract multicultural discourse prevalent in neoliberal globalization, stressing that challenging white supremacy is the most pressing and significant task for Black political theologies. Building on this, Lloyd (2016) calls on all political theologies – not just Black ones – to critically engage with and dismantle the ideology of whiteness, which he argues to be a form of idolatry. In a similar vein, J. Kameron Carter (2008) discusses the process of whitening Jesus, noting that the figure of Christ could only be reimagined as a religious symbol of the West after a process of deracialization, during which his Jewish and Semitic origins were systematically erased and forgotten.

2.4.3. Decolonial political theologies

Although I cannot fully explore this issue here, it is important to emphasize that I use the term 'decolonial' and not 'postcolonial' because I consider it to be more robust in terms of philosophical criticism. This approach is informed by the work of scholars such as Catherine Walsh (2009), Aníbal Quijano (1992) and Santiago Castro-Gómez and Ramón Grosfoguel (2007), who claim that the postcolonial dimension, while significant, is historically and politically limited. It primarily addresses the formal dismantling of colonialism as a political, legal and economic system. In contrast, the concept of *coloniality*, emerging from a decolonial perspective, refers to a far broader, more pervasive and subjectivizing meta-structure that encompasses linguistic, material and symbolic dimensions persisting in postcolonial contexts and perpetuating ontological, epistemic and material forms of domination at every level. There is a coloniality of power, knowledge and being that continues to divide the world into centre and periphery, and it is against this complex of dominations that decolonial critique arises. In this regard, the theory of the encryption of power is accurate in identifying colonialism as the site *par excellence* of the rigid division between *potestas* and *potentia*, where the former is imposed upon the latter in a way that encrypts power, establishing a naturalized and rigid reality in which democracy, in its representational guise, is reduced to a mere simulacrum (Sanín-Restrepo 2016: 106).

I would also like to emphasize that I am distancing myself from postcolonial theories advanced by thinkers such as Homi K. Bhabha and Gayatri Spivak. On the one hand, their frameworks are detached from the Latin American context that I aim to engage with more directly, and on the other hand, they do not offer significant reflections on theological-political issues. Postcolonialism, since its 'foundation' in the work of Frantz Fanon (1925–61), has not primarily addressed religious themes (Sugirtharajah 2012: 2), often viewing them as mere ideological constructs of colonialism. Moreover, as South African theorist Gerald West argues, postcolonialism is 'not sufficiently attentive to the structural and systemic dimensions of power, particularly at the macroeconomic level of global neoliberal capitalism' (2008: 153).

As will be seen in the following pages, this critique does not apply in any way to decolonial political theologies, whose main currents are closely linked to the so-called liberation theology. This theological movement was conceived by Catholic thinkers such as the Peruvian Gustavo Gutiérrez, the Brazilians Leonardo Boff and Frei Beto, the Uruguayan Juan Luis Segundo, the Salvadoran Jon Sobrino and the Ecuadorian Leonidas Proaño. Among Protestant theologians, key figures include the Brazilian Rubem Alves and the Argentine José Míguez Bonino.[32]

Initially, it seems significant to me that, even if unconsciously and underdeveloped, decolonial thought emerged from the theological sphere rather than the other way around. Indeed, liberation theology is one of the first and most legitimate decolonial manifestations in Latin America, having arisen long before the concept of decoloniality was articulated in the contemporary academic discourse. From the late 1960s onward, liberation theology began to be cautiously received in Europe under the label of 'theology of revolution'.[33] While the term 'liberation theology' became widely known only after Gustavo Gutiérrez's work in 1971,[34] I find it at least curious that a theological-political critique born in Latin America under the sign of liberation had to be translated into the word 'revolution' to be recognized in Europe. While 'revolution' is a concept more easily understood within Marxist frameworks, 'liberation' carries deeper theological and spiritual connotations. This shift points to the challenges of translating theological concepts into secular political discourse.

Beyond these minor details, liberation theology can be defined as a broad Latin American Christian movement that developed theological and political theories and practices aimed at understanding and confronting the region's social and economic inequalities. It often combined theological constructions with Marxist theories, a synthesis that was facilitated by the Second Vatican Council. Subsequently, in 1984 and 1986, the movement was condemned by the Catholic Church through the actions of the administrative body that succeeded the medieval Inquisition, now known as the Congregation for the Doctrine of the Faith, then headed by Cardinal Joseph Ratzinger, who would later become Pope Benedict XVI.[35] However, the greatest threat faced by priests and scholars associated with liberation theology did not come from Rome but from the Latin American dictatorships of the 1960s to the 1980s, which regarded them as Marxist agitators and subjected them to persecution, torture and murder. A notorious and tragic example of this repression is the massacre of six Jesuits on 16 November 1989, carried out by the Salvadoran military dictatorship at the residence of Central American University.[36] On that occasion, a university employee and her fifteen-year-old daughter were also killed. Among the murdered was the university's dean, Ignacio Ellacuría (1930–89), one of the most brilliant thinkers of liberation theology. Along with Jon Sobrino, Ellacuría co-authored a work titled *Mysterium Liberationis*, which, despite its Latin title, was written for a broad audience and addresses themes such as creation, grace, eschatology, sacraments and Christology.

The seemingly contradictory foundational theses of liberation theology were articulated in Gutiérrez's 1971 work. For him, God loves all equally and gratuitously, yet has a *preferential* love for the poor. As a result, Christians are called to promote the liberation of the oppressed – and also of the oppressors, who dehumanize themselves through the exploitation of others' lives and labour – on three levels: political liberation, psychological-anthropological liberation and spiritual liberation from sin. Interpreting Gutiérrez's ideas, Roberto Goizueta (2019: 282) sees no inconsistency in them because God's universal love is not neutral. In fact, God is not an ahistorical abstraction but a presence that reveals Itself in the troubled and unjust history of humanity. This is why God sides with the poor. If God were to remain neutral, He would effectively legitimize the injustices of the world. Furthermore, it is only by preferentially loving the poor – and actively working on their behalf, as liberation theology does not hierarchize contemplation, prayer and service – that one can genuinely love all people. The preference for the poor is, in a literal sense, *preferential*, not exclusive.

According to Gutiérrez, poverty, whether material or spiritual, does not possess any ontological significance. Liberation theology thus turns to the poor not because they are inherently 'better' than the powerful, but because of theological imperatives clearly demonstrated in the *Gospels*. In fact, the *Gospels* reveal that God incarnated, grew and died in this world among the dispossessed (Goizueta 2019: 283). Therefore, the preference for the poor is theocentric, as Gutiérrez (1987) explains in his important work on Job, an archetypal theological-political figure that symbolizes the apparent cosmic injustice suffered by the innocent, a theme that will be explored further in the conclusion of this book. From the perspective of the preferential love for the poor, the spirit of liberation theology can be encapsulated in a statement by Jon Sobrino, a Spanish theologian who has lived in El Salvador since 1957. Deviating a phrase by Origen and Cyprian, who famously said '*extra ecclesiam nulla salus*' ('outside the Church there is no salvation'), Sobrino asserts that '*extra pauperes nulla salus*', meaning 'outside the poor there is no salvation' (2008: 69).

Liberation theology can be understood in terms of three generations of theologians. The first one includes the aforementioned Latin American 'founding fathers', who were deeply engaged in grassroots work with marginalized communities and were avid readers of Marxist thinkers. The second generation consists of theologians who studied with the founders, such as the Mexican Elsa Tamez and the Chilean Pablo Richard. These authors move beyond Marxism to develop their theological-political critiques and begin to engage with Black and feminist theologies. The third generation, working within a much more radical post-structuralist and hermeneutical philosophical context, further intensifies this dialogue. Indeed, third-generation liberation theologians extend their engagement beyond the ecclesiastical and academic spheres, actively participating in NGOs, social movements and broader civil society formations (Aguilar 2019: 294–5). Their connections with decolonial theory and post-structuralist thought are particularly pronounced, as they develop post-foundational theories that contest the idea of an ultimate, fixed foundation for understanding the sacred (Panotto 2016a, b; 2020). These constructions resonate with the concept of *an-archy* discussed in section 2.2. In her work on gender, for example, Argentine theologian Marcella Althaus-Reid (2005) calls for a queer liberation theology that is indecent and rooted in the right to be abnormal. Similarly,

Argentine theologian Iván Petrella (2004) contends that liberation theology must break with the Church and the university, seek non-canonical sources and engage in identity politics while positioning itself against the prevailing capitalist economic system. This perspective has been further developed by Jun Mo Sung (1998), a Korean Catholic theologian based in Brazil since 1966, who argues that faith in the capitalist market contradicts the values of the kingdom of God, as human dignity cannot depend on one's participation in the market.

According to Andrade and Panotto (2023: 2–3), the specific sociopolitical context that gave rise to liberation theology in Latin America during the 1960s and 1970s no longer exists, but this does not diminish its relevance. On the contrary, given the recent intensification of colonial patterns of domination, the insights of liberation theology have proven to be not only theoretically sound but also socially urgent. This is especially true when linked to decolonial thought to denounce: (1) the reconfiguration of the coloniality of power in both theological and social-scientific discourses; (2) the reinforcement of capitalist racism, *machismo* and patriarchy; (3) the necropolitical dynamics driving environmental destruction; and (4) the consolidation of neoliberal consumerist culture. Thus arises the possibility of a renewed decolonial theology of liberation that deepens and profanes the Schmittian perception according to which all theological thought is determined by specific spatiotemporal conditions. Today, it is essential to update categories such as 'poverty', which are no longer limited to the lack of economic resources but also encompass issues related to gender, race and anthropocentric perspectives. Therefore, the preferential option for the poor, a defining characteristic of liberation theology, now extends to include the struggles for women, Black people and the planet. As the authors assert: 'in the face of the *Thanatos* of modern and colonial civilization, the theologies of liberation – theologies of life! – have much to contribute in the search for alternatives that banish the idols of death and put the Gods of life back at the center' (Andrade and Panotto 2023: 6).

Perhaps the most compelling example of the intersection between decolonial political theologies and liberation theology is the work of the Argentine philosopher and historian Enrique Dussel (1934–2023), who recently passed away in his exile in Mexico. Dussel integrates his theological expertise with a profound critique of Modernity, arguing that it is a category constructed by Europeans at the expense of the colonized peoples. He asserts that colonialism not only provided material support to the metropolises of the Old World but also shaped their epistemological and ontological foundations.

In *Politics of Liberation* (2007), Dussel critically re-examines history to challenge its Eurocentric centralization in Greece and Europe in general, denouncing the division of history into periods defined by Western criteria. He deconstructs, among other concepts, the notions of secularism and progress, revealing how these ideas were shaped by colonialism and continue to serve its power structures.

In the specifically theological-political terrain, Dussel argues in several of his works that post–Second World War theology and philosophy were not only reformist but also failed to confront the fundamental structures of capitalism. He asserts that these intellectual movements delegitimized radical critiques of the system by labelling them as anarchic or fanatical utopias. In contrast, Dussel contends that a true reading of the *Gospels* reveals a profound need to align with the majority of humanity – the oppressed – and denounce what he refers to as the 'ethics of hegemonic minorities'. This ethical framework, according to Dussel, is grounded in philosophical apparatuses like the theory of argumentation, which aim to create 'consensus' while excluding the victims of European Modernity. Modernity, in this view, divided the world into centre and periphery, establishing a global order where identity and consensus were, and continue to be, constructed through exclusionary processes. In this logic, the 'other' is both produced and oppressed, often erased from the very communicative communities that claim to represent universal interests (1973: 97–156, 2013: 309–11).

Dussel defends a 'barbaric' and impure theology, one that is capable of reinterpreting tradition – just as he did with Marxist thought – to develop forms of social liberation across political, pedagogical and sexual dimensions, with particular emphasis on the role of women. For Dussel, Christianity is animated by a prophetic and liberating spirit, which, drawing on Marx's theory of commodity fetishism, identifies capitalism as a form of idolatry akin to that denounced by the ancient prophets of Israel. This theological approach emphasizes the need to defy contemporary modes of oppression and domination, seeing in capitalism not just an economic system but a deeply entrenched idol that must be dismantled for true human liberation to occur.

Positions such as those of Petrella, Sung and Dussel are particularly relevant and urgent in the current context, when a theological-political version of neoliberalism is emerging with increasing force. In various Neo-Pentecostal movements, rather than adopting a preferential option for the poor, neoliberal political theologies view power and wealth as theological indicators of salvation, while poverty is framed as a sign of damnation. This leads to the development of individualistic, anti-communitarian, authoritarian and aporophobic forms of subjectivation, processes that I will address in the next chapter. For now, it is important to recognize that decolonial political theologies encompass more than just liberation theology. Therefore, a brief mention of other strands within this tradition is warranted, many of which intersect with feminist and Black political theologies, as noted earlier.

Since a detailed analysis of the various authors currently engaged in decolonial political theologies is not feasible here, it seems useful to at least outline the general contours of their contributions. These thinkers begin with a necessary critique of the 'founding fathers' of the movement, such as Gutiérrez, arguing that they universalized and homogenized the category of the poor. In contrast, they emphasize that each human group, even when oppressed by similar economic conditions, organizes itself socially, religiously and politically in distinct ways, thus giving rise to specific and diverse traditions of the oppressed, rather than a singular, unified tradition. This critique also emphasizes the need to decentralize theological-political reflection, which has traditionally treated the *Bible* and Christianity as *a priori* elements, compelling indigenous, African and Eastern belief systems to conform to European standards, thereby producing unequal processes of syncretism.

From this perspective, the Botswanan feminist theologian Musa Dube (2010) proposes exploring the established biblical theological-political tradition for what she terms 'zones of contact', interrogating how relationships are formed within them and how ideologies related to gender, class, age, race, and so on are articulated. She also seeks to identify possible reinterpretations that could foster genuine cultural interdependence in these zones. The counterpoint approach, inspired by musical theory and championed by Palestinian theorist Edward Said (1935–2003), seems to be even more powerful. In counterpoint, there is no dominant voice; instead, different voices continually interweave, creating a more harmonious and complex musical whole (Said 1993). Building on this, Sinhalese biblical hermeneut Rasiah Sugirtharajah (2012) suggests reading the life of Jesus in close dialogue with the life of Buddha, allowing the two narratives to complement, critique and enhance one another. In summary, contemporary decolonial political theologies have four interrelated tasks (Brazal 2019: 519–21): *deconstructing*, *reconstructing* and *critiquing* the dominant readings produced by the Global North, while remaining committed to *resisting* theological-political models based on either sovereignty or the market, as discussed in the next and concluding chapter.

3

Antagonisms

God is a man-eater.

(*Gospel of Philip*, 110, 35–36)

3.1. The capitalist religion

Political theologies that aspire to be democratic and radical need to be plural and situated, singular and relative to a specific epochal context that is both conflictual and concrete. Currently, this context is rooted in capitalism, which means that any political theology – whether conservative or libertarian – must begin from this dimension, much like Schmitt, Benjamin and Taubes started from sovereignty to either justify or depose it.

More than merely an economic mode of production, capitalism functions as a religion, that is, a factory of subjectivities.[1] As Benjamin stated in his dense 1921 fragment titled *Capitalism as Religion*, capitalism represents a restless cult religion, characterized as a liturgy centred on the dimension of glory and its inherent emptiness (Heron 2008). It is structured like a grand and infinite feast (1991 [VI]: 100–93) in which there are no dogmas, as any aspect of capitalism can be critiqued, provided that the cult – namely, consumption – remains constant and unreflective. Its product is guilt, not dogma. In this, capitalism reveals itself as a parasite that has become autonomous from Christianity, the most powerful of the guilt-inducing religions. When a religion produces dogmas, these can be questioned and eventually transcended. However, if it relinquishes dogma – which serves as a mediation to the sacred – all that remains is the empty shell of guilt, which also signifies debt, as suggested by the German word *Schuld*, capable of conveying both meanings. In the case of capitalism, guilt/debt compels the faithful to consume incessantly in an expiatory ritual that offers no possibility of redemption, condemning humanity to the 'house of despair', where guilt manifests as a debt inscribed in the hell of the faithful consumer's unconscious. Thus, capitalism becomes, in a theological-political-economic sense, synonymous with guilt without expiation – eternally and gloriously.

In his enigmatic manner, Benjamin realized that capitalism is not just a mode of wealth production or a specific worldview (*Weltanschauung*) but rather a metaphysics, a view that many contemporary authors also support (Gunjević 2015: 82). In this regard, he radicalized the insights of classical thinkers such as Karl Marx and Max Weber, who, while not fully equating capitalism with religion – unlike Benjamin, who did so without reservation – acknowledged significant connections between these two realms.

Within his sociopolitical context, Marx was a vehement critic of religion, engaging in polemics with Ludwig Feuerbach by asserting that it is insufficient to merely denounce the religious phenomenon; rather, it is far more urgent to liberate human beings from the material conditions that facilitate and necessitate religious experience. For Marx, religion represents the inverted and idealized image of class society, which is why the struggle must focus on the material conditions that sustain such a society rather than on religion itself. He posited that religion is not only an ideological expression of the process of alienation but also a form of protest against social oppression, functioning as 'the sigh of the oppressed creature, the heart of a world without heart, the spirit of a spiritless situation' (1956: 378).

Nevertheless, this instrumental view of religion – one with which I clearly do not concur – did not prevent Marx from acknowledging its significant role in the self-constituting logic of capital. In fact, at the outset of the fourth part of the first chapter of *The Capital*, Marx reflects on the commodity, describing it as a very difficult thing, full of metaphysical subtleties and theological refinements, an assessment that cannot be explained solely by the author's proverbial irony. What is at stake is the concept of fetishism. Originally rooted in anthropology and the sociology of religion, fetishism describes how social relations are mediated through objects. In this context, the commodity fetishism theorized by Marx allows for the objectification of people and the subjectification of objects, creating an illusory dimension that operates as if it were more real than reality itself.

In a satirical extension of Marx's insights, Paul Lafargue (1842–1911), Marx's son-in-law, authored an article in 1887 titled *The Religion of Capital*. In this work, he depicts a gathering of capitalists who, parodying the Council of Nicaea, convene a world congress to establish the tenets of the religion of capital. They assert that capital is the God everyone knows, sees, touches, smells and tastes; it exists for all our senses. Lafargue (1916) concludes that it is the only God who has yet to encounter an atheist.

In turn, at the beginning of the last century, Max Weber, in his seminal work *The Protestant Ethic and the Spirit of Capitalism*, identifies significant connections between the individualistic structure of Protestantism and the historical development of capitalism in Northern Europe. Unlike Marx, who interprets religion as an ideological superstructure arising from an economic base, Weber argues that capitalism itself is rooted in religious foundations. He posits that capitalism embodies a process of rationalization that stems from the secularization of Protestantism. Unlike Catholics, Protestants do not distinguish between holy days and workdays; for them, all of life is a time for rational capitalist production, a point that Marx had previously observed. Nonetheless, the crucial element linking capitalism – which Weber regards as the quintessential expression of Modernity – to Protestantism is the doctrine of predestination. According to this doctrine, the faithful are not saved by their works, as maintained by Catholicism.

Thus, for example, according to some interpretations of Calvinist belief, all human beings are predestined for heaven or hell from birth, irrespective of their actions. But it is possible to ascertain who is destined for salvation and who is condemned to flames of hell through their economic success in this life, which serves as a sign of divine favour. This perspective can lead to a disregard for traditional Christian morality and conventional social responsibilities, as those marked for paradise may feel justified in prioritizing personal gain over communal obligations. Weber argues that the accumulation of capitalist wealth serves as retrospective evidence – at least from God's perspective, *sub specie aeternitatis* – of one's eternal salvation. This notion is encapsulated in the famous 'entrepreneurial spirit' of capitalism, which arises from worldly asceticism. In this framework, capitalists produce wealth not for spending but as a clear and increasingly indicator of their divine favour and salvation, remaining distant from any notions of excess or gift exchange. Conversely, poverty is seen as a confirmation of eternal damnation, a condition ordained by God that cannot be contested, thereby delegitimizing any state-sponsored social welfare efforts for the economically disadvantaged. At this juncture, the alignment between the vocation for salvation and the vocation for entrepreneurship becomes evident, ideas that in German can be expressed by a single word: *Beruf*.

Additionally, it is crucial to recognize that, for John Calvin (1509–64), salvation is not only predestined but also individual, rendering any challenge to God's designs impossible, who chooses to save a select few while condemning the majority. The secular manifestation of this individualistic theology is the capitalist market, where each person must pursue their own advantage, operating under the assumption of universal competitiveness that remains beyond reproach, as it reflects an ontological and metaphysical truth akin to the 'natural' and ultimately just world system established by God. Over time, capitalism has evolved into neoliberalism, transitioning from a means of salvation into the 'iron cage' described by Weber, a self-sustaining system that has emerged as a religion in its own right, as noted by Benjamin.

In relation to this theme, it is pertinent to reference the viewpoint of Spanish theorist José Luis Villacañas, who, while espousing a different conception of political theology than that which informs this book, agrees that neoliberalism represents its most perfected manifestation in contemporary society. For Villacañas (2020, 2024), political theology refers to the compact government of populations wherein the psychological experiences of the governed are not divided into autonomous political and religious spheres; rather, they are unified within a singular, distinctly theological-political dimension that encompasses the drives of death, pleasure and knowledge as identified by Freud. In this regard, neoliberalism emerges as one of the most powerful expressions of political theology, since it subordinates all social spheres to the economy. By economizing domains such as science, art, health, politics and religion, participation in any of these social spheres necessitates mediation through the economy and its logic rooted in guilt, predestination and debt. While I find Villacañas' broad definition of political theology – emphasizing the unidimensionality of power and subjective agglutination without adequately addressing the role of transcendence – to be somewhat reductive, his analysis aligns with the argument presented in this chapter: neoliberalism is inherently theological-political.

In the context of capitalist religion, money appears as the true incarnation of the divine. Its symbolic and quantitative materiality transforms money into a magical-religious phenomenon, making it comprehensible and contestable only within that same framework. This insight was notably articulated by Alan Moore, a renowned graphic novelist and self-proclaimed wizard, who reflected on the seemingly insane actions of Bill Drummond and Jimmy Cauty. Operating under the alias KLF (Kopyright Liberation Front), they garnered approximately one million pounds from their electronic music ventures in England, only to incinerate this substantial sum on 23 August 1994, on the island of Jura in Scotland. Cauty and Drummond could not explain why they did this and quickly expressed regret, especially after facing backlash from those who viewed the video documenting the money burning. They even preserved the ashes of the incinerated banknotes in a suitcase, presenting this 'proof' to their bewildered audience.[2] However, Alan Moore, unlike the others, refrained from indignation and provided a compelling interpretation of Cauty and Drummond's performance, one that I find particularly insightful.

As the warlock explains, money is a magical phenomenon. Burning it is not the same as burning food or people, as it consists merely of paper that symbolizes value. Therefore, if money functions as a symbol, the only way to combat it is to adopt an equally symbolic stance. By burning money, Cauty and Drummond declared in the most radical way their disbelief in capitalist magic, thereby creating space for others to question this same illusion, which serves as a cornerstone of neoliberal political theology. The gesture of incinerating one million pounds was not simply an act of amusement, madness or a misguided attempt at self-promotion; rather, it was a magical act – I would argue, a theological-political one – imbued, like every magical act, with a social dimension that transcends the individual sphere. According to Alan Moore, the duo was seeking an answer through their performance: 'It was a powerful magical event [. . .]. I can't see any other explanation for it. You're dealing with a form of language, a conversation – but you're not sure what the conversation is . . . you're waiting for a reply' (*in* Higgs 2012: 61).

It is important to emphasize Moore's main argument: magic can only be countered on its own terrain. This perspective aligns with the argument I develop in this book, suggesting that political theology must be challenged within the framework of political theology itself. Simply denying or repressing it, as the 'secular' and 'rationalist' liberal tradition often does, is both ineffective and potentially dangerous. Thus, the first step in dismantling political theology is to recognize that it is neither monolithic nor necessarily authoritarian. In fact, the convergence between capitalism and religion can also foster critical responses, such as liberation theology. Despite all the limitations inherent in a socio-religious movement, it has established the category of idolatry to indicate that the disenchantment of the world, as described by theorists of supposed modern secularization, amounts to nothing more than the functional replacement of the celestial God with a terrestrial deity known as capital. This hidden God demands blind worship, and it is clear that economic idolatry is rooted in a sacrificial ideology (Assmann and Hinkelammert 1989). The God-capital remains concealed by the continuous process of its glorification yet fully operational, a strategy that renders it imperceptible as a divine entity and hinders the necessary critique of religion. Consequently, capital is understood as irresistible and omnipresent, without recognizing that these attributes are divine and can only be decrypted and destituted through radical criticism.

Within this horizon of critical closure, any demonstrating of the intrinsic unsustainability of the capitalist economic system – together with the so-called 'science' that underpins it – remains ineffective unless accompanied by a coherent theological-political decryption. Capitalism functions as a cult religion and must be confronted as such. Criticism cannot be confined to its technical and economic dimensions; while these aspects are integral to capitalism's operation, they ultimately rely on its religious foundation. Thus, both the basis and the crisis of capitalism are fundamentally ethical and metaphysical rather than purely economic, social or political. A trivial yet significant example: to eliminate the global scarcity of potable water, an investment of only $29 billion would be sufficient, while in 2014 alone, Americans spent $77 billion on soft drinks (Huici 2016: 12–13). This indicates that capitalism possesses the technical and logistical capability to eradicate extreme poverty but chooses not to do so for several reasons, some of which are undoubtedly theological-political. In this context, the problem of Evil must be re-examined from ontological, ethical and metaphysical perspectives, an endeavour that only a democratic-radical political theology can effectively undertake.

Capitalism corresponds to a cult in which both its God and dogmas remain concealed, offering visible and conscious emphasis only to its ritualistic dimension, which is strongly subjectivizing. This ritual is enacted with every seemingly innocuous transaction, each purchase and sale performed tirelessly by its devoted adherents. Today, 'an uninterrupted cult is celebrated whose liturgy is work and whose object is money. God has not died, he has become Money. The Bank [. . .] has taken the place of the Church and its priests and, governing credit [. . .], manipulates and manages faith – the scarce, uncertain trust – that our time still brings with it' (Agamben 2012).

Despite the apparent simplicity of capitalist rituals such as buying, selling and borrowing, capitalism, like any religion, elevates the contingent to the status of the necessary, effectively ontologizing its own history by framing money and the market as intrinsic to human nature (Huici 2016: 143–6). Simultaneously, the capitalist religion seeks to reshape reality to conform to its own dogmas. It disregards the distinction between the sacred and the profane spheres – an essential feature of all historical religions – blurring these boundaries under the deceptive guise of a materialism that lacks genuine materiality, as it is rooted in a complex metaphysics with medieval Christian origins. Within this framework, Being and praxis are divided, situating the ontological foundation of Being in the Father while attributing its economic and administrative functions to the Son. This religious paradigm underlies the notion of a 'liberal' economy, which claims to operate free from regulation or limits (Agamben 2011: 261–87).

Agamben contends that 'economic theology', rather than 'political theology', more accurately captures the ideological foundation of capitalism (2011: 66). This shift complicates the struggle against capitalism, as economic theology obscures its dominant nature beneath the guise of the 'naturalness' and 'voluntariness' of economic relations. According to neoliberal discourse, these relations are not characterized by violence, impositions or authoritarian commands, but by the hypothetical individual freedom inherent in contracts and commerce. While in political theology God appears as the creator and the imperator of the world, in economic theology He assumes the ostensibly more 'natural' role of the world's administrator. This brings forth the concept of economy – derived from the Greek *oikonomía* (οἰκονομία) – as a form of administration tied to salvation (2011: 53–67) and encapsulated in the well-known image from political economy: the invisible hand of the market.[3]

To substantiate his thesis, Agamben (2011: 277) distinguishes between two types of sovereignty, each corresponding to a different theological version: the dynastic sovereignty of divine right comes from the theological-political paradigm, whereas popular-democratic sovereignty derives from the theological-providential paradigm. I agree with the Italian philosopher only in terms, given that all economic theology is inevitably political in a broad sense, as it involves an existential decision. As Heidegger (1954) notes, there is nothing less technical than technique in its essence, particularly when it involves a decision for technique. In the context of the purported economic theology, this is evident in the neoliberal apparatus for self-administration and market governance. Furthermore, to support, as Agamben argues, that the *oikonomic* paradigm founds popular-democratic sovereignty, I believe it is necessary to emphasize that this occurs in the form of the encryption of democracy, a strategy intrinsic to political liberalism that involves apparatuses such as political representation, elections, public opinion, Constitution, and so on. Without this crucial distinction, which Agamben overlooks, genuinely radical-democratic theologies appear unattainable. As demonstrated in section 2.4, this perception is far from accurately reflecting reality.

Finally, a brief reference to the theological-economic formation of the neoliberal subject seems necessary, a theme on which Agamben offers particularly useful clues. He illustrates how the Greek concept of *oikonomía*, initially understood as the arrangement and management of the household (*óikos*, οἶκος), gradually evolved into a salvific and mysteriological meaning in the early centuries of Christianity (Agamben 2011: 17–52). Theologians such as Justin, Theophilus of Antioch, Tatian, Irenaeus, Hippolytus and Tertullian, each in their own way, still regarded *oikonomía* – translated into Latin sometimes as *dispensatio*, sometimes as *dispositio* – as a form of household management. This concept, originally derived from Aristotle, was transformed so that the house became a metaphor for the world, with God as the *despótes* (δεσπότης), the administrator. However, through a complex process that cannot be fully retraced here, at a certain point, particularly from the work of Clement of Alexandria onward, the administration of the world became internalized within God and linked to the notion of providence. This shift indicated the very self-administration of the divine 'body', which was subsequently divided into three persons. Consequently, there was a transition from the *economy of the mystery*, referring to God's often incomprehensible administration of the world, to the *mystery of the economy*, which pertains to the enigmatic problem of God's self-management. This transition offers a justification to the exotic Christian idea of a God who, being at the same time unique and transcendent in relation to creation, still requires intervention in the immanent world to administer it. But the shift from the administration of the world to the self-administration of the divine Self does not imply a separation between these spheres. Instead, God's *oikonomía* serves as the necessary prerequisite for the incarnation of the Son and His passion, making possible human salvation and guiding the *oikonomía* of the world toward its ultimate purpose and fulfilment.

Thus, economics, even in its modern sense, is profoundly theological. As Blaise Pascal (1623–62) aptly notes in his *Thoughts* of 1670, it lacks any ontological foundation; consequently, the only way to establish economics is to obscure its origins (1962: 51). This mirrors the way the theological and glorious *oikonomía* operates, dividing the divine substance into Being (the Father) and praxis (the Son), thereby encrypting the *an-archy* that is (dis)constitutive of both. In this process, it is essential to highlight an aspect that Agamben seems to overlook: the formation of the paradigm of the 'entrepreneur of oneself', typical of neoliberalism. The *oikonomía* internal to God, who self-manages by dividing into Father, Son and Holy Spirit, corresponds to a form of individualistic 'care of the self' akin to the strategies that shape the neoliberal subject into an entrepreneur of their own Self. Consequently, the neoliberal body is as a secularized theological body that has internalized the management and control of the world, effectively transforming into an economic body. It is a totally administered body and, therefore, incapable of conceiving an outside, as both its interior and exterior are governed by *oikonomía*.

A central question then arises: Why do individuals, despite being subjectified by *oikonomía* and transformed into enterprises of themselves, continue to comply with a political, economic and legal system that inflicts significant harm on the world and contradicts the ideals of many secular (e.g. human rights) and religious (e.g. Christianity) moralities that ostensibly inspire 'developed' societies? The answer is straightforward: people obey because they believe. Capitalism is a religion in which its adherents hold uncritical beliefs; thus, the issue of obedience does not even manifest at the level of consciousness, as is the case with all other religions. Even though the capitalist narrative – focused on the notion that individual effort and hard work guarantee success and happiness – is both implausible and empirically false, it continues to be accepted so uncritically that it resembles a blind, idolatrous faith that enforces universal competition and constrains the radical-democratic space. To overcome capitalism and the apparatuses that currently operationalize it within the neoliberal model, we must recognize these as theological mechanisms. This requires us to subvert faith in capital and pave the way for *an-archic*-democratic convictions.

As noted in section 1.3, the English historian Edmund Morgan argues in his book *Inventing the People* that the legitimization of political power relies on shared fictions and processes of 'make-believe'. Such processes enable capitalism to assume the role of religion in the contemporary world. To effectively confront this powerful ideology, struggles and antagonisms are crucial in both material and symbolic realms. Unfortunately, the latter task has yet to be fully recognized by many so-called progressive or left-wing movements. In contrast, the right-wing spectrum – particularly its most extreme factions – exploits the theological-political dimension extensively to further its objectives, a topic I will explore in the next two sections.

3.2. Christofascism and the capture of political theology by the extreme right

The discussion regarding the religious-based ideologies that fuel the far-right today is vast and extremely complex and cannot be fully reproduced in this and the next section, which is limited to some aspects of the extreme right's capture of Christian political theology. However, to grasp the complexity of the broader context in which far-right ideologies intersect with religious beliefs, it is instructive to consider the role of Traditionalism in the political landscapes of the United States, Russia and Brazil. Dangerous ideologues such as Steve Bannon, Aleksandr Dugin and the late Olavo de Carvalho serve as representative examples of this interplay.

Although not a religion in the conventional sense, Traditionalism – founded in the early twentieth century by René Guenón (1886–1951), a French mystic who converted to Islam – combines elements from various spiritual traditions, including Islam, Hinduism, Zoroastrianism and pre-Christian beliefs. It critiques Modernity, viewing it as a period of decadence in which materialism has supplanted the true spiritual values of elite cultures (Teitelbaum 2021: 9–12). This racist perspective was further developed by Guenón's successor, the Italian Julius Evola (1898–1974), who proposed a true revolt against Modernity in favour of an aristocratic, anti-egalitarian, anti-liberal and anti-democratic social order. Evola advocates the need to recognize the superiority of the Aryan race, the dominance of men over women and the preeminence of the Global North over the Global South (Teitelbaum 2021: 12–13).

Traditionalism seeks to recover an idealized, often mythologized past, aiming to impose a hierarchical and authoritarian social order. Rooted in an upper-class oriented and spiritualist worldview, the movement rejects Modernity, secularism and democracy, advocating for the superiority of specific cultural and religious traditions (Sedgwick 2023). Despite its mystical origins, Traditionalism has skillfully appropriated contemporary tools and platforms to disseminate its ideas, paradoxically leveraging the very technologies it critiques. While positioning itself as an elitist movement, Traditionalism often appeals to populist and nationalist sentiments, striving to cultivate a support base among segments of society disillusioned with the *status quo*. In summary, Traditionalism is a contradictory phenomenon: it is mystical yet politically focused, elitist yet populist and anti-modern yet media-savvy. Its ultimate goal is to oppose secularism, democracy and identity movements like feminism, seeking to restore a purported natural order that divides humanity into rulers and ruled.

In this sense, although it has important religious roots, Traditionalism is not a modern political theology, insofar as it explicitly rejects the basic functional assumption posited by Carl Schmitt. Moreover, Traditionalism's relationship with Christianity are problematic and ambiguous, particularly given the Christian tenet of the inherent equality of all human beings. Thus, as previously indicated, I will limit my analysis in the following pages to the specifically modern theological-political landscape inspired by Christianity. However, I recognize that in the real world these divisions are fluid and it is often difficult to discern where the boundaries of Traditionalism and political theology begin and end, especially within the inherently contradictory context of far-right movements, in which both may overlap with numerous other spiritual movements.

Having confined my inquiries to the domain of political theology, a crucial issue to initiate this discussion is the convergence between Christianity and fascism, a recent phenomenon examined by several scholars, including Baker (2021) and Foertsch and Pieper (2023). In 1987, the German theologian Dorothee Sölle introduced the expression 'Christofascism' in one of the essays from her book *The Window of Vulnerability: A Political Spirituality*. This term highlights the spurious alliance between political conservatism, mass media (including television) and the commodification of Christianity, all of which are characteristic features of the American far-right.

According to Sölle, the three primary values that underpin Christofascism in the United States are: an exacerbated nationalism, manifested in the notion of American exceptionalism; patriarchal familism, which necessitates the submission of women, relegating them to roles as reproducers, mothers and housewives, positions supposedly ordained by God; and the glorification of work, the free market and capitalism, coupled with a condemnation of any form of social solidarity toward the economically vulnerable, which is viewed as not only counterproductive but also unbiblical (Sölle 1990: 135–7). For illustrative purposes, consider an excerpt from *Listen, America!* by Jerry Falwell, an ultraconservative Baptist televangelist closely aligned with Ronald Reagan's policies in the 1980s:

> The system of free enterprise is clearly prescribed in the Bible, in the Proverbs of Solomon. Jesus Christ makes clear that the work ethic is part of his plan for mankind. Private property is biblical. Business competition is biblical. Ambitious and successful business practice is clearly prescribed as part of God's plan for his people. (*in* Sölle 1990: 137–8)

In 1968, Sölle had already noted in her work *Beyond Mere Obedience: Reflections on a Christian Ethic for the Future*, dedicated to critiquing the notion that

Christianity demands absolute obedience, that various Christian sectors historically provided significant support for both Hitler and Mussolini. This was particularly true among Lutheran evangelicals, who perceived the secular and pluralistic German Weimar Republic (1918–33) as an irreligious structure that needed to be destroyed. For Sölle, Christofascism continues to thrive today, inspiring, for example, American white supremacist movements, an assessment supported by theologians and scholars such as Tom Faw Driver (1981) and Douglas John Hall (2013). In Brazil, the term was adopted by theologian Fábio Py to describe the truculent and authoritarian far-right government of Jair Bolsonaro (2019–2022) and the theological-political positions of the churches that supported him, a topic that will be addressed in the next section.[4]

The Christofascist interpretive framework proves useful for elucidating many seemingly contradictory theological-political phenomena that have emerged in recent times, as long as one understands not only its genesis but also its meaning and limits. Initially, it may appear shocking to associate Christianity – often characterized as a religion of love – with fascism, one of the most brutal political movements of the last century. But Christianity has never constituted a unified doctrine. The variant that aligns with fascist ideals emphasizes the divine, glorious and vengeful aspects of Christ, while discarding the preferential option for the poor that underpins liberation theology, thereby nullifying the human complexity of Jesus. It is an encrypted Christianity that relies on certain literal and violent passages from the Old Testament while paradoxically rejecting elements that are distinctly Jewish, including revolutionary prophecy. This results in a kind of exclusivist, intolerant and triumphalist Christomonism. As Dorothee Sölle observed, this tendency manifests powerfully in the animosity directed toward the poor, foreigners and various minority groups, particularly those related to gender.

Another important aspect to consider is the meaning of 'fascism' within the term 'Christofascism'. This usage does not directly refer to the specific far-right political movement founded by Benito Mussolini and Giovanni Gentile in Italy during the 1920s. Instead, significant philosophical and sociological studies define fascism not as a specific, historically determined political movement but as a broader political category, which is how Sölle employs the term.

Umberto Eco (1932–2016), for instance, outlines the characteristics of what he ironically calls 'Ur-Fascism' or eternal fascism. These traits include traditional values, irrationalism, an emphasis on action for its own sake, suppression of criticism, promotion of contradictory thinking, fear of difference, appeals to frustrated middle classes, obsession with conspiracy, xenophobia, anti-pacifism, contempt for the weak, a cult of heroism and death, misogyny, populism and the use of an Orwellian newspeak (Eco 2018).

In a similar vein, in the introduction to the American edition of *Anti-Oedipus* by Deleuze and Guattari, Foucault offers insights on living a non-fascist life. He argues that fascism is more than a political doctrine; it embodies a lifestyle and existential attitude grounded in negative categories that seek to suppress multiplicity, difference and flow. This perspective encapsulates a defining characteristic of fascism in a broad sense, which, in my understanding, lies in an obsessive ideal of purity. Despite its length, Foucault's passage deserves to be quoted, as his reflections seem increasingly pertinent today:

> Paying a modest tribute to Saint Francis de Sales, one might say that *Anti-Oedipus* is an *Introduction to the Non-Fascist Life.* This art of living counter to all forms of fascism, whether already present or impending, carries with it a certain number of essential principles which I would summarize as follows if I were to make this great book into a manual or guide to everyday life:
>
> - Free political action from all unitary and totalizing paranoia.
> - Develop action, thought, and desires by proliferation, juxtaposition, and disjunction, and not by subdivision and pyramidal hierarchization.
> - Withdraw allegiance from the old categories of the Negative (law, limit, castration, lack, lacuna), which Western thought has so long held sacred as a form of power and an access to reality. Prefer what is positive and multiple, difference over uniformity, flows over unities, mobile arrangements over systems. Believe that what is productive is not sedentary but nomadic.
> - Do not think that one has to be sad in order to be militant, even though the thing one is fighting is abominable. It is the connection of desire to reality (and not its retreat into the forms of representation) that possesses revolutionary force.
> - Do not use thought to ground a political practice in Truth; nor political action to discredit, as mere speculation, a line of thought. Use political practice as an intensifier of thought, and analysis as a multiplier of the forms and domains for the intervention of political action.
> - Do not demand of politics that it restore the 'rights' of the individual, as philosophy has defined them. The individual is the product of power. What is needed is to 'de-individualize' by means of multiplication and displacement, diverse combinations. The group must not be the organic bond uniting hierarchized individuals, but a constant generator of de-individualization.
> - Do not become enamored of power. (1983: XIII–XIV)

Fascism rejects the different, the foreigner and the abnormal, always perceiving them as impure and inferior individuals who must be dominated or, in extreme cases, purged. This results in a particularly violent form of biopower, that is, a political power that directly impacts both the biological and psychological aspects of human life, disciplining individuals according to specific rules deemed 'normal', whether those are evolutionary, religious, scientific, and so on (García Collado and Matos 2021). When this perspective intertwines with the supremacist, divinized and triumphalist version of Christianity previously mentioned, Christofascism is born.

In the face of an unpredictable and ever-changing world, such simplistic doctrines provide an illusory sense of security to those who perceive their traditional ways of life as being threatened. Yet, as Sölle points out – highlighting another contradiction inherent in Christofascism – transformation and change are fundamental to Christianity itself. The Christian faith is rooted in the belief that God became human, entered this world, experienced incarnation, suffering, death and resurrection. It is a history of profound transformations. For this reason, Christianity emphasizes the necessity of a change of mind, the *metánoia* (μετάνοια) which Christ frequently references and demands in the *Gospels*. This concept is fundamentally at odds with a dogmatic and unchanging faith (Sölle 1982: 8). For Sölle, those who uncritically accept the version of Christ that has been bequeathed to them by tradition are already betraying and manipulating Jesus, for the only Christ of significance is the one who challenges individuals, teaching them in a way that sensitizes and transforms their conscience (1982: 5).

In summary, Christofascism embodies the intersection of nationalist, racist, sexist and authoritarian ideologies with certain Christian principles, either interpreted literally or creatively reimagined to serve the extreme right's interests. It marks a significant revival of 'classical' political theology, where sacred beliefs are employed to legitimize oppressive and exclusionary practices. In fact, Christofascism distorts and decontextualizes the Christian message to create a narrative that provides divine justification for political domination. By claiming a mandate from God, its proponents assert moral authority over critical issues such as immigration, gender, sexuality, education and race. This appropriation closely mirrors the historical roles of classical political theology, particularly in medieval contexts and, to some extent, in Schmittian political theology. Notwithstanding, Christofascism aspires not only to a functional relationship between political and religious spheres, as Schmitt suggests, but also to establish substantial dominance of political institutions by religious doctrine.

The principal mechanisms through which Christofascism appropriates Christianity include: (1) the political exploitation, simplification and corruption of Christian symbols, language and rituals; (2) the establishment of rigid dichotomies – such as 'us' against 'them', the pure versus the impure – that categorize individuals and groups as either allies or adversaries; and (3) the mobilization of segments of society through fear, transforming perceived threats to the 'Christian nation' into media spectacles often associated with immigrants, secularism, Islam, African religions, and so on. As a result, this form of mobilization frequently leads to calls for authoritarian measures purportedly aimed at protecting Christians. The ultimate outcome of Christofascism is the moral legitimization of violence, manifesting as a grotesque holy war against all 'non-Christian' society. These ideas starkly contrast with the essential ideas of Christianity, which, despite its historical complexities and paradoxes, has emphasized love, tolerance and peace among all individuals throughout its 2,000-year doctrine.

Nevertheless, the contradictions inherent in the concept of Christofascism are of little consequence, as it is a theological-political construct that lacks commitment to abstract reason. In this context, examining its development within the Brazilian political landscape can be quite enlightening. Indeed, in the absence of a reaction in the strictly theological field from Brazilian political forces that call themselves 'progressive' and 'left-wing' – many of which are hostile to any religious experience, viewing it as a pre-modern and irrational dimension – Christofascism has currently become a significant theological-political force in Brazil. This situation is further aggravated by the near extinction of liberation theology and the lack of robust democratic-radical theological traditions in the country, such as those rooted in Black[5] and feminist movements discussed in the previous chapter.

Now, a brief justification is necessary to confine the following pages to the Brazilian sociopolitical context, which may seem somewhat obvious in a book rooted in the theory of the encryption of power, a framework that is explicitly decolonial. Therefore, the choice to focus on a Latin American region, rather than a European or American one, should not seem unusual. Nonetheless, I believe it is important to clarify my research assumptions once more, especially as a Brazilian intellectual.

At this final stage of the book, as I aim to briefly illustrate some of the ideas presented here through a sort of 'case study', it would be artificial and inconsistent to describe realities I do not personally experience and that I can only access through readings. Moreover, centring my more 'sociological' considerations – understood through a personal point of view, of course – on Brazil offers certain epistemic advantages, given my intimate familiarity with the context. In fact, this approach allows English-speaking readers to engage with a critical theological-political perspective focused on a country they may not know well, thereby avoiding the monotonous and repetitive analyses often centred on the major Western countries. Finally, it is important not to overstate the specificity of the Brazilian case, as it is part of a much broader context. For instance, Brazilian Pentecostalism originated from American movements, though it quickly developed its own distinctive characteristics. Consequently, many of the analyses presented in this and the following section can be extrapolated to other situations, provided that appropriate methodological care is taken.

Well, after this decolonial *nihil obstat*, it is important to note that the characteristic uncritical and ahistorical concern with maintaining, recovering or achieving fictitious purity is evident in the Brazilian version of Christofascism. Uniting strands of conservatism and Christian fundamentalism – both Catholic and Protestant (including Evangelicals, Baptists, Neo-Pentecostals, etc.) – Brazilian Christofascism perceives itself as a religious authority superior to the corrupt and liberal political power, which is supposedly dominated by communists and minorities who threaten the traditional Brazilian Christian family and its values. From this perspective, the speech delivered in 2017 by former federal prosecutor and former congressman Deltan Dallagnol – one of the main individuals responsible for the imprisonment of incumbent president Luiz Inácio Lula da Silva in 2018 and for the demonization of the left-wing – at the Lagoinha Baptist Church in Belo Horizonte, in defence of the so-called ten measures against corruption, is significant. In his address, Dallagnol advocated for the symbolic construction of a wall, similar to that of the biblical character Nehemiah, to separate the pures from the corrupts.[6]

Although some scholars identify a theocratic bias in Brazilian Christofascism, I interpret it as a genuine form of political theology. The main religious denominations advocating for Christofascist proposals do not abandon the notion of political representation and maintain a strong presence in institutions, which they see as a decisive arena in the struggle between Good and Evil. Despite its pronounced individualism reconfigured in the form of a violent and patriarchal familism, Brazilian Christoascism has cultivated a solid public base of representation, now embodied in the Evangelical Parliamentary Front (FPE).[7] This front includes 202 federal deputies and 26 senators, according to official data from 2023, and has been vital to the viability of Jair Bolsonaro's far-right government. The FPE represents a powerful political force, given that Brazil has a total of 513 federal deputies and 81 senators.

Another striking and contradictory feature of Brazilian Christofascism is its contempt for the poor and its vehement rejection of public policies aimed at including minorities, despite many adherents who hold Christofascist beliefs being economically and socially vulnerable (Corten 1996). These individuals often perceive their situation not as a result of structural issues within the capitalist system, but rather as consequences of moral and individual failures – such as disbelief, laziness, sin, curses and demonic possessions – that can be overcome through increasing psychic and material surrender to their churches. This leads to the development of true rituals of suffering (Paravidini and Gonçalves 2009), which are interpreted as 'contracts with God' within the entrepreneurial organization of the faithful's existence grounded in the theology of prosperity, a topic explored in the next section.

3.3. Neo-Pentecostalism in Brazil: A political-economic theology

3.3.1. Theology of prosperity

As Fábio Py states, 'to alienate oneself from theological agendas is to fail to engage in the dispute over the terms and semantics that involve a fundamental segment of the Brazilian population. This is the key problem for progressive sectors today: they fail to recognize that the peripheries yearn for theologies' (2020: 6–7). This reality is demonstrated not only by various academic works (e.g. Baptista 2009; Birman and Machado 2012) but also by something more fundamental, intangible and vital: the daily interactions with individuals who constantly invoke God and the divine not in a formal or customary way, but with existential commitment. It indicates that the primary socialization processes for this population do not occur – or no longer occur – through the State, schools or traditional religions, but rather through a very specific circuit centred on faith communities, which has been successfully leveraged in Brazil by Neo-Pentecostalism.

The aim of this brief subsection is not to provide a historical-sociological analysis of Neo-Pentecostalism, but merely to illustrate, through a contemporary and relevant example, that the authoritarian political theology conceived by Schmitt remains alive, albeit in a radically modified form. If each era is linked to a dominant metaphysical image that manifests in concepts, institutions and political practices, then the current era – characterized by the instrumentalization and colonization of politics by the economy rather than its decline – can be understood as a theological-economic period. Ultimately, this context encompasses political dynamics that tend to be repressed, making it exceedingly difficult not only to engage in meaningful debate but also to acknowledge that we are situated within what Michael Löwy (1996) referred to as a 'struggle of the gods'.

The theology now on the brink of political hegemony[8] adopts economic forms derived from neoliberalism, such as the prosperity theology, which is central to Neo-Pentecostalism. In this way, it claims to be apolitical, asserting that it follows the 'naturalness', 'objectivity' and 'biblicalness' of economic relations and facts. Nevertheless, this perspective itself constitutes a political position, as it locates the economy within a given or 'revealed' dimension. Consequently, the economic theology of Neo-Pentecostalisms must be recognized and challenged for what it truly is: a political theology that, while not purely Schmittian – since it does not centre on the idea of sovereignty and is not functional but rather substantial – assumes in the present day its conservative and authoritarian tasks.[9]

Neo-Pentecostalism gained significant visibility in my country in 2016 due to the significant involvement of Neo-Pentecostal leaders in the impeachment of President Dilma Rousseff and their subsequent almost unconditional support for the far-right government of Jair Bolsonaro. However, Brazilian Neo-Pentecostalisms are more complex than it may initially appear, having even maintained strong ties and alliances with the centre-left Workers' Party (*Partido dos Trabalhadores*) during the 2000s. Furthermore, as Gedeon Alencar (2005) suggests, it is essential to adopt all necessary methodological precautions to avoid reproducing racist and aporophobic prejudices, as many Brazilian Neo-Pentecostal adherents, like Evangelicals in general, are Black and poor.

According to sociologist Paul Freston (1994: 108), the history of Brazilian Pentecostalism can be divided into three 'waves'. The first is 'classical Pentecostalism', which encompasses the first four decades of the last century, with the Congregational Church (founded in 1910) and the Assembly of God (founded in 1911) as its primary denominations. The second wave spans from the 1950s to the

1980s, marked by the fragmentation and dynamization of Pentecostalism across various Brazilian cities, with key denominations including the Quadrangular Church (1951), Brazil for Christ (1955) and God Is Love (1962). The 'third wave', known as Neo-Pentecostalism, aligns with the homonymous movement in the United States and represents a dissent from the evangelical current, emerging between the 1970s and 1980s. The main organizations of Neo-Pentecostalism in Brazil today include the Universal Church of the Kingdom of God (*Igreja Universal do Reino de Deus*), the International Grace of God Church (*Igreja Internacional da Graça de Deus*), the World Church of God's Power (*Igreja Mundial do Poder de Deus*), the Reborn in Christ Church (*Igreja Renascer em Cristo*), the Fountain of Life Apostolic Church (*Igreja Apostólica Fonte da Vida),* the Heal Our Land Evangelical Community (*Comunidade Evangélica Sara Nossa Terra*) and the Peace and Life Christian Community (*Comunidade Cristã Paz e Vida*).

'Pentecostalism' is a broad term that encompasses a variety of religious denominations, organizations and beliefs embraced by approximately 600 million people worldwide. Its distinctive feature is the pursuit of a special and direct relationship with the Christian God, symbolized by the descent of the Holy Spirit upon the apostles during the feast of Pentecost, as narrated in the second chapter of the *Acts of the Apostles* of Luke. As I have previously noted, and contrary to the assertions of some journalists and scholars (e.g. Passos 2020), Pentecostalism is not a theocratic religious movement. Although it preaches and aspires to a direct connection with divinity, in practice this requires not only participation in faith communities but also the indispensable mediation of representatives (bishops, ministers, pastors, etc.), positioning it as a theological-political movement.

Brazilian Neo-Pentecostalisms amplify certain characteristics of the original American model, as the pursuit of a direct relationship with God encompasses not only a spiritual dimension but also the attainment of material success (Oro 2001 and Taussig 1987). As Max Weber noted, wealth is considered an essential element of spiritual salvation. However, Neo-Pentecostals do not embrace the asceticism inherent in Weber's 'spirit of capitalism'. Instead, they aim to enjoy their material possessions in an intense and worldly manner, sometimes resulting in consumerist and ostentatious practices (Mariano 1996: 42–4). This characteristic suggests that Neo-Pentecostalism is linked to a specific neoliberal political-economic theology rather than a generic 'capitalist system'.

Furthermore, although they do not acknowledge this sociological fact, Brazilian Neo-Pentecostalisms have inherited traditions and rituals from religions of African origin (Birman 1994; Fry and Howe 1975; Oro 1997; Silva 2005). As a result, they present a worldview that is supernatural, magical and anti-intellectual (Vondey 2013: 37), believing in a spiritual battle between God and the devil (Mariz 1999; Mariano 2003) in which human beings actively participate. Neo-Pentecostals believe that individuals can be subject to possession and curses, but with proper personal and familial dedication – often manifested through investments in oneself, which may include miraculous healings, exorcisms and financial contributions – people can also become soldiers or elects of God. This perspective highlights the integrity of the Neo-Pentecostal subject, viewed as someone complete and pure, happy and materially, socially and personally fulfilled due to their submission to God.

In this context, the so-called *prosperity theology* assumes significant importance. Developed in the United States in the 1940s, it was received in Brazil with some reservations during the 1970s but has since come to dominate the Neo-Pentecostal landscape in the country (Mariano 1996: 27–8). Proposed by pastors such as Esek William Kenyon and Kenneth Hagin in the United States and extensively promoted in Brazil by figures like Edir Macedo, this doctrine is based on the premise that individuals can – and should – enter into a contractual relationship with God, viewing Him as a 'partner' for the faithful. Through the power of the spoken word, adherents believe they can create a life that is rich, happy, healthy and peaceful (Romeiro 1993). This attitude is known as 'positive confession', which asserts that believers possess the power to realize their desires through true faith by determining, declaring and decreeing them aloud. In this way, by consistently verbalizing their spiritual and material aspirations, perceived as 'contractual rights', the faithful believe they can compel God to fulfil these desires, under the penalty of breaking the contract, which seems unthinkable to them. This helps explain, for instance, the extremely popular phrase 'God is faithful' that Neo-Pentecostals display on their T-shirts, cars and various objects, a notion that would be incomprehensible to a Catholic sensibility, which cannot perceive in its transcendent and inexplicable God a mere contractual dimension. In contrast, in the Pentecostal world, God emerges as an economic partner and, therefore, demands fidelity, as He Himself is contractually faithful to His worldly associates. In this context, the words of Edir Macedo, leader of the most prominent Brazilian Neo-Pentecostal organization, the Universal Church of the Kingdom of God, are particularly telling:

> God desires to be our partner. [. . .] The bases of our partnership with God are the following: what belongs to us (our life, our strength, our money) now

> belongs to God; and what is His (the blessings, peace, happiness, joy, and all that is good) now belongs to us. (1990: 85–6)

If a believer's financial situation does not improve, prosperity theologians do not attribute this to the capitalist system or the unequal economic structures in which he or she lives; instead, they blame the individual's lack of faith. Indeed, the extreme faith required of Neo-Pentecostal subjects must be demonstrated ostentatiously, whether through tithing to the community or, more spectacularly, by engaging in 'challenges to God'. In these challenges, believers are encouraged to make substantial offerings that could jeopardize their already precarious financial situations, being led to donate to church goods such as cars, trucks, jewellery, salaries, inheritances, and so on. This act serves to illustrate the absolute nature of their faith in the contract with God (Mariano 1996: 36–40).

3.3.2. Theology of dominion

Another crucial element of Neo-Pentecostalism, although not exclusive to this movement, is the theology of spiritual battle – a belief that emphasizes the active participation of the faithful in the war between God and the devil. Unlike other Christian groups, Neo-Pentecostals advocate for an offensive stance against demons, fostering a faith that is expansive in nature, as it is imperative to convert as many individuals as possible. Furthermore, Neo-Pentecostal faith tends to be intolerant, viewing religions such as Candomblé, Umbanda, Spiritism and even the Catholic veneration of saints and Mary as manifestations of demonic power and control. Consequently, Neo-Pentecostals believe these practices must be denounced and combated, potentially including concrete measures of persecution (Mariz 1999; Silva 2007).

The Neo-Pentecostal worldview operates within a dimension populated by evil beings who are everywhere, leading to the interpretation that all personal, social, political, health and other problems faced by the faithful are the result of demonic actions. In this context, missionary R. R. Soares, leader of the World Church of God's Power, asserts: 'Behind religion, intellectualism, poetry, art, music, psychology, human understanding and everything we come into contact with, Satan hides' (1984: 103). Similarly, Edir Macedo states that signs of demonic possession include symptoms such as nervousness, headaches, insomnia, fainting, fear, suicidal thoughts, attacks, addictions and depression (2002: 64–70), that is, nearly all negative health conditions afflicting individuals exploited by the capitalist system.

With this magical and all-encompassing worldview characteristic of Neo-Pentecostalism, the believers' life becomes depoliticized, leading them to overlook any economic, structural or historical causes of their suffering, interpreting their existence solely through a theological lens. However, as we know, this approach – disregarding politics or viewing it as a realm dominated by Evil – constitutes a political position in itself, and a profoundly serious one. It underpins the proselytism and intolerance that define the aforementioned theology of spiritual battle, which can be seen as a variation of the *theology of dominion* that emerged in the United States between the 1960s and 1980s. Its central thesis posits that politics should be aligned with biblical practices, particularly those found in the Old Testament, as God is believed to have granted dominion over the Earth to humanity in the following terms:

> And God made man in his image, in the image of God he made him: male and female he made them. And God gave them his blessing and said to them, Be fertile and have increase, and make the earth full and be masters of it; be rulers over the fish of the sea and over the birds of the air and over every living thing moving on the earth. (*Genesis*, 1:27-28)

According to Rousas John Rushdoony (1916–2001), the founder of reconstructionism – a particularly radical variant of dominion theology – true Christians bear the responsibility of reconstructing the political landscape in alignment with biblical commandments. This approach, known as theonomy, begins with the private education of children to shield them from the perceived corruption fostered by public education (McVicar 2015). The proposed 'new' theonomic law, which would be enacted by Christian legislators and enforced by Christian judges, is intended to reflect the institutions of biblical Israel. This includes measures such as the death penalty, debt slavery and the persecution of those who fail to adhere to prescribed 'Christian' social standards (Pereira 2023: 151). Thus, what may initially appear as an apolitical stance – the theology of spiritual battle – ultimately translates into a highly political agenda – the theology of dominion. This political theology has been explicitly endorsed and promoted by the Bolsonaro government in Brazil (Pereira 2023: 161–8).

Key political figures in the Bolsonaro government, including former First Lady Michelle Bolsonaro, Senator Damares Alves and Congressman Nikolas Ferreira, are associated with the theology of dominion, which explicitly aims to 'liberate' individuals from the dominion of Evil by subordinating state powers to Neo-Pentecostal faith. To achieve this objective, it is essential to wrest power from established institutions, a strategy advocated by prominent reconstructionist theorist and American economic historian Gary North (1942–2022). North also supports neoliberalism in the economic sphere, illustrating the intricate interplay between political and economic theologies. Contrary to Agamben's perspective, these two domains do not oppose one another but rather complement each other.

According to Gary North (1982, 1989), who advocates for the death penalty by stoning for homosexuals and for children who curse their parents (1986: 59), and who was a member of the Mises Institute as well as a proponent of a radically 'libertarian' biblical economy, the project of dominion theology will unfold in two stages. In the first one, taking advantage of the secular nature of the liberal State, it is essential to capitalize on all opportunities to increase the number of adherents and disseminate the reconstructionist doctrine. This process began in Brazil in 1977 with the establishment of the Universal Church of the Kingdom of God and gained further momentum following the country's redemocratization in 1988, a political context that enabled the election of Neo-Pentecostal parliamentarians who were fully aware of the objectives of dominion theology, as elucidated in Edir Macedo's book *Plan of Power*.

In this work, Macedo adopts a vaguely intellectual position, citing philosophers such as Hobbes, while portraying God as a capable statesman and an exemplary entrepreneur. He suggests that, in the *Book of Genesis*, God provided humanity with 'a lesson in planning, organization and execution of an idea' (Macedo and Oliveira 2008: 8). This underscores the inseparability of economic and political theology, which is particularly evident in Macedo's discussion of the need for evangelicals to take institutional control of political power. He also addresses the lack of political representation for his followers and concludes the book by outlining the foundations of the 'nation of our dreams'. His intentions appear unequivocal:

> Remember: we are dealing with a dispute over spaces and the consolidation of these spaces [. . .]. What do Christians lack to establish themselves politically? In fact, the answer to this question is quite complex, but we can summarize it: well-coordinated actions, which begin with political awareness, strategies and unity around this noble cause, which depends in part on the religious leaders who are at the head of God's flock. (Macedo and Oliveira 2008: 45–6, 51)

Macedo further details the objectives of the second phase of the power project linked to dominion theology, in which its leaders would have successfully infiltrated the political and legal institutions. At this stage, they would be positioned to enact crucial changes aimed at transforming the liberal State into a kind of Old Testament community, which, as Gary North acknowledges, would inherently lack a secular character:

> We must use the doctrine of religious liberty, to gain independence for Christian schools until we train up a generation of people who know that there is no religious neutrality, no neutral law, no neutral education, and no neutral civil government. Then they will get busy in constructing a Bible-based social, political and religious order which finally denies the religious liberty of the enemies of God. (North 1982: 25)

These ideas are not, as some might assume, mere ramblings of a lunatic without real-world influence. North's project is gradually taking shape, not only in his own country but also in Brazil. This was clearly demonstrated by Michelle Bolsonaro's speech on 25 February 2024, at a pro-Bolsonaro political demonstration on Paulista Avenue, arguably the most prominent space in the country for media coverage today. During this event, the former First Lady of the Bolsonaro dynasty openly acknowledged the necessity of transcending the secular State, despite this being an unconstitutional and potentially criminal proposal in Brazil. Here is what she said:

> For a long time, we were negligent, yes, to the point of saying that we could not mix politics and religion. And Evil took over. Evil occupied the space. Now, the time has come for liberation. 'You will know the truth, and the truth will set you free'. That was the verse he [Jair Bolsonaro] used throughout the campaign, and I believe that this was generated in the spiritual world. Because I believe in a living God, an all-powerful God who is capable of restoring, of healing our nation. Do not give up, women, men, youth, children: do not give up on our country. Keep praying, keep crying out because I know that our God, from the highest heavens, will grant us help. (ICL Notícias 2024)

As can be seen, Michelle Bolsonaro unambiguously preaches the need to mix politics and religion to combat 'Evil', further asserting that her husband Jair Bolsonaro's campaign was inspired by the spiritual realm. At this point, it is revealing to note that Jair Messias Bolsonaro, a former Army captain who has, among many absurd and controversial statements, defended torture (Poder 360 2021), coups d'État (CNN Brasil 2022; Terra Brasil 2024) and the closure of the National Congress and the Supreme Federal Court (El País 2020; Folha de S. Paulo 2021; Veja 2022), was the first Brazilian president elected (in 2018) through the support of the Neo-Pentecostal vote, since the difference in votes that led him to victory corresponds exactly to the (growing) portion of this electorate (Instituto Humanitas Unisinos 2018).

In such a scenario, space opens up in Brazil for the implementation of the second phase of the theology of dominion, evident in the intense politicization and demonization of issues related to gender, abortion, early childhood education, prison and drug policies, among others. Although Bolsonaro lost the 2022 election by a narrow margin of just over 1 per cent of valid votes (Tribunal Superior Eleitoral do Brasil 2022), powerful Neo-Pentecostal parliamentary majorities are now in control, actively promoting the policies characteristic of dominion theology with almost crusader zeal. Furthermore, a significant portion of the Brazilian populace is either consciously or unconsciously aligned with this project, as evidenced by the attempted coup d'État on 8 January 2023, when thousands of pro-Bolsonaro militants tried to seize the institutional headquarters of the three branches of government in Brasília (Agência Brasil 2024). This event bore a grotesque resemblance to the attack on the Capitol by Donald Trump supporters on 6 January 2021.

In summary, while acknowledging certain historical, sociological and theological boundaries, one could argue that, in Brazil, Neo-Pentecostal movements represent a theological-political inversion of liberation theology. Indeed, liberation theology is characterized by its intellectual rigour, collectivist orientation, New Testament focus and strong critique of capitalism, positioning itself within the political left. In contrast, Neo-Pentecostalism tends to be anti-intellectual, individualistic and rooted in Old Testament teachings, aligning itself with right-wing politics and serving as a site for the divinization of capitalism.

This interpretation gains further credence when considering how both theological orientations address the issue of poverty. As discussed in section 2.4.3, liberation theology emphasizes its option for the poor, positing that, in a certain sense, all human beings experience poverty, whether materially or spiritually. This perspective resonates with contemporary philosophers such as Judith Butler (2004b), who argues that existential precarity defines what it means to be human. Conversely, Neo-Pentecostal movements view poverty as a consequence of sin, curses or demonic influence, believing that God's will encompasses universal prosperity, health and happiness. Thus, the incarnation of Christ among the poor is interpreted not as a mandate to sustain their condition but as a way to equip them with the tools necessary to transcend poverty (Mariano 1996: 33). First-wave Pentecostals, known for their more ascetic approach, also held a negative view of poverty, rejecting its status as a Christian virtue and aspiring to escape it through heavenly reward (Loreto 1994: 158–9). While their perspective was somewhat moderated, the early Pentecostal movement still regarded poverty with suspicion. Conversely, contemporary Neo-Pentecostalism, influenced by neoliberal ideologies, marks a radical departure from this earlier tradition. By emphasizing individual prosperity and equating material success with spiritual fulfilment, Neo-Pentecostalism has transformed money into an object of idolatry, fundamentally altering the theological understanding of poverty.

Conclusion

Life in Common and Radical-Democratic Faith

> [. . .] *that God may be all in all.* [. . .] *let vs eate and drinke, for to morrowe wee die.*
>
> (1 *Cor.* 15, 28; 32)

Brazilian historian Sérgio da Mata argues that the political theology of the Bolsonaro government involves a shift toward a form of 'Brazilian Hebraism'. While this hypothesis is fundamentally accurate, it appears to be incomplete as it does not account for the significant theological-economic dimension. Nevertheless, his conclusion holds merit, particularly in his assertion that 'God is too important a subject to be left solely to those who believe in Him' (2020: 67). From this perspective, there is an urgent need to reclaim the democratic potential of emerging theological-political currents. Only by doing so can we effectively challenge sovereign and neoliberal political theologies on their own terrain: the realm of social narratives and the contestation of meanings. This task cannot be achieved solely through rational, scientific or supposedly neutral discourses and arguments. Within politics, there exists a dimension of transcendence that has neither been nor will be surpassed by Modernity. This dimension must be engaged with, critiqued, subverted and reconstructed in the pursuit of politically democratic, philosophically libertarian and economically equitable goals. Democratic political theologies can offer valuable tools for these endeavours.

I believe that the field of political theology can adopt new frameworks today, distinct from those envisioned by Carl Schmitt, which led him to justify the institutions of his historical context. To achieve this, radical-democratic (a)theologies must detach themselves from the 'real' world and its systems of legitimation, much like Jesus did on numerous occasions. This approach would fulfil a critical-radical function, enabling these theologies to point toward alternative social experiences that, rather than reinforcing the idolatry of capital, align themselves with the marginalized and defeated. Indeed, Jesus contested the established political-economic power – the oikonomic *potestas* of his time – most notably in the emblematic episode of the expulsion of the temple merchants, which is recounted in *all* four *Gospels* (*Mark* 11:15-19; *Matt.* 21:12-17; *Luke* 19:45-48; *John* 2:13-16). He also denounced false and misogynistic moralities in the scene of the stoning of the adulterous woman (*John* 8:1-11) and celebrated the common good and the infinite productivity of life on several occasions, such as at the wedding at Cana (*John* 2:1-11) and during the multiplication of loaves and fishes,[1] miracles that can easily be read from a radical-democratic matrix.

In this context, the miracle no longer serves as the theological-political simile of the state of exception that suspends normality, as Schmitt envisioned. Instead, it emerges, in the words of Hannah Arendt, as an irruption of the new and the original, disrupting the predictable processes of the world. This is exemplified by the miracles of life on Earth and the manifestations of intelligence in organic beings (Arendt 2005: 111–12). Moreover, beyond the *Gospels*, numerous passages and concepts in other books of the New Testament can be read and reinterpreted today as powerful anticapitalist manifestos. One notable example is chapter 18 of the *Book of Revelation*, which is crafted to denounce the 'sorceries' of the 'great ones of the Earth', the merchants who have deceived all nations.

From a more historiographical and less theological perspective, it is important to heed the often-overlooked warning offered by Frederico Lourenço in the introduction to his remarkable translation of the *Greek Bible* into Portuguese (2016: 21). Lourenço contends that the *Gospels* are texts quite different from those read by the Hellenistic elite of the first century AD. Rather than depicting heroic battles or wars, or containing refined philosophical digressions and seductive princesses and queens, the *Gospels* emphasize the rejected and the marginalized. They highlight the experiences of the common people, the rabble ranging from housewives to prostitutes, lepers, the mentally ill, the physically disabled and fishers. Thus, the original foundation of what later became a conservative, authoritarian and sovereign political theology corresponds to a common, multitudinous and popular dimension, one that is fundamentally loving, as broadly defined by Hardt and Negri (2009: 179–88) in their reinterpretation of Spinoza and Deleuze. This non-sovereign approach of the *Gospels* was beautifully embodied in the peasant and plebeian rendition of the *Gospel of Matthew* brought to the screen by Pier Paolo Pasolini in 1964.[2]

Starting from the consideration of a weak god who communicates with the humiliated and the oppressed, it seems feasible to construct an alternative conception of the political, one centred on sociability, encounter and multiplicity. This perspective would update one of Walter Benjamin's most enigmatic theological-political theses, the second one, in which he speaks of a weak messianic force ('*eine schwache messianische Kraft*') (1991 [I]: 694) that emerges in the struggle against the fascist exception that has become the norm. This force promotes, through the revival of the tradition of the oppressed (*Unterdrückten*), an effective exception (*wirkliche Ausnahmezustand*) capable of decrypting *potestas* and redeeming history (1991 [I]: 697). In this context, it is important to recall God's response to Paul when the latter asked Him to remove the thorn from his flesh: 'My grace is enough for you, for my power is made complete in what is feeble' (2 *Cor.* 12:9).

Weakness stands in opposition to the vanity of the powerful, creating a context in which sovereignty – understood as an unrestricted *potestas* – can be decrypted, allowing for the emergence of democratic multiplicity and its logic of life in common. This configuration resonates with the disruptive framework announced by Paul when he states that God chooses the weak things of the world to shame the strong; the foolish things to confound the wise; and the things that are not to nullify the things that are (1 *Cor.* 1:27-28). This establishes a dynamic movement that continuously shifts from potency to act and from act to potency, affirming not the One and the stable, but the multiple and the transient.

In the realm of affects, this implies choosing the side of pain over fear. In his interpretation of the *Book of Job*, Antonio Negri (2002) presents pain – not merely individual suffering, but collectively experienced pain as a possibility of ethical-radical participation in the other – as a central democratic political affect. He contrasts this with fear, which is associated with the sovereignty that emanates from above. Indeed, Hobbes himself knew very well that fear is fundamental to maintaining the majesty of the laws imposed on human beings (1965 [II, 27]: 229). On the other hand, pain and suffering, arising from the grassroots, serve as common grounds for the formation of democratic communities. Unlike fear, which fosters passivity in the face of the divine, pain and suffering manifest as catalysts for active struggle, denunciation and rebellion. Fear shapes passive, amorphous subjects who surrender themselves to power. Conversely, pain represents the first step toward radical social transformation, as suggested by Job's rebellious attitude, always imprecating and provoking an immeasurable power (God? capitalism?) that torments a human being plunged into the abyss of an equally boundless production (of pain? of labour?).

Furthermore, the *Book of Job* constitutes the first piece of the complex anti-sacrificial machine that would evolve into Christianity, as noted Jean-Pierre Dupuy (2008). Following Job, the narrative tradition surrounding sacrifice shifted from an impersonal and collective perspective to one that centres on the individual victim. In this context, it is the victim who speaks and, by discursively assuring his innocence as a paradoxical condition of sacrifice – as Christ does – renders this apparatus inoperative, depriving the sacred of its power and bringing it to the sphere of human gestures. With the denial of the tradition of sacrifice – now increasingly portrayed from the perspective of the victims – something like a tradition of the oppressed becomes possible. This shift disrupts the monopoly of the victors – the sacrificers – over the act of storytelling and, consequently, the power to shape worlds. It is from these and many other 'defeats' of the weak that the struggle for the excessive experience of radical democracy can be re-engaged.

Democracy is fundamentally a promise. Its core value resides in the belief that human beings can honour agreements without reliance on superior external authorities – such as the State, God, the People or Reason – which, being abstract, can never truly disappoint anyone. In contrast, the possibility that individuals might fail to uphold their commitments is paradoxically essential for fostering trust. This dynamic gives rise to what I term 'democratic faith'. Trust can only be meaningfully discussed when we acknowledge the potential for its denial through the breach of promises (Lummis 2016). This may clarify why radical democracy is the most challenging form of political engagement to envision. Nonetheless, it is present everywhere, albeit often encrypted and disempowered. Without trust, contemporary society – indeed, any society – would be untenable. Rooted in the concepts of promise and trust, radical democracy provides no guarantees, in stark contrast to state violence, religious doctrines and bureaucratic systems. If radical democracy were to function on a global scale, its objective would be to illuminate the small, everyday actions that underpin communal living, revealing what society *could be* by drawing on what it *already is* in a peripheral and often unconscious manner. This is also the conclusion reached by Sanín-Restrepo and Machado-Araujo within the paradigm of the theory of the encryption of power:

> Is there a path towards another world? This book tries to prove that there is, nevertheless, it not only proves that another world is possible, but, more importantly, that such a world already exists. It has been marginalized and lies below the clutter of hegemony, but it breathes and produces the truth of

> difference. We simply need another arrangement of the sensible for registering it, another perception to allow its sway to show us the way. This is perhaps the golden thread that binds the whole book together, and we can formulate it with simplicity: The world we live in is the world of difference and immanent becoming, it is occluded and negated by the simulacrum of power as *potestas* that systematically imposes its fallacious model of man (through constitutions, the market, the rule of law) into the world. (2025b: 197)

At this point, it is essential to emphasize that democracy is not merely a form of government; rather, it constitutes the fundamental substrate necessary for any governance structure, including the most autocratic regimes. Claude Lévi-Strauss (1955) recognized this during his months spent living among the Nambikwara Indians in Brazil. He noted that the foundation of all political societies lies in consent, which serves as both the origin and the limit of power. In small and simple societies, this consent is readily observable as both a sociological and psychological reality. In turn, in contemporary States, consent manifests as differentiated systems of mutual guarantees, loans and counterloans that individuals extend to one another.[3]

Every government – whether 'primitive' or 'modern' – must presuppose some degree of trust between the governors and the governed, who are, after all, human beings rather than mere objects that can be controlled solely by force. This essential minimum of trust, which also embodies a basic equality, is what the governor must extend to each individual governed; without it, no political relationship can exist. This constitutes the democratic minimum and the foundational trust that underpin the existence and functioning of societies. Symmetrically, as Hobbes recognizes, there is no ruler powerful enough to be immune from physical elimination by the governed.[4] This dynamic highlights the biopolitical substrate of equality, which asserts that human beings must be treated as such in order to be governed rather than annihilated – a scenario in which no government could exist, as there would be no subjects of power. Furthermore, it is from this very biopolitical substrate that the mortality of the sovereign and their institutions arises. This substrate forms the basis of democracy and equality, enabling any and all government.

Radical democracy is not a scandalous or impractical novelty; rather, it is a political project aimed at decrypting, maximizing and liberating the minimum levels of democracy, equality and trust that already exist within society. This effort seeks to free these values from elitist-liberal constraints and restrictions, revealing them as manifestations of the excessive, permanent and inexhaustible production of the common for the common. I am not proposing to transform the minimum of democracy necessary for any society into an autonomous form of government, which would make democracy dependent on the glorious *oikonomía*. This is precisely what the 'founding fathers' of the United States achieved when they established representative democracy and constitutionalism, effectively encrypting, colonizing and controlling the masses' desire for freedom and equality, redirecting it into patterns acceptable to capital and private property. To be clear, my aim is to maximize not the government, always *oikonomic*, but the minimum democracy that all governments must recognize, thereby creating a non-governmental space, that is, a truly political sphere and not an economic one.

As both promise and trust, radical democracy embodies the messianic structure of becoming, oriented toward the future and its unpredictable reconfigurations between being and what ought-to-be, reality and justice, actuality and ideality, operating within the realm of desire. This does not imply the impossibility of democracy; rather, it underscores its radical processuality, which requires that its defenders adopt a form-of-life that, while grounded in the world, consistently points toward its transcendence, reflected in an inexhaustible desire for self-transformation (*metánoia*). This entails living, as Paul advised, in a reality that is more real than reality itself. In this hyperreality, the gesture is accomplished at the same time as it denies itself:

Τοῦτο δέ φημι, ἀδελφοί, ὁ καιρὸς συνεσταλμένος ἐστίν· τὸ λοιπὸν ἵνα καὶ οἱ ἔχοντες γυναῖκας ὡς μὴ ἔχοντες ὦσιν, καὶ οἱ κλαίοντες ὡς μὴ κλαίοντες, καὶ οἱ χαίροντες ὡς μὴ χαίροντες, καὶ οἱ ἀγοράζοντες ὡς μὴ κατέχοντες, καὶ οἱ χρώμενοι τὸν κόσμον ὡς μὴ καταχρώμενοι· παράγει γὰρ τὸ σχῆμα τοῦ κόσμου τούτου. θέλω δὲ ὑμᾶς ἀμερίμνους εἶναι	Therefore, I say to you, brothers and sisters, the time is short: what remains is for those who have wives to live as if they had none, and those who mourn as if they did not mourn, and those who rejoice as if they did not rejoice, and those who buy as if they owned nothing, and those who use the world, as if not abusing it. For the figure of this world is passing away. I want you to be free from anxieties (1 *Corinthians* 7, 29-32).[5]

The formula 'as if not' (*hôs mé*, ὡς μὴ) employed by Paul indicates a particular theological-messianic strategy: to depose without abdicating. This approach entails rendering the law inoperative without abolishing it, which is why Paul uses the Greek verb *katargéo* (καταργέω), meaning 'to render inoperative' or 'to deactivate' (*argós*, ἀργός). In this context, deactivating the law means extracting it from the realm of archaic command and *potestas* without destroying it, thereby transforming it into a law of faith, that is, of a democratic wager. Through this theological-messianic figure, Agamben proposes that the apparatus of citizenship could be reinterpreted within the framework of radical democracy as 'being a citizen as if one were not'. According to the Italian philosopher, the factical political and juridical condition in which one finds themselves – for example, that of slave or master – cannot be simply negated or transformed, as a naïve perspective, whether revolutionary or reformist, might suggest. What is at stake here is a much more radical and nuanced approach: to use the factical condition in which each person finds themselves without appropriating it, while avoiding the hypostatization that leads to the creation of new identities (2014b: 86–7).[6]

The Pauline passage cited above is structured as a parodic critique of Roman property law, specifically the *ius utendi et abutendi*, which is reflected in the phrase 'those who use the world as if not abusing it'. In this manner, Paul counters the legal apparatus of property – the right to use, exploit and even destroy – by advocating for a use of the world that recognizes it as something unappropriable. In this way, a being emerges who, by using – that is, deactivating – the world and its contingent conditions, opens up new social possibilities that are currently unimaginable under the iron law of capitalism and its neoliberal political theology. Living in the dimension of 'as if not' necessitates the ongoing deposing of the social conditions in which one lives, engaging with them without appropriation and, crucially, without annihilating them. Such annihilation would merely inaugurate a new cycle of power encryption, as negation corresponds to the reverse of affirmation (Agamben 2014b: 345–7). Thus, to live from the perspective of the 'as if not' requires a kind of unfolding of life into two dimensions that, however, do not oppose each other but rather potentiate one another: the life we live daily (*vita quam vivimus*), with all its particularities and imperfections, its small and large victories and tragedies, and the life for which we live (*vita qua vivimus*), which is the aspect that gives meaning to our existence, making life liveable (Agamben 2011: 248).

It is a psychic, social and existential experience similar to that of religious faith, which enables one to act in the world with the hope that things will improve, thereby realizing the 'new arrangement of the sensible' referred to by Sanín-Restrepo and Machado-Araujo. One should not shy away from using this term, which has been banished from the 'serious' and 'rational' academic discourse: faith, that is, 'substance of things hoped for, and the sign that the things not seen are true' (*Heb.* 11:1). Faith is an integral aspect of all political action and thought. However, for several reasons – including the quantitative technicization of political knowledge, which has become confined to the rigid academic boundaries of 'political science' – faith has been confiscated by religions.

It is necessary to overcome this appropriation and to recognize the open, collective and transformative nature of faith – or, if one prefers, of the wager – as possessing a radical dimension that enables activities capable of creating worlds through words, promises and commitments. After all, both religion and politics are belief systems that involve a set of convictions that are empirically unverifiable; it remains uncertain whether these convictions are true or false (in fact, this question may not even be relevant in this context). Nonetheless – and perhaps precisely for this reason – religion and politics have the capacity to provide meaning and coherence to both collective and individual human existence (Hervieu-Léger 1993: 105). As Lucien Goldmann argues, faith should not be conflated with its transient and contingent manifestations tied to specific positive religions; instead, it should be understood as a total and shared experience inherent to social utopias. Both faith and utopia are oriented toward transindividual values that challenge the *status quo* (Goldmann 1955: 99).

Nevertheless, the similarities between religious faith and political faith – or democratic faith, as I refer not to technocratic cabinet-level politics but to the political in its very substrate of ungovernability – do not erase their significant differences. Religious faith invariably points toward transcendence, toward another world where Jesus' promise will be fully realized, thus embodying the idea that hope is exhaustible in the process of its fulfilment. Theologians such as Jürgen Moltmann (1964) and Johann Baptist Metz (1997) played a significant role in shaping what became known as the 'new political theology' in the latter half of the twentieth century, a movement that posits hope as the fundamental Christian experience. They argue that Christian faith is oriented toward the future, pointing to the second coming of Christ and His kingdom, an event that stands in opposition to the political powers of this world. Consequently, the new political theology asserts that the Christian community lives in exile and that the present world lacks true substance when confronted with the radical eschatological nature of becoming, which is anchored in the memory of Jesus' sacrifice, promise and expectation (Rizzi 1991).

In turn, I consider the faith involved in the form-of-life typical of a radical democracy to be far more demanding than the hope of the 'new political theology'. It requires a trust in *this* world that cannot be exhausted, being excessive and constantly productive. Armed with this faith, the hidden people can use the flawed, contradictory and empirical democracies *as if they were not* imperfect, but per-fect (from the Latim *per-fectum*, i.e., done, finished, 'real'), for only in the dimension of inexhaustibility and excess does radical democracy can truly flourish, thus overcoming the separation between the simulated Sovereign People and the hidden people that grounds it as it is subjected to the dialectical machine of the supposed 'reality' and 'objectivity'. In this dimension, as Jean-Luc Marion (2013) indicates, an alternative emerges that allows us to think of God beyond Being and the ontological difference as a kind of *impossibility of impossibility*, which, without any romantic or idealistic feature, shapes a negative certainty. This stands in opposition, in a way, to the Heideggerian notion of death, which for the *Dasein* appears as the radical *possibility of impossibility*. For Marion, the question of God survives any argument regarding the impossibility of experiencing Him because God, by definition, pertains to what is impossible for us. In a similar manner, the concept of grace and its empirical manifestations in forgiveness and sacrifice are not based on any condition that would make their occurrence possible, as they transcend the logic of exchanges characteristic of capitalist religion. According to Marion (2010), it is likely that these negative certainties, which no future theory or experience can correct or refute, provide us with much greater confidence than any other form of certainty.

At this point, the differentiation between *the life we live* and *the life for which we live* reveals all its potency, for one can live in imperfect democracies without settling for their limitations, always aiming for another democracy, namely, the life for which and in the name of which one lives. This is reflected in the democratic excess, in the *immeasurable potential* that opposes the measureless value characteristic of *oikonomía*. Ontologically, this excess is conceived as the potency of Being in the face of chaos and the indeterminacy of existence, preserving the possibility of perceiving and embodying the Messiah, of opening the door of history through acts that are always overflowing, as they are co-institutive and always open to the other: revolutionary *caritas*, that is, friendship of the human being with God, but with a god who is human himself and much more: life itself.

The excessive and ever-demanding nature of democracy does not lead to its destruction; rather, it fosters its infinite perfectibility. When one recognizes the limitations of 'real democracy', it is easy to become disillusioned and turn to systems of governance grounded in wealth, force or tradition, which lack the radical dimension of ideality. In contrast, radical democracy manifests in the same gesture that, while denying actual and self-exhausting abuses, points to an insurmountable *rest* that sustains alternative societal projects. Thus, it becomes a matter of living in the world *as if there were no* world. Without this perspective, I believe it is impossible to transform it.

Thus, far more than merely a form of government, democracy is a *collective existential state* founded on promise and trust. This implies that there is no a specific moment in time when one will, either miraculously or through the most arduous social struggles, 'achieve' democracy, as if it were a point on a straight line that, once reached, would reveal 'true democracy'. While it is possible to conceptualize varying degrees of democratic collective experiences based on certain institutional and procedural standards, democracy itself – beyond being conflated with these instruments – will never present itself as an accomplished, guaranteed or static reality. For this reason, the form-of-life engendered and demanded by radical democracy constitutes a paradoxical expression of an (a)theological and *an-archic* sociability, that is, a worldview without foundation or command. Therefore, democratic life is the collective form-of-life that, recognizing and fully aware of the permanent void on which it is founded, does not succumb to despair nor seeks to establish metaphysical or functional authorities to encrypt *an-archy* by transforming it into glory. Instead, the democratic void is embraced as an opportunity for *creation*, in line with Deleuze's thought, for whom potency refers to an openness to the new that, far from being mere inactivity, reflects the state of a world without specific purposes or destinations to be achieved. We are all placed in the real, 'thrown' into the Here (*Da*) of Being (*Sein*), so that this existential abandonment unites us in our weakness, in the intrinsic precariousness of all humanity – indeed, of all life – even if it can be, and often is, socially maximized to the detriment of some, as Judith Butler (2004b) argues.

But here it is worth remembering that 'precarious' comes from the Latin word *praex*, meaning 'prayer'. In this context, beyond its intrinsic transience as a mere being of words, prayer can only have a transindividual meaning, as it is always directed towards others, even if mediated by the great Other who, long before being objectified as a psychoanalytic concept, was already experienced in the form of a God who transcends his creation. Ultimately, prayer turns towards ourselves, collectively transfigured in the form of God. Thus, it is the common fragility inherent in all human beings that allows us to escape the guilt/debt imposed by the political theologies of sovereignty and capital. By deactivating these forces, we can establish a *common debt* (Esposito 2013: 221–8) which represents a life in common, understood as a shared *munus* rather than as an afflictive and enslaving legal-economic bond, constituting an interpersonal relationship that is not reducible to guilt or to egoistic processes of reciprocal immunization.

It is important to recall here the passage from the first dissertation in Nietzsche's *Genealogy of Morals* (1989) in which he argues that the creation of gods occurs when the weak anthropomorphize the guilt and resentment they feel toward the strong, thereby giving rise to an unpayable debt. Now, cancelling the debt would thus mean eliminating the distinction between the weak and the strong and, recognizing that all of us are ontologically weak, establishing a debt that is not resented, but rather felt as a common belonging of living beings to finitude, death and the potent *an-archic* void that (de)grounds us. From then on, the challenge will be to establish a common use of oneself that is also a common use of the world.

As I have explored in other works (Matos 2020: 355–408, 2024b), every democratic political theology is an (a)theology, a field of tensions in which even the existence of the divine is situated within the realm of the undecidable, thereby fostering criticism and openness. This reveals democracy as the political instantiation of the death of God, that is, the demise of the unified, closed, ahistorical, patriarchal and guilt-inducing discourse that sustains the encryption of power. In this context, forms of popular self-organization become democratic to the extent that they embrace the dispersion and diffusion of political power as an *an-archic* reality, not allowing themselves to be encrypted by apparatuses that reduce plurality to the theopolitical rule of the One, thus enabling the experience, for example, of a Latin American, Black, female Jesus, and so on.

However, it is insufficient to merely multiply the incarnations of the divine; it is equally essential to grasp their simultaneous universal and contingent, performative and unfounded, fabulous and historical nature. This understanding challenges the traditional subjectivizing machine of theological-political capture, which today adopts neoliberal economic features by promising wealth, health and peace to all. It is up to feminist, Black, decolonial and many other (a)theologies to not simply criticize such promises, which stem from desires that are in themselves legitimate, but to demonstrate their unattainability in the context of societies that, being racist, xenophobic, sexist and homophobic, are also unequal and unjust. In doing so, perhaps it can be shown to people that their societies have never been and will never be pure, as the Christofascism claims.

In this sense, the primary task of a democratic-radical political theology is to demonstrate to people that the desire for a good life is not economic, but political. This means that all neoliberal mechanisms aimed at privatizing happiness are not just ethically condemnable but also ineffective. One can only live well in the *pólis*, that is, with others, despite others, by being an other. It is a qualitative framework – and therefore political – that cannot be subsumed under a mathematical operation of an economic nature. Only through the restoration of the *political dimension of happiness* can the existential guilt that feeds prosperity theologies be transformed into a common debt of humanity to itself and to all living beings. This transformation enables a break from the individualistic cycle of guilt-frustration-consumption-guilt and points toward a genuinely political – and not merely economic – experience of coexistence with others. To achieve this, it is essential not only to take seriously the Christian ideas of redemption and liberation from guilt and debt but also to remember the *common* and *political* promise of Jesus: 'Where two or three are come together in my name, there am I among them' (*Matt.* 18:20). This perspective seeks to transform the 'weak messianic power' of the *mikrói* referenced by Benjamin not into a bureaucratic and State-controlled revolution, but into forms-of-life, into existential gestures that transubstantiate William Blake's (1790: 27) verse in *The Marriage of Heaven and Hell*: 'For every thing that lives is Holy'.

Notes

Introduction

1 As I explore in greater depth in my book *Representation Against Radical Democracy: An (A)theological Archaeology of Separated Power*. Here I present a condensed summary of these arguments for a broader readership.

2 'Now laws remain in credit not because they are just, but because they are laws. That is the mystic foundation of their authority; they have no other. And that is a good thing for them. They are often made by fools, more often by people who, in their hatred of equality, are wanting in equity; but always by men, vain and irresolute authors' (Montaigne 1958 [III, 13]: 821).

Chapter 1

1 Unless otherwise indicated, all translations in this book are my own.

2 Indeed, the notion of origin adopted in this work is devoid of any metaphysical connotation; rather, it suggests an archaeological-philosophical approach, as defined by Agamben, capable of transcending historiographical linearity and pointing towards a kind of constant presence in things, which never finish beginning in their multiple historical incarnations, just as theology has always been included in politics. Walter Benjamin's words are fundamental to understanding this proposal: 'Origin [*Ursprung*], although an entirely historical category, has, nevertheless, nothing to do with genesis [*Entstehung*]. The term origin is not intended to describe the process by which the existent came into being, but rather to describe that which emerges from the process of becoming and disappearance. [. . .] That which is original is never revealed in the naked and manifest existence of the factual; its rhythm is apparent only to a dual insight. On the one hand it needs to be recognized as a process of restoration and reestablishment, but, on the other hand, and precisely because of this, as something imperfect and incomplete. There takes place in every original phenomenon a determination of the form in which an idea will constantly confront the historical world, until it is revealed fulfilled, in the totality of its history. Origin is not, therefore, discovered by the examination of actual findings, but it is related to their history and their subsequent development [*Vor- und Nachgeschichte*]' (1998: 45–6).

3 To comprehend Foucault's understanding of 'Enlightenment', which diverges from the definitions found in history textbooks, see Foucault (1984).

4 The *Theological-Political Treatise* was deemed impious by Thomasius. Published in 1670, it was swiftly banned in the Netherlands, and in 1679 it was added to the list of books prohibited by the Church. Even Hobbes confessed that he would not have dared to write with such boldness. For a historical overview of the reception of this remarkable book, see Nadler (2013).

5 For in-depth discussions of the meaning and scope of political theology throughout its historical development and in contemporary times, see Bailey, Cavanaugh and Hovey (2012); Borghesi (2013); Böckenförde (1983); Castrucci (1981); Cavanaugh and Scott (2019); Dean, List and Schwarzkopf (2023); Fiorenza, Tanner and Welker (2013); Galli (2024); Newman (2018); Nicoletti and Sartori (1991); Preterossi (2022); Phillips (2012); Silva (2019); and Wiedenhofer (1976).

6 I will not delve into this discussion in detail, but for further exploration I recommend the article by Béatrice Han entitled 'L'*a priori* historique selon Michel Foucault: difficultés archéologiques'.

7 The complex and often tense relations between the Holy Roman Empire and the papacy, always interpreted through creative readings of the theory of the two swords, are explored by the young Hans Kelsen in his 1905 doctoral thesis, which focused on analysing the concept of the State in the thought of Dante Alighieri. For a legal history perspective on the same subject, see Calasso (1951).

8 For a general overview of this initial historical period of political theology, see Momigliano (1975); Scatolla (2009); and Villacañas (2016).

9 Just like Pitkin, who translates the term 'representation' as 'to make present again' (1972: 8–9); Gerhard Leibholz (1996) also makes the same mistake.

10 As explained in Hofmann (1974: 38); Leibholz (1989: 70); and Rausch (1977: 78). For further reading on the general topic of political representation, see: Bußhoff (2000); Costa (2004); Duso (2003); Fisichella (1996); Galli (1987); Haller (1987); Matos (2020); Podlech (1978) and Rausch (1968).

11 For a comprehensive examination of contemporary developments in radical political theology, see Robbins' previously cited work and Crockett's 2013 book.

12 It is not the purpose of this book to discuss the complex history of the idea of 'political spirituality' in Foucault's work, which is often misunderstood by readers who are not always inspired by good faith. For analyses on this topic, weighing the pros and cons, see Afary and Anderson (2005) and Ghamari-Tabrizi (2016).

13 A comprehensive examination of Simone Weil's intricate and compelling ideas on 'spiritual politics' falls beyond the scope of this work. It suffices to note here that I have categorized her approach as 'charitable' due to its rejection of any legal means of enforcing justice.

14 This is one of the themes that would be elucidated within the so-called unwritten doctrines of Plato, as described by Reale (1991).

15 'What is at stake is the capture and inscription in a separate sphere of the inoperativity that is central to human life. The *oikonomia* of power places firmly at its heart, in the form of festival and glory, what appears to its eyes as the inoperativity of man and God, which cannot be looked at. Human life is inoperative and without purpose, but precisely this *argia* and this absence of aim make the incomparable operativity [*operosità*] of the human species possible. Man has dedicated himself to production and labor [*lavoro*], because in his essence he is completely devoid of work [*opera*], because he is the Sabbatical animal par excellence. [. . .] This inoperativity is the political substance of the Occident, the glorious nutrient of all power' (Agamben 2011: 245–6).

16 'What is in question is nothing less than a new and unheard of concentration, multiplication, and dissemination of the function of glory as the center of the political system. [. . .] Contemporary democracy is a democracy that is entirely founded upon glory, that is, on the efficacy of acclamation, multiplied and disseminated by the media beyond all imagination. [. . .] As had always been the case in profane and ecclesiastical liturgies, this supposedly "originary democratic phenomenon" is once again caught, orientated, and manipulated in the forms and according to the strategies of spectacular power' (Agamben 2011: 256).

17 It is important to note, following Scholem, that some of the earliest Kabbalists did not distinguish between the *Ayin Sof* understood as God and the first *sefirah*, which would be the Nothingness from which the world emerges, thus approaching a pantheistic view. In contrast, later Kabbalists, especially those of the sixteenth century such as Moses Cordovero and Isaac Luria, drew a distinction between God and the abyss of Nothingness that is said to have emerged from Him to make creation possible, thereby preserving the radical transcendence between the Creator and the world (Biale 1985: 79–80). A particularly interesting example is provided by Abraham Cohen de Herrera (1570–c. 1635) in his treatise *The Gate of Heaven*, where he identifies the Nothingness that separates God from His creation with the Aristotelian category of potency (2010: 295). As can be seen, this discussion is extremely complex and cannot be fully addressed within the narrow scope of this book. Moreover, for the purposes of my argument, it matters little whether what lies at the beginning is a Nothingness or a hidden, ineffable and unmanifest God who first 'creates' Nothingness and then the world. In both cases, there is an *an-arkhé* in a principle position. As I discuss shortly in the main text, it is a *necessary contradiction* within the economy of Kabbalah, that is, it is not truly a contradiction.

18 See also, for more articulate critiques, Sanín-Restrepo 2016's book: p. 47–70 (against Deleuze), p. 71–114 (against Agamben) and p. 114–208 (against Negri).

19 The text was subsequently republished as an introduction to a collective work that has made significant contributions to the development of the concepts of encryption and decryption of power. See Sanín-Restrepo and Méndez-Hincapié (2018).

20 To this end, see the insightful chapter IV of Sanín-Restrepo's 2016 work, which provides a clear and accessible explanation of Aristotle's complex theory of act and potency, as well as its subsequent developments, challenges and innovative interpretations in contemporary thought.

21 To be honest with Agamben, it is important to note that, outside of his *Homo Sacer* project, in one of his most recent works – *The Unrealizable: Towards a Politics of Ontology* – he explicitly admits that act and potency are co-originating, emphasizing that the error of Western metaphysics does not lie in distinguishing them, but rather in thinking that potency preexists separately, thus creating the false problem of the transition to act (2022: 71). In this regard, drawing on numerous authors, particularly some 'minor' figures in the Western canon, such as Dante and Nicolaus of Cusa – the latter, in his *De Possest*, advocates for the coincidence of existence and possibility – Agamben arrives at the notion of self-affection, understood as a ontological-modal dimension where the encounter between object and subject, existence and essence, and, finally, act and potency occurs.

22 An excellent study on the role of negativity – and, in some ways, of potency – in Hegel's thought is Andrew Cole's *The Birth of Theory*, which has the merit of attempting to bring Hegel closer to authors who are hostile to him, such as Nietzsche and Deleuze. Furthermore, Cole demonstrates that the idea of theory in contemporary philosophy emerges thanks to Hegel's efforts, so that, in one way or another, all current thought is indebted to him.

23 'Encryption is a primal form of "solidification" of power based on the prohibition of the creation, access, and uses of any and every form of communication through the establishment of transcendent models and inscrutable languages. Encryption is finally the denial of politics through the stratifications and occultation of language. Power in a solid state is the technology that absorbs energy from its exterior and transforms it to a hierarchization of subjectivities; it is the contracture of all circulation where every relation becomes prefixed' (Sanín-Restrepo 2018: xvi).

24 In *Contributions to Philosophy: From Event*, Heidegger uses the old German spelling – *seyn* – of the verb *sein* (to be), with an y instead of an i, to denote that, in this phase of his philosophical development, he is addressing the question of the *truth of Being*, distancing himself from the metaphysical tradition that focuses on the inquiry into the *essence of Being*. He takes this path because he realizes that the question of the essence of Being can only be answered through the *Dasein*, a being/entity that, inevitably anthropologizing, leads to the presupposition

of something like a supreme being, that is, God, thus concealing Being. In contrast, Heidegger's *Seyn* assumes the impossibility of a human thematization of Being, appearing as a mysterious ontological-temporal formation devoid of any anthropocentric foundation. I will revisit this discussion in section 2.2.1.

25 '[. . .] to be is to be against nothingness; to be is to be possible. To be possible is to exercise power. Hence, to be is always exercised through some kind or other of power that is essentially tapped into a primal presupposition, be it called idea, substance, logos, nature, society, man, epistemology, mind, judgment, or concept. "To be is to exercise power" is then the deceptive frontispiece of the grand edifice of Western politics' (Sanín-Restrepo 2018: xiv).

26 This is a good example of a situationist *détournement*. Hegel's original sentence, characteristic of his idealist dialectic, states that 'the false is a moment of the true'. In the ninth paragraph of *The Society of the Spectacle*, Debord simply inverts the subject and predicate to characterize the present era with acuity and precision, when, in fact, 'the true is a moment of the false'.

27 For a discussion of the linguistic roots from which the Greek words that today indicate the classical forms of government were constructed, cf. Cesare (2024).

28 '*Nur noch ein Gott kann uns retten*'. This famous statement by Heidegger comes from his lengthy interview with the German newspaper *Der Spiegel* on 23 September 1966, in which he also reflected obliquely on his Nazi past. The philosopher authorized the publication of the interview only posthumously, leading to its release in May 1976. For an English translation, see Heidegger (1981b).

Chapter 2

1 The bibliography on Schmitt's political theology is so extensive that a thorough review is beyond the scope of this work. However, some classic studies warrant particular mention, including Beaud (1993); Bignotto (2008); Bravo (2011); D'Ors (1976); Festa (1987); Freund (1989); Galli (1981, 1996: 331–459), Mouffe (1999) and Nicoletti (1990). On the historical-political dimension of Schmitt's *Political Theology*, see the introduction by Alexandre Franco de Sá (2024) to his excellent Portuguese translation.

2 The comparison is drawn from the 1h13m20s mark in the outstanding seminar on political theology presented by Galli at the Istituto Italiano per gli Studi Filosofici: <https://www.youtube.com/watch?v=_1AuJsLz210&ab_channel=AccademiaIISF>.

3 Interestingly, this famous sentence of Hobbes does not appear in the first English edition of *Leviathan* from 1651; it is found only on page 133 of the revised second

edition from 1668, which is presented in Latin. This edition can be accessed online here: <https://archive.org/details/leviathansivedem00hobb/page/132/mode/2up>.

4 According to Alexandre Franco de Sá, the Kelsenian *Rechtsstaat*, insofar as it represents the fusion of creator (State) and creature (law), would constitute a kind of juridical paganism in which God becomes immanent to nature, thus resembling Spinoza's *Deus sive natura* (Sá 2024: 41).

5 The text of this book was completed in 1964 but was published only posthumously in 2012 due to complex issues surrounding censorship in McCarthyist America, where Kelsen relocated in 1940 in response to the rise of Nazism in Europe. See Matos (2013) for further details.

6 In his 1944 essay *The Rise of Secular Religions*, Aron defines secular religions as follows: 'I propose to call "secular religions" the doctrines that occupy in the minds of our contemporaries the place of a vanished faith and transfer the salvation of humanity to a form of social order to be established in the remote future'. This article was later republished in Aron (1990). For further discussion on secular or political religions, see Gentile (2001); Ley (2003); Maier (1996–2003) and Rivière (1988).

7 In the same vein: 'Christianity is a historical religion, not only because it is based on a historical figure and events that are considered to have actually occurred, but also because it assigns to time, conceived as linear and irreversible, a soteriological meaning. Moreover, by linking its own destiny to history, it interprets and conceives itself from a historical perspective, and develops and carries with it a kind of philosophy or, more precisely, a theology of history' (Puech 1978: 35).

8 'All changes, all shifts from the old to the new are accessible to us only insofar as they allow themselves [. . .] to be drawn into a constant frame of reference by means of which demands can be defined, in which an identical "position" has to be satisfied. The fact that the new in history cannot in each case be random, but rather is under the pressure of preexisting expectations and needs, is the condition for having something like a "knowledge" of history. The concept of "reoccupation" designates, in its implications, the minimum of identity that, even in the most moving movements of history, must be found or that can at least be presupposed and sought. [. . .] "reoccupation" means that different statements can be understood as answers to identical questions' (Blumenberg 2021: 541).

9 'The awareness of a decisive separation from the past, the way in which it shaped the beginning of Modernity, cannot be demanded of any other epoch in such a comparable way. This does not in any way characterize the formation of the Middle Ages, because medieval legitimacy was sought directly in the connection of the Middle Ages to the intellectual system of Antiquity and in the construction of an identity with it. Since Modernity sought to define and realize itself as a world epoch,

there can be no advantage for Modernity in defining itself in relation to the Middle Ages, which, on the contrary, tried to hide the fact that it was something other than Antiquity, because Antiquity was considered an anticipation of Christianity. Precisely when "Modernity" wanted to be literally a new era, dissociating itself from the previous period as the "Middle Ages", interpolating this period between itself and "classical Antiquity", for historical knowledge such a declarative claim cannot mean anything real without further ado. If, for the emerging Middle Ages, the meaning of the reception of ancient materials consisted in hiding the foundation of this reception, for the emerging Modernity, resolute as it was in relation to the historical rupture, the issue consisted in hiding the primacy of "reoccupation" in its referentiality to a constant matrix of needs' (Blumenberg 2021: 537–8).

10 'The state of exception has a meaning for the science of law analogous to that of miracle for theology' ('*Der Ausnahmezustand hat für die Jurisprudenz eine analoge Bedeutung wie das Wunder für die Theologie*') (Schmitt 1996: 43). In the 'classical' theology of Thomas Aquinas (2008, I, q. 105, a. 7), miracles are understood as events that transcend the normal order established by God (*praeter ordinem rerum*). They belong to the domain of special providence, which, being exceptional, serves to complement the regular normativity of general providence. This interplay not only reinforces the structure of divine governance but also imbues human freedom with meaning.

11 'Don't let anyone deceive you in any way, for that day will not come until the rebellion occurs and the man of lawlessness is revealed, the man doomed to destruction. He will oppose and will exalt himself over everything that is called God or is worshiped, so that he sets himself up in God's temple, proclaiming himself to be God. Don't you remember that when I was with you I used to tell you these things? And now you know what is holding him back, so that he may be revealed at the proper time. For the secret power of lawlessness is already at work; but the one who now holds it back will continue to do so till he is taken out of the way. And then the lawless one will be revealed, whom the Lord Jesus will overthrow with the breath of his mouth and destroy by the splendor of his coming' (2 *Thessalonians*, 3–8).

12 For an examination of Benjamin's messianic political theology, see Costa (2023); Gagnebin (1999); Gentili (2020); Guerra and Tagliacozzo (2020); Fazio and Lijoi (2019); Jacobson (2003); Martel (2011); Raulet (1997); Seminari di Studi Benjaminiani (2010) and Wohlfarth (1986).

13 The influence of Catholicism on Schmitt's thought should not be underestimated. In this regard, adopting a methodology that would likely resonate with the German jurist – who believed that an idea can only be fully understood within the context of an intellectual confrontation taken to its extremes – it is particularly illuminating

to consider the 2019 volume *Critique of Political Theology: Hebrew Voices on Carl Schmitt*, edited by Giorgio Fazio and Federico Lijoi. The book features texts and testimonies from five prominent Jewish thinkers – Walter Benjamin, Hans Kelsen, Leo Strauss, Karl Löwith and Jacob Taubes – who challenged Schmitt's Catholic political theology. For a discussion on the possibility of a Jewish political theology, see Taub (2017).

14 'In every era the attempt must be made anew to wrest tradition away from a conformism that is about to overpower it. The Messiah comes not only as the redeemer, he comes as the subduer of Antichrist. Only that historian will have the gift of fanning the spark of hope in the past who is firmly convinced that *even the dead* will not be safe from the enemy if he wins. And this enemy has not ceased to be victorious' (Benjamin 1968: 255).

15 Here is part of Benjamin's original text: '*Dann wird uns als unsere Aufgabe die Herbeiführung des wirklichen Ausnahmezustands vor Augen stehen*' (1991 [I]: 697). Harry Zohn translates the German adjective *wirklich* as 'real', which does not seem appropriate to me. While this translation highlights the epistemological dimension at stake in the eighth thesis, it fails to capture the effective and dynamic nuance of the term, which resonates clearly with Hegelian thought. Indeed, Hegel employed the German word *Realität* to denote simple reality in its given and seemingly (i.e. falsely) unchangeable state, whereas *Wirklichkeit* refers to the processual and dialectical nature of the real. Therefore, I prefer to translate *wirklich* as 'effective'.

16 One of the most comprehensive summaries of the various interpretations of Benjamin's enigmatic essay can be found in the chapter dedicated to the philosopher in Bernstein (2013). For further insights on the concept of pure violence, see Martel (2012) and Silva (2018).

17 For a more in-depth analysis of the notion of 'means without ends', see the essay of the same title by Agamben (1996).

18 In 1940, confronted with the looming Nazi barbarity that threatened to imprison him in a concentration camp, this alternative re-emerged forcefully in Benjamin's life, when his desperate escape from France on foot toward Portugal – where he planned to embark for the United States – passing through the Pyrenees seemed to have reached its end at the Spanish border, more specifically in the Catalan city of Portbou. There, he and the others who accompanied him were detained by the Francoist guards, leaving him no option – or so he seems to have thought – but to end his own life on the night of 25–26 September. Ironically, this act appears to have frightened the guards, who, the morning after Benjamin's death, released his companions to continue their journey (Tackels 2012: 501–16). His body was buried in an unknown location, and today a poignant symbolic memorial stands on the seafront in Portbou, remembering not only Walter Benjamin's words but also his sacrifice.

19 On Taubes' political theology, see Bielik-Robson (2014); Faber (2022); Faber, Goodman-Thau and Macho (2001); Løland (2020); Muller (2022); Spegne (2016); Stimilli (2019); Treml (2012) and Weigel (2019).

20 Horkheimer spoke out harshly about Zionism on several occasions. For example: 'The creation of the State of Israel, which materialized due to the persecution and in order to rescue Jewish individuals, is the symbol of the current crisis of Judaism. However, this crisis points towards the end of the "spiritual reality" of Judaism. This is a fatal dialectic, nevertheless characteristic for our age' (1985–96 [18]: 643). 'The Jewish people were not nationalistic at all, they were suffering for the sake of all Humanity. Israel, on the contrary, is a nation-State, at its base structured like all others. Thus, the original messianic thought had to vanish for the sake of national existence' (1985–96 [14]: 326). 'Whatever will happen to Eichmann in Israel, demonstrates the lack of power and not the power of the Jews, who are self-conscious and conscious of their rights. It demonstrates the pretension of authority and not the practice of authority by the State of Israel. Everyone knows that Israel's totalitarian affectations, which recall Benito and the Russians, were tolerated this time only with respect to New York' (1985–96 [6]: 348). On the subject, see Neubauer (2012).

21 'It is a matter of choosing between the dictatorship that comes from below and the dictatorship that comes from above; I choose the one that comes from above, because it originates from cleaner and more serene regions; it is, in the end, a choice between the dictatorship of the dagger and the dictatorship of the saber; I choose the dictatorship of the saber, because it is more noble' (Donoso Cortés 1854: 274).

22 'Whether we are dealing with a being, an idea, a knowledge, or a praxis, in every case the beginning is not a simple preamble, which then disappears into what follows. On the contrary, the origin never ceases to begin, that is, to command and govern what it has put into being' (Agamben 2019: 52–3).

23 Meister Eckhart (1260–1328), the medieval German theologian, is often regarded as a precursor to many modern philosophical and mystical ideas, especially in terms of his conception of the divine and the self. His influence extended beyond his own time, inspiring later thinkers, including the Renaissance priest and mystic Angelus Silesius (1624–77). Silesius is perhaps best known for his *an-archic* verse: '*Die Rose ist ohne warum; sie blühet weil sie blühet*' ('The rose is without a reason; it blooms because it blooms'). This line, from his work *The Cherubic Pilgrim* (I.289), captures the essence of *an-archy*, an existence that unfolds without reference to a higher, external principle or justification. The verse resonates deeply with Schürmann's philosophical project, which emphasizes the idea of *an-archy* as a movement away from foundational and hierarchical structures of power. It is significant that the epigraph of Schürmann's *magnum opus* is a Latin quotation from Meister Eckhart:

'*Hoc enim proprie vivit quod est sine principio*', that is: 'Only that which is without a principle properly lives'.

24 It is important to emphasize that the focus of my analysis is not Heidegger's thought per se, but rather that of Schürmann, who should be regarded as an independent thinker and not merely a commentator on the German philosopher's ideas. This distinction pertains to methodological concerns, but it should not be taken to suggest that an engagement with Heidegger is unnecessary. On the contrary, his status as one of the most influential anti-foundationalist philosophers of the past century warrants a direct reading of his work. That said, before proceeding, it is crucial to decrypt the terminology of this complex and controversial author, especially considering the theological-political dimensions his work often entails. For this purpose, the reference text is *Being and Contingency: Decrypting Heidegger's Terminology*, in which Ricardo Sanín-Restrepo concludes, in a completely *an-archic* way: '[. . .] everything is contingent, and contingency means that only when beings exist, not as a necessity, is the meaning of being necessary' (2021: 147). Additionally, a helpful resource for navigating Heidegger's specialized language is the synoptic table of terms and their English translations compiled by William Blattner – author of *Heidegger's 'Being and Time': A Reader's Guide* – available at: <https://faculty.georgetown.edu/blattnew/heid/Heidegger-jargon.html>

25 The original title of the book is *Beiträge zur Philosophie (Vom Ereignis)*. According to Franco Volpi, the '*Vom*' in the subtitle does not mean 'about', but rather 'from', meaning that it is not a complement of argument but of origin (2011: 278). The implicit idea is that the text was not written by the subject named Martin Heidegger, but emanated directly from the event. Therefore, the traditional English translation 'of the event' seems incorrect to me, which is why I propose 'from the event'.

26 In a similar way, at the beginning of his *Science of Logic*, Hegel already noted that Being is identical to Nothing because both are indeterminate.

27 I make no pretense of offering an original, immanent or autonomous interpretation of Nietzsche. Rather, my aim is to juxtapose and critically evaluate the interpretations of Nietzsche provided by Heidegger, Schürmann and Deleuze, highlighting both areas of agreement and points of divergence.

28 For an in-depth discussion on post-anarchism, see Evren (2011); Koch (2011); May (1994, 2011) and Newman (2011, 2015). For a more concrete examination of contemporary anarchist practices and their complex relationship with the left, refer to Klausen and Martel (2011).

29 'And it is precisely this that we read in the Bible. In the Greek translation made by the rabbis of Alexandria in the third century BC, the book of Genesis opens with the phrase "*en archē*, in the beginning God created the heavens and the earth";

but as we read immediately afterward, he created them by means of a command, which is to say an imperative: *genēthētō*, "And God said: let there be light". The same thing happens in the Gospel of John: "*en archē*, in the beginning was the *logos*, the word". But a word that is in the beginning, before everything, can only be a command. Thus I believe that perhaps the most correct translation of this famous *incipit* should be not "in the beginning was the word" but "in command – that is, in the form of a command – was the word". If this translation had prevailed, many things would be more clear, not only in theology, *but also and above all in politics*' (Agamben 2019: 52).

30 I use the label 'post-structuralist' in a strictly chronological sense, referring only to authors who followed the structuralist generation of Benveniste, Jakobson, Lévi-Strauss, Meillet, Saussure and others, without assuming any overarching idea or unified theory that connects them.

31 On the subject of Black political theologies in general, see Cleage Jr. (1968); Cone (1969, 1970); Copeland (2019); Hopkins (2005); Katongole (2011); Jones (1998); Roberts (1974) and Silva (1998).

32 For a comprehensive overview of liberation theology, see Aguilar (2007, 2008a, b); Claffey and Egan (2009); Ellacuría and Sobrino (1990); Löwy (1996) and Rabinovich (2023).

33 Two examples of anthologies and analyses of texts by liberation theology authors that were published in Europe under the title – much more commercial and marketable, obviously – of 'theology of revolution' are Tödt and Rendtorff (1968), which is not limited to Latin American liberation theology, and Vaccari (1969).

34 Interestingly, Rubem Alves had anticipated the widespread use of the term 'liberation theology' in his 1968 doctoral thesis, *Towards a Theology of Liberation: An Exploration of the Encounter Between the Languages of Humanistic Messianism and Messianic Humanism*, which was later published as *A Theology of Human Hope* (1969). This precedes Gutiérrez's influential work by three years, highlighting the independent development of similar theological concerns among Latin American thinkers. For further discussion on this topic, see Linhares (2014). Additionally, Harvey Cox's *The Secular City* (1965) should also be cited. Although not directly connected to liberation theology, its ideas on secularization, the role of the Church and the relationship between faith and society resonate strongly with this genuinely Latin American movement. In his book, Cox argues that secularization should not be seen as an inherently negative or destructive force, but rather as a complex phenomenon capable of fostering new forms of religious expression and spiritual living. He stresses the importance of Christians aligning with the dispossessed, who are marginalized and rendered invisible in today's technologically advanced societies.

35 Even before becoming Pope, Ratzinger – who was, in fact, a prominent intellectual – rejected the political dimension of theology. Accordingly, he could not avoid condemning liberation theology, although he acknowledged some 'golden particles' within it. However, his profoundly conservative judgement is categorical, condemning not only the politicized liberation theology but also any kind of political theology. This is clearly illustrated in the following excerpt from *Eschatology*, a work first published in 1977: 'The Kingdom of God is not a political concept and, therefore, cannot serve as a basis for constructing a political praxis or for critiquing certain political actions. The realization of the Kingdom of God is not a political process, and conceiving it in this way means falsifying both politics and theology. The result of this is the emergence of false messianisms which, by their very essence and the internal logic of their messianic claims, lead to various forms of totalitarianism' (2020: 81). As can be seen, Ratzinger conflates political theology with political (or civil/secular) religion.

36 See the dossier *Martyrs of El Salvador* from the Humanitas Institute of Unisinos available at: <https://www.ihuonline.unisinos.br/artigo/2948-martires-de-el-salvador>. For a literary recreation of this dramatic event, refer to *Senselessness*, an impressive and tragicomic novel by Horacio Castellanos Moya.

Chapter 3

1 The bibliography on the religious character of capitalism and its contemporary form, neoliberalism, continues to expand each year. Notable contributions include Gentili, Ponzi and Stimilli (2010), Kotsko (2018), Jongen (2007), Preterossi (2022: 204–77), Raschke (2019), Stimilli (2020) and Villacañas (2020).

2 The performance is titled *K Foundation Burn a Million Quid* and can be viewed on YouTube: <https://www.youtube.com/watch?v=a3dcXzPFLOc&ab_channel=KiLN>.

3 It is striking how most authors fail to recognize the entirely theological character of the invisible hand that Adam Smith speaks of in book IV, chapter 2, paragraph 9 of the famous – but little read – 1776 work, *The Wealth of Nations*. The metaphor finds various and exact parallels in theological literature: 'According to Augustine, God governs and administers the world, from the great to the small things, with an occult hand sign' ('*omnia, maxima et minima, occulto nutu administranti*': Augustine, *The Literal Meaning of Genesis*, 3, 17, 26); in Salvian's treatise on the government of the world, empires and provinces, but also the smallest details of private homes are led by '*quasi quadam manu et gubernacula*' (Salvian, *On the Government of God*); Thomas Aquinas (*Summa Theologiae*, q. 103, a. I, ad 2, p. 5) speaks in the same way of a *manus gubernatoris* that governs the created without being seen; in Luther (*De*

servo arbitrio), the creature is itself a hand (*Hand*) of the hidden God; finally, in Bossuet, 'Dieu tient du plus haut des cieux les rênes de tous les royaumes; il a tous les coeurs en sa main' (Bossuet 1936, Part III, Chapter 7, pp. 1024–1025)" (Agamben 2011: 284).

4 However, Py (2020: 29) is mistaken in his assertion that the term 'Christofascism' appears in Sölle's 1970 work *Beyond Mere Obedience: Reflections on a Christian Ethic for the Future*, which is a translation of the original German text *Phantasie und Gehorsam* from 1968. In reality, 'Christofascism' is a neologism that titles one of the essays (p. 133–41) in Sölle's collection referenced at the beginning of this section, which was published in Germany in 1987 under the title *Das Fenster der Verwundbarkeit: Theologisch-politische Texte.*

5 However, I cannot overlook the significant – and unfortunately exceptional – theological-political dimension present in the final writings (1880–2) of the great Brazilian abolitionist Luiz Gama (1830–82), who argued that 'slaves are like Lazarus: they need to be resurrected'. This resurrection, he suggested, could occur actively when a slave, acting in accordance with 'natural law', kills their master. As Bruno Rodrigues de Lima – editor of Gama's complete works (2023) – states: 'He kills, inevitably, to resurrect'.

6 See, from minute eleven, the video on YouTube: <https://www.youtube.com/watch?v=MA6-UM03s6M&ab_channel=X%C3%AAro>.

7 Regarding the FPE as the political-institutional arm of Brazilian Christofascism, see Py (2020: 12–24). However, it is essential to clarify that neither Py nor I are claiming that every Evangelical belief or individual is Christofascist. Instead, there exists a notable affinity between the Christofascist principles outlined here and those of the FPE. For a more in-depth understanding of the FPE's ideology and its power project, refer to the works of Dip (2018) and Duarte (2012).

8 For discussions on the growth of Neo-Pentecostalism in relation to Catholics – who remain the largest religious group in Brazil, although their total representation has been declining in each census – and regarding its political agency, see, in addition to the classic work by Pierucci (1989), the following studies: Burity and Machado (2006), Camurça (2013, 2019, 2020), Mariano (2011) and Trevisan (2013).

9 For insights on the conservative character of Neo-Pentecostalism, see Almeida (2017), Almeida and Toniol (2018), Antoniazzi (1994), Fernandes (1988) and Mariano (2005).

Conclusion

1 This miracle is presented in the *Bible* in two versions: 'feeding the 5,000' (*Matt.* 14:13-21; *Mark* 6:31-44; *Luke* 9:10-17; *John* 6:5-15) and 'feeding the 4,000' (*Mark* 8:1-9; *Matt.* 15:32-39).

2 From this perspective, I contend that it is possible to extract from Pasolini's literary and cinematic work a powerful theological-political-pornographic fresco, as discussed in Matos (2024a).

3 Lévi-Strauss presents this insightful and eloquent reflection at the conclusion of chapter VII (section 29) of his monumental travel autobiography of 1955, *The Sad Tropics*.

4 'Nature hath made men so equall, in the faculties of body, and mind; as that though there bee found one man sometimes manifestly stronger in body, or of quicker mind then another; yet when all us reckoned together, the difference between man, and man, is not so considerable, as that one man can thereupon claim to himselfe any benefit, to which another may not pretend, as well as he. For as to the strength of body, the weakest has strength enough to kill the strongest, either by secret machination, or by confederacy with others, that are in the same danger with himselfe' (Hobbes 1965 [I, 13]: 94).

5 I translate this biblical passage into English through the mediation of Giorgio Agamben's Italian version (2014b: 346), as he faithfully preserves the apparent contradictions of the Greek original and engages with them philosophically.

6 It is important to note that the notion of 'as if not' – central to the closure of Agamben's *Homo Sacer* project, as it gives rise to the figure of the form-of-life that opposes the exception – owes much to the winter course of 1921–2 titled *Introduction to the Phenomenology of Religion* by the young Heidegger. At that time, still without his own developed vocabulary, Heidegger reads Paul's letter in order to identify what he calls factical life, that is, life as it is (*Was*) in its everydayness, which he contrasts with an authentic life grounded in its historical-temporal 'how' (*Wie*), an idea that will later be translated as *Dasein*. In this sense, perhaps Agamben's greatest innovation in his reading of Paul, consistent with his emphasis on inoperativity as something intrinsic to the human, was to shift the discussion from the 'how' to the 'how not'.

References

Adorno, T. W. (1984), 'Cultural Criticism and Society', in *Prisms*, 17–34, Massachusetts: Massachusetts Institute of Technology.

Afary, J. and K. B. Anderson (2005), *Foucault and the Iranian Revolution: Gender and the Seductions of Islamism*, Chicago: University of Chicago Press.

Agamben, G. and G. Deleuze (2011), *Bartleby: La Formula della Creazione*, trans. S. Verdicchio, Macerata: Quodlibet.

Agamben, G. (1982), *Il Linguaggio e la Morte: Un Seminario sul Luogo della Negatività*, Torino: Einaudi.

Agamben, G. (1995), *Il Potere Sovrano e la Nuda Vita*, Torino: Einaudi.

Agamben, G. (1996), *Mezzi Senza Fine: Note sulla Politica*, Torino: Bollati Boringhieri.

Agamben, G. (2001), 'Il Cinema di Guy Debord', in E. Ghezzi and R. Turigliatto (ed.), *Guy Debord Contro il Cinema*, 103–7, Milano: Il Castoro.

Agamben, G. (2000), *Il Tempo che Resta: Un Commento alla «Lettera ai Romani»*, Torino: Bollati Boringhieri.

Agamben, G. (2008), Signatura Rerum*: Sul Metodo*, Torino: Bollati Boringhieri.

Agamben, G. (2009), 'On the Limits of Violence', trans. L. Fabbri and E. Fay, *Diacritics*, 39 (4): 103–11. https://10.1353/dia.2009.0034.

Agamben, G. (2011), *The Kingdom and the Glory: For a Theological Genealogy of Economy and Government*, trans. L. Chiesa and M. Mandarini, Stanford: Stanford University Press.

Agamben, G. (2012), 'Giorgio Agamben, Intervista a Peppe Savà: Amo Scicli e Guccione', *Ragusa News*, 16 August 2012, https://www.ragusanews.com/articolo/28021/giorgio-agamben-intervista-a-peppe-sava-amo-scicli-e-guccione

Agamben, G. (2013), *Il Mistero del Male: Benedetto XVI e la Fine dei Tempi*, Bari-Roma: Laterza.

Agamben, G. (2014a), 'Estado de Exceção e Genealogia do Poder', trans. D. Nascimento, *Revista Brasileira de Estudos Políticos*, 108: 21–39.

Agamben, G. (2014b), *L'Uso dei Corpi*, Vicenza: Neri Pozza.

Agamben, G. (2018a), 'Auschwitz: L'Archivio e il Testimone', in *Homo Sacer: Edizione Integrale (1995–2015)*, 760–881, Macerata: Quodlibet.

Agamben, G. (2018b) '*Stasis*: La Guerra Civile Come Paradigma Politico', in *Homo Sacer: Edizione Integrale (1995–2015)*, 251–310, Macerata: Quodlibet.

Agamben, G. (2019), 'What is a Command?', in *Creation and Anarchy: The Work of Art and the Religion of Capitalism*, 51–65, trans. A. Kotsko, Redwood: Stanford University Press.

Agamben, G. (2022), *L'Irrealizzabile: Per una Politica dell'Ontologia*. Torino: Einaudi.

Agamben, G. (2023a), 'Che Cos'É il Contemporaneo?', in *La Mente Sgombra: Profanazioni. Nudità. Il Fuoco e il Racconto*, 90–9, Torino: Einaudi.

Agamben, G. (2023b), 'Creazione e Salvezza', in *La Mente Sgombra: Profanazioni. Nudità. Il Fuoco e il Racconto*, 81–9, Torino: Einaudi.

Agamben, G. (2024a), '*Aion* e *Chronos*. Nuove Tesi sul Concetto della Storia', in *La Lingua che Resta: Il Tempo, la Storia, il Linguaggio*, 3–39, Torino: Einaudi.

Agamben, G. (2024b), *Quaderni. Volume 1: 1972–81*, Macerata: Quodlibet.

Agência Brasil (2024), 'Relembre o Passo a Passo da Tentativa de Golpe no 8/1', 08 January 2024, https://agenciabrasil.ebc.com.br/politica/noticia/2024-01/relembre-o-passo-passo-da-tentativa-de-golpe-no-81.

Agência IBGE Notícias (2023), 'Censo 2010: Número de Católicos Cai e Aumenta o de Evangélicos, Espíritas e Sem Religião', 23 June 2023, https://agenciadenoticias.ibge.gov.br/agencia-sala-de-imprensa/2013-agencia-de-noticias/releases/14244-asi-censo-2010-numero-de-catolicos-cai-e-aumenta-o-de-evangelicos-espiritas-e-sem-religiao.

Aguilar, M. I. (2007), *The History and Politics of Latin American Theology. Vol. I: The Problem of Theological Generations*, London: SCM.

Aguilar, M. I. (2008a), *The History and Politics of Latin American Theology. Vol. II: Theology and Civil Society*, London: SCM.

Aguilar, M. I. (2008b), *The History and Politics of Latin American Theology. Vol. III: A Theology of the Periphery*, London: SCM.

Aguilar, M. I. (2019), 'Liberation Theology 2: Developments and Reception', in W. T. Cavanaugh and P. Scott (eds.), *The Wiley Blackwell Companion to Political Theology*, 293–306, Oxford: Blackwell.

Alencar, G. (2005), *Protestantismo Tupiniquim: Hipótese Sobre a (Não) Contribuição Evangélica à Cultura Brasileira*, São Paulo: Arte.

Almeida, R. and R. Toniol, eds. (2018), *Conservadorismos, Fascismos e Fundamentalismos: Análises Conjunturais*, Campinas: Editora da Universidade de Campinas.

Almeida, R. (2017), 'A Onda Quebrada: Evangélicos e Conservadorismo', *Cadernos PAGU*, 50: 5–30.

Althaus-Reid, M. (2001), *Indecent Theology: Theological Perversions in Sex, Gender, and Politics*, London: Routledge.

Althaus-Reid, M. (2005), 'From Liberation Theology to Indecent Theology: The Trouble with Normality in Theology', in I. Petrella (ed.), *Latin American Liberation Theology: The Next Generation*, 20–38, New York: Orbis.

Altizer, T. J. J. (1966), *The Gospel of Christian Atheism*, Louisville: Westminster John Knox.

Altizer, T. J. J. (2000), *The New Apocalypse: The Radical Christian Vision of William Blake*, Aurora: The Davies Group.

Alves, R. (1969), *A Theology of Human Hope*, Washington: Corpus.
Andrade, L. M. and N. Panotto, eds. (2023), *Decolonizing Liberation Theologies: Past, Present, and Future*, London: Palgrave Macmillan.
Antoniazzi, A., ed. (1994), *Nem Anjos Nem Demônios: Interpretações Sociológicas do Pentecostalismo*, Petrópolis: Vozes.
Aquinas, T. (2008), *Summa Theologiae*, trans. English Dominicans, Cambridge: Cambridge University Press.
Arendt, H. (2005), *The Promise of Politics*, New York: Schocken.
Aristotle (1984), *The Complete Works of Aristotle: The Revised Oxford Translation*, 2 vols., ed. Jonathan Barnes, Princeton: Princeton University Press.
Aron, R. (1990), *Chroniques de Guerre: La France Libre (1940–45)*, Paris: Gallimard.
Assmann, A., J. Assmann and W.-D. Hartwich (2007), 'Epílogo', in Taubes, J., *La Teología Política de Pablo*, trans. M. G-B. López, 123–53, Madrid: Trotta.
Assmann, H. and F. Hinkelammert (1989), *A Idolatria do Mercado: Ensaio sobre Economia e Teologia*, trans. J. A. Clasen, Petrópolis: Vozes.
Assmann, J., ed. (1992), *Politische Theologie zwischen Ägypten und Israel*, München: Siemens Stiftung.
Assmann, J. (2000), *Herrschaft und Heil: Politische Theologie in Ägypten, Israel und Europa*, München: Hanser.
Aubenque, P. (1966), *Le Problème de l'Être chez Aristote*, Paris: Presses Universitaires de France.
Badiou, A. (1998), *Saint Paul: La Fondation de l'Universalisme*, Paris: Presses Universitaires de France.
Bailey, J. W., W. T. Cavanaugh and C. Hovey, eds. (2012), *An Eerdmans Reader in Contemporary Political Theology*, Grand Rapids: Wm. B. Eerdmans.
Baker, C. (2021), *Confronting Christofascism: Healing the Evangelical Wound*, Berkeley: Apocryphile.
Bakounine, M. A. (1871), *La Théologie Politique de Mazzini et la Internationale*, Paris: Comission de Propagande Socialiste.
Baptista, S. (2009), *Pentecostais e Neopentecostais na Política Brasileira: Um Estudo sobre Cultura Política, Estado e Atores Coletivos Religiosos no Brasil*, São Paulo: Annablume/Instituto Metodista Izabela Hendrix.
Bauerschmidt, F. C. (1999), 'Aesthetics: The Theological Sublime', in J. Milbank, C. Pickstock and G. Ward (eds.), *Radical Orthodoxy: A New Theology*, 201–19, London: Routledge.
Beaud, O. (1993), 'Carl Schmitt ou le Juriste Engagé', in Schmitt, C., *Théorie de la Constitution*, 5–113, Paris: Presses Universitaires de France.
Beckford, R. (1998), *Jesus Is Dread: Black Theology and Black Culture in Britain*, London: Darton, Longman & Todd.
Beckford, R. (2001), *God of the* Rahtid: *Redeeming Rage*, London: Darton, Longman & Todd.

Beckford, R. (2014), *Documentary as Exorcism: Resisting the Bewitchment of Colonial Christianity*, London: Bloomsbury.

Benjamin, W. (1968), *Illuminations*, ed. H. Arendt, trans. H. Zohn, New York: Schocken.

Benjamin, W. (1979), *One-Way Street and Other Writings*, trans. E. Jephcott and K. Shorter, London: Harcourt Brace Jovanovich.

Benjamin, W. (1991), *Gesammelte Schriften*, vols. I, II, IV and VI, ed. H. Schweppenhäuser, R. Tiedemann and T. Rexroth, Frankfurt am Main: Suhrkamp.

Benjamin, W. (1998), *The Origin of German Tragic Drama*, trans. J. Osborne. London: Verso.

Benjamin, W. (2006), 'Theological-Political Fragment', in H. Eiland and M. W. Jennings (eds.), *Selected Writtings. Vol. 3 (1935–38)*, 305–6, trans. E. Jephcott, Cambridge: Harvard University Press.

Bernstein, R. J. (2013), *Violence: Thinking Without Banisters*, Cambridge: Polity.

Biale, D. (1985), 'Gershom Scholem's Ten Unhistorical Aphorisms on Kabbalah: Text and Commentary', *Modern Judaism*, 5 (1): 67–93.

Bielik-Robson, A. (2014), 'The Identity of the Spirit: Taubes Between Apocalyptics and Historiosophy', in *Jewish Cryptotheologies of Late Modernity: Philosophical Marranos*, London: Routledge.

Bignotto, N. (2008), 'Soberania e Exceção no Pensamento de Carl Schmitt', *Kriterion: Revista de Filosofia*, XLIX (118): 401–16.

Bingemer, M. C. and I. Gebara (1989), *Mary: Mother of God, Mother of the Poor*, New York: Orbis.

Birman, P. and C. Machado (2012), 'A Violência dos Justos: Evangélicos, Mídia e Periferias da Metrópole', *Revista Brasileira de Ciências Sociais*, 27 (80): 55–69.

Birman, P. (1994), 'Cultos de Possessão e Pentecostalismo no Brasil: Passagens', *Religião e Sociedade*, 17 (1–2): 90–109.

Blake, W. (1790), *The Marriage of Heaven and Hell*, original illuminated manuscript from 1790, https://archive.org/details/the-marriage-of-heaven-and-hell/mode/2up.

Blattner, W. (2023), *Heidegger's 'Being and Time': A Reader's Guide*, London: Bloomsbury.

Bloch, E. (1921), *Thomas Müntzer als Theologe der Revolution*, München: Kurt Wolff.

Bloch, E. (1954–59), *Das Prinzip Hoffnung*, 3 vols., Frankfurt am Main: Suhrkamp.

Bloch, M. (1993), *Apologie Pour l'Histoire ou le Métier d'Historien*, Paris: Armand Colin.

Blumenberg, H. (1971), 'Wirklichkeitsbegriff und Wirkungspotential des Mythos', in M. Fuhrman (ed.), *Terror und Spiel: Probleme der Mythenrezeption*, 11–66, Munich: Wilhelm Fink.

Blumenberg, H. (2021), *Die Legitimität der Neuzeit*, Frankfurt am Main: Suhrkamp.

Böckenförde, E. W. (1983), 'Politische Theorie und politische Theologie', in J. Taubes (ed.), *Der Fürst dieser Welt: Carl Schmitt und die Folgen*, Munich: Wilhelm Fink.

Bodin, J. (1993), *Les Six Livres de la République: Un Abrégé du Texte de l'Édition de Paris de 1583*, ed. G. Mairet. Paris: Librairie Générale Française.

Boesak, A. (1976), *Farewell to Innocence*, New York: Orbis.

Borghesi, M. (2013), *Critica della Teologia Politica: Da Agostino a Peterson*, Bologna: Marietti 1820.

Bravo, R. C. (2011), 'Catolicismo Romano y Forma Política: Manifiesto Político-Eclesial y Pieza del Engranaje Decisionista', in C. Schmitt, *Catolicismo Romano y Forma Política*, IX-LXXXVIII, trans. P. Madrigal, Madrid: Tecnos.

Brazal, A. M. (2019), 'Postcolonialism', in W. T. Cavanaugh and P. Scott (eds.), *The Wiley Blackwell Companion to Political Theology*, 516–30, Oxford: Blackwell.

Briggs, S. (1997), 'A History of Our Own: What Would a Feminist History of Theology Look Like?', in R. Chopp and S. G. Daveney (eds.), *Horizons in Feminist Theology: Identity, Tradition, and Norms*, 165–78, Minneapolis: Fortress.

Brunner, O., W. Conze and R. Koselleck, eds. (1972–97), *Geschichtliche Grundbegriffe: historisches Lexikon zur politisch-sozialen Sprache in Deutschland*, 8 vols., Stuttgart: Klett-Cotta.

Burity, J. and M. das D. Machado, eds. (2006), *Os Votos de Deus: Evangélicos, Política e Eleições no Brasil*, Recife: Massangana.

Burnet, J. (1892), *Early Greek Philosophy*, London-Edinburgh: Adam and Charles Black.

Bußhoff, H. (2000), *Politische Repräsentation: Repräsentativitat und Norm von Politik*, Baden-Baden: Nomos.

Buthelezi, M. (1976), 'Toward Indigenous Theology in South Africa', in S. Torres and V. Fabella (eds.), *The Emergent Gospel: Theology from the Underside of History*, 56–75, New York: Orbis.

Butler, J. (2004a), 'What is Critique? An Essay on Foucault's Virtue', in S. Salih (ed.), *The Judith Butler Reader*, 302–22, Oxford: Blackwell.

Butler, J. (2004b), *Precarious Life: The Powers of Mourning and Violence*, London: Verso, 2004.

Byttebier, P., J. Dale and P. Figurski, eds. (2022), *Political Liturgies in the High Middle Ages: Beyond the Legacy of Ernst H. Kantorowicz*, Turnhout: Brepols.

Cacciari, M. (2013), *Il Potere che Frena*, Milano: Adelphi.

Calasso, F. (1951), *I Glossatori e la Teoria della Sovranità: Studio di Diritto Comune Pubblico*, Milano: Giuffrè.

Câmara dos Deputados do Brasil (2023), 'Frente Parlamentar Evangélica do Congresso Nacional', https://www.camara.leg.br/internet/deputado/frenteDetalhe.asp?id=54477.

Camurça, M. A. (2013), 'O Brasil Religioso que Emerge do Censo de 2010: Consolidações, Tendências e Perplexidades', in F. Teixeira and R. Menezes (eds.), *Religiões em Movimento: O Censo de 2010*, 63–87, Petrópolis: Vozes.

Camurça, M. A. (2019), 'Religião, Política e Espaço Público no Brasil: Perspectiva Histórico/Sociológica e a Conjuntura das Eleições Presidenciais de 2018', *Estudos de Sociologia*, 2 (25): 125–59.

Camurça, M. A. (2020), 'Um Poder Evangélico no Estado Brasileiro? Mobilização Eleitoral, Atuação Parlamentar e Presença no Governo Bolsonaro', *Revista NUPEM*, 12 (25): 82–104.

Canfora, L. (2012), *La Democrazia: Storia di un'Ideologia*, Bari-Roma: Laterza.

Cannon, K. G. (1988), *Black Womanist Ethics*, Oxford: Oxford University Press.

Caputo, J. D. (2006a), 'Atheism, A/Theology and the Postmodern Condition', in M. Martin (ed.), *The Cambridge Companion to Atheism*, 267–82, Cambridge: Cambridge University Press.

Caputo, J. D. (2006b), *The Weakness of God: A Theology of the Event*, Bloomington: Indiana University Press.

Caputo, J. D. (2007), *What Would Jesus Deconstruct? The Good News of Postmodernism for the Church*, Grand Rapids: Baker.

Carter, J. K. (2008), *Race: A Theological Account*, Oxford: Oxford University Press.

Castro, E. V. de (2014), *Cannibal Metaphysics*, ed. P. Skafish, Minneapolis: Minnesota University Press.

Castro-Gómez, S. and R. Grosfoguel, eds. (2007), *El Giro Decolonial: Reflexiones para una Diversidad Epistémica más allá del Capitalismo Global*, Bogotá: Siglo del Hombre/IESCO/Pensar.

Castrucci, Emanuele (1981), 'Teologia Politica e Dottrina dello Stato', in G. Dilcher and L. L. Vallauri (eds.), *Cristianesimo, Secolarizzazione e Diritto Moderno*, vol. 1, 731–54, Milano: Giuffrè.

Cavanaugh, W. T. and P. Scott, eds. (2019), *The Wiley Blackwell Companion to Political Theology*, Oxford: Blackwell.

Césaire, A. (1950), *Discours sur le Colonialisme*, Paris: Réclame.

Cesare, D. di (2014), *Israele: Terra, Ritorno, Anarchia*, Torino: Bollati Boringhieri.

Cesare, D. di (2024), *Democrazia e Anarchia: Il Potere nella Polis*, Torino: Einaudi.

Chen, Y. A. (2022), *Toward a Micro-Political Theology: A Dialogue Between Michel Foucault and Liberation Theologies*, Eugene: Pickwick.

Chopp, R. S. (1995), 'Feminist Queries and Metaphysical Musings', *Modern Theology*, 11 (1): 47–63.

Chopp, R. S. (1996), 'Theological Methodology', in J. S. Clarkson and L. M. Russell (eds.), *Dictionary of Feminist Theologies*, 180–2, Louisville: Westminster John Knox.

Claffey, P. and J. Egan, eds. (2009), *Movement or Moment? Assessing Liberation Theology Forty Years After*, Bern: Peter Lang.

Cleage Jr., A. B. (1968), *The Black Messiah*, New York: Sheed & Ward.

CNN Brasil (2022), 'Presidente Jair Bolsonaro Defende Golpe de 64 e Daniel Silveira', 31 March 2022, https://www.youtube.com/watch?v=zDSJwaUcErQ.

Coccia, E. (2024), *Hiérarchie: La Société des Anges*, trans. J. Gayraud. Paris: Rivages.

Cole, A. (2014), *The Birth of Theory*, Chicago: University of Chicago Press.

Comaroff, J. L. (2009), 'Reflections on the Rise of Legal Theology: Law and Religion in the Twenty-First Century', *Social Analysis*, 53 (1): 193–216.

Cone, J. H. (1969), *Black Theology and Black Power*, New York: Seabury.

Cone, J. H. (1970), *A Black Theology of Liberation*, Philadelphia: Lippincott.

Cone, J. H. (2011), *The Cross and the Lynching Tree*, New York: Orbis.

Copeland, M. S. (2019), 'Black Political Theologies', in W. T. Cavanaugh and P. Scott (eds.), *The Wiley Blackwell Companion to Political Theology*, 271–87, Oxford: Blackwell.

Corten, A. (1996), *Os Pobres e o Espírito Santo: O Pentecostalismo no Brasil*, Petrópolis: Vozes.

Costa, M. T. (2023), *Il Carattere Distrutivo: Walter Benjamin e il Pensiero della Soglia*, Macerata: Quodlibet.

Costa, P. (2004), 'El Problema de la Representación Política: Una Perspectiva Histórica', trans. A. Agüero and M. J. Sola, *Anuario de la Facultad de Derecho de la Universidad Autónoma de Madrid*, 8: 15–61.

Cox, H. (1965), *The Secular City: Secularization and Urbanization in Theological Perspective*, New York: Collier.

Crockett, C. (2013), *Radical Political Theology: Religion and Politics After Liberalism*, New York: Columbia University Press.

D'Ors, Á. (1976), 'Teología Política: Una Revisión del Problema', *Revista de Estudios Politicos*, 205: 41–77.

De Vries, H. (2006), 'Introduction: Before, Around, and Beyond the Theologico-Political', in De Vries, H. and L. Sullivan, *Political Theologies: Public Religions in a Post-Secular World*, New York: Fordham University Press.

Dean, M., L. List and S. Schwarzkopf, eds. (2023), *Political Theology Today: 100 Years After Carl Schmitt*, London: Bloomsbury.

Debord, G. (2006), *The Society of the Spectacle*, trans. D. Nicholson-Smith, Zone: New York.

Deleuze, G. (1968), *Différence et Répétition*, Paris: Presses Universitaires de France.

Deleuze, G. (1969), *Logique du Sens*, Paris: Les Éditions de Minuit.

Deleuze, G. (1985), 'Les Plages d'Immanence', in A. Cazenave and J. F. Lyotard (eds.), *L'Art des Confins: Mélanges Offerts à Maurice de Gandillac*, 79–81, Paris: Presses Universitaires de France.

Deleuze, G. (1986), *Nietzsche and Philosophy*, trans. H. Tomlinson, London: Continuum.

Deleuze, G. (1990), *Pourparlers (1972–90)*, Paris: Minuit.

Deleuze, G. (1993), 'Pour en Finir Avec le Jugement', in *Critique et Clinique*, 158–69, Paris: Les Éditions de Minuit.

Deleuze, G. (2003), 'L'Immanence: Une Vie…', in *Deux Régimes de Fous*, 359–63, Paris: Minuit.

Derrida, J. (1989–90), 'Force of Law: The «Mystical Foundation of Authority»', trans. M. Quaintance, *Cardozo Law Review*, 11: 920–1045.

Didi-Huberman, G. (2018), *Atlas ou o Gaio Saber Inquieto: O Olho da História*, trans. M. Arbex e V. C. Nova, Belo Horizonte: Editora da Universidade Federal de Minas Gerais.

Diels, H. and W. Kranz, eds. (1951), *Die Fragmente der Vorsokratiker*, 6. ed., Berlin: Weidmannsche.
Dip, A. (2018), *Em Nome de Quem? A Bancada Evangélica e seu Projeto de Poder*, São Paulo: Civilização Brasileira.
Dogliani, M. (2014), 'La Rappresentanza Politica come Rappresentanza del «Valore» di uno Stato Concreto', *Democrazia e Diritto*, 2/2014: 7–26.
Donoso Cortés, J. (1854), 'Discurso sobre la Dictadura', in *Obras de Don Juan Donoso Cortés*, vol. III, Madrid: Tejado.
Driver, T. F. (1981), *Christ in a Changing World: Toward an Ethical Christology*, New York: Crossroad.
Duarte, T. dos S. (2012), 'A Participação da Frente Parlamentar Evangélica no Legislativo Brasileiro: Ação Política e (In)Vocação Religiosa', *Ciencias Sociales y Religion/Ciências Sociais e Religião*, 14 (17): 53–76.
Dube, M. (2010), 'Intercultural Biblical Interpretations', *Swedish Missiological Themes*, 98 (3): 361–88.
Dupuy, J.-P. (2008), *La Marque du Sacré*, Paris: Carnets Nord.
Duso, G. (2003), *La Rappresentanza Politica: Genesi e Crisi del Concetto*, Milano: Franco Angeli.
Duso, G. (2012), 'Ripensare la Rappresentanza alla Luce della Teologia Politica', *Quaderni Fiorentini per la Storia del Pensiero Giuridico Moderno*, 41: 9–47.
Dussel, E. (1973), *Para una Ética de la Liberación Latinoamericana*, Buenos Aires: Siglo XXI.
Dussel, E. (2007), *Política de la Liberación: Historia Mundial y Crítica*, Madrid: Trotta.
Dussel, E. (2013), *Ética de la Liberación en la Edad de la Globalización y de la Exclusión*, Buenos Aires: Docencia.
Echeverría, B. (2000), *La Modernidad de lo Barroco*, México: Era.
Eco, U. (2018), *Il Fascismo Eterno*, Milano: La Nave di Teseo.
El País (2020), 'Bolsonaro Invoca Intervenção Militar Contra o STF e Flerta com Golpe', 29 May 2020, https://brasil.elpais.com/brasil/2020-05-29/bolsonaro-invoca-intervencao-militar-contra-o-stf-e-flerta-com-golpe.html.
Ellacuría, I. and J. Sobrino, eds. (1990), Mysterium Liberationis*: Conceptos Fundamentales de la Teología de la Liberación*, 2 vols., Madrid: Trotta.
Eschweiler, K. (1931–32), 'Politische Theologie', *Religiöse Besinnung*, IV (2): 72–88.
Esposito, R. (2012), 'Palabra', in *Diez Pensamientos acerca de la Política*, 193–218, trans. L. P. López, México: Fondo de Cultura Económica.
Esposito, R. (2013), *Due: La Macchina della Teologia Politica e il Posto del Pensiero*, Torino: Einaudi.
Esposito, R. (2020), *Pensiero Istituente: Tre Paradigmi di Ontologia Politica*, Torino: Einaudi.
Esposito, R. (2023), *Vitam Instituere*, Torino: Einaudi.
Eusebius, P. C. E. (1857), 'Commentaria in Psalmos', in J. P. Migne (ed.), *Patrologiae Cursus Completus: Series Graeca*, Tomus XXIII, Paris.

Evren, S. (2011), 'Introduction: How New Anarchism Changed the World (of Opposition) After Seattle and Gave Birth to Post-Anarchism', in S. Evren and D. Rouselle (eds.), *Post-Anarchism: A Reader*, 1–19, London: Pluto.

Fabella, V. and M. A. Oduyoye, eds. (1988), *With Passion and Compassion: Third World Women Doing Theology*, New York: Orbis.

Faber, R., E. Goodman-Thau and T. Macho, eds. (2001), *Abendlandische Eschatologie:* Ad *Jacob Taubes*, Würzburg: Konigshausen.

Faber, R. (2022), Ad *Jacob Taubes: Historischer und politischer Theologe, moderner Gnostiker*, Hamburg: Europäische Verlagsanst.

Fazio, G. and F. Lijoi, eds. (2019), *Critica della Teologia Politica: Voci Ebraiche su Carl Schmitt*, Macerata: Quodlibet.

Fernandes, R. C. (1988), *Novo Nascimento: Os Evangélicos em Casa, na Igreja e na Política*, Rio de Janeiro: Mauad.

Festa, S. (1987), 'Monoteismo come Problema Politico? Sulla «Teologia Politica» di Carl Schmitt', in R. Racinaro (ed.), *Tradizione e Modernità nel Pensiero Politico di Carl Schmitt*, 139–55, Napoli: Edizioni Scientifiche Italiane.

Fiorenza, E. S. (1996), *The Power of Naming: A Concilium Reader in Feminist Liberation Theology*, New York: Orbis.

Fiorenza, F. S., K. Tanner and M. Welker, eds. (2013), *Political Theology: Contemporary Challenges and Future Directions*, Louisville: Westminster John Knox.

Fisichella, D. (1996), *La Rappresentanza Politica*, Roma/Bari: Laterza.

Flusser, V. (2007), *Bodenlos: Uma Autobiografia Filosófica*, São Paulo: Annablume.

Flusser, V. (2010), *A Escrita: Há Futuro para a Escrita?*, trans. M. J. da Costa, São Paulo: Annablume.

Foertsch, S. and C. M. Pieper (2023), 'A Social History of Christofascism', in D. Hiebert (ed.), *The Routledge International Handbook of Sociology and Christianity*, 93–100, London: Routledge.

Földényi, L. (2006), *Dostoyevski Lee a Hegel en Siberia y Rompe a Llorar*, trans. A. K. Meszaros, Barcelona: Galaxia Gutenberg.

Folha de S. Paulo (2021), 'Bolsonaro Ameaça o STF de Golpe, Exorta a Desobediência à Justiça e Diz que Só Sai Morto', 07 September 2021, https://www1.folha.uol.com.br/poder/2021/09/na-paulista-bolsonaro-repete-ameacas-golpistas-ao-stf-e-diz-que-canalhas-nunca-irao-prende-lo.shtml.

Foucault, M. (1963), *Naissance de la Clinique: Une Archéologie du Regard Médical*, Paris: Presses Universitaires de France.

Foucault, M. (1964), 'La Prose d'Actéon', *Nouvelle Revue Française*, 12 (135): 444–59.

Foucault, M. (1966), *Les Mots et les Choses: Une Archéologie des Sciences Humaines*, Paris: Gallimard.

Foucault, M. (1969), *L'Archéologie du Savoir*, Paris: Gallimard.

Foucault, M. (1970), 'Theatrum Philosophicum', *Critique: Revue Générale des Publications Françaises et Étrangères*, 26 (282): 885–90.

Foucault, M. (1983), 'Preface', in G. Deleuze and F. Guatarri, *Anti-Oedipus: Capitalism and Schizophrenia*, XI-XIV, trans. R. Hurley, M. Seem and H. R. Lane, Minneapolis: Minneapolis University Press.

Foucault, M. (1984), 'Qu'Est-ce que les Lumières?', *Magazine Littéraire*, 207: 35–9.

Foucault, M. (2001), 'À quoi Rêvent les Iraniens?', in *Dits et Écrits*, vol. II (1976–88), 688–94, Paris: Gallimard.

Foucault, M. (2015), 'Qu'Est-ce que la Critique?', in H. P. Fruchaud and D. Lorenzini (eds.), *Qu'Est-ce que la Critique? Suivi de « La Culture de Soi »*, 33–70, Paris: Vrin.

Foucault, M. (2020), 'Political Spirituality as the Will for Alterity: An Interview with the *Nouvel Observateur*', trans. S. V. Bremner, *Critical Inquiry*, 47: 121–34.

Freston, P. (1994), 'Uma Breve História do Pentecostalismo Brasileiro: A Assembléia de Deus', *Religião & Sociedade*, 16 (3): 104–29.

Freund, J. (1989), 'La Teologia Politica Secondo Carl Schmitt', *Behemot*, 6: 33–40.

Fry, P. H. and G. N. Howe (1975), 'Duas Respostas à Aflição: Umbanda e Pentecostalismo', *Debate e Crítica*, 6: 75–94.

Fulco, R. (2017), 'Le Rapport entre Politique et Religion', *Cahiers Simone Weil*, XXXX (3): 325–44.

Fulco, R. (2024), '¿Política Espiritual *Versus* Teologia Política?', trans. A. Pradera, *La Maleta de Portbou* 65: 109–115.

Gagnebin, J.-M. (1999), 'Teologia e Messianismo no Pensamento de W. Benjamin', *Estudos Avançados*, 13 (37): 191–206.

Galeano [Subcomandante Insurgente] and Subcomandante Insurgente Moisés (2016), 'A Story to Try to Understand', https://enlacezapatista.ezln.org.mx/2016/11/26/a-story-to-try-to-understand/.

Galimberti, U. (2023), 'Senza Parole: Lo Spaesamento e l'Etica del Viandante', *Festival Filosofia* (Carpi), 17 September 2023, https://www.youtube.com/watch?v=tqkmJUokWE0&ab_channel=Festivalfilosofia

Galli, C. (1981), 'La Teologia Politica in Carl Schmitt: Proposte per una Rilettura Critica', in G. Duso (ed.), *La Politica oltre lo Stato*, 127–37, Venezia: Arsenale.

Galli, C. (1987), 'Immagine e Rappresentanza Politica', *Filosofia Politica*, 1: 9–30.

Galli, C. (1996), *Genealogia della Politica: Carl Schmitt e la Crisi del Pensiero Politico Moderno*, Bologna: Il Mulino.

Galli, C. (2015), *Janus's Gaze: Essays on Carl Schmitt*, ed. A. Sitze, trans. A. Minervini, Durham: Duke University Press.

Galli, C. (2020), *Forme della Critica: Saggi di Filosofia Politica*, Bologna: Il Mulino.

Galli, C. (2022), *Ideologia*, Bologna: Il Mulino.

Galli, C. (2024), 'Eclipse y Regreso de la Teologia Política', trans. A. Pradera, *La Maleta de Portbou*, 65: 99–104.

Gama, L. (2023), *Liberdade (1880–82)*, Obras Completas, Vol. 8, ed. B. R. de Lima, São Paulo: Hedra.

García Collado, F. (2024), *Phobiopolítica: Democracia, Psicología y Ética en la Era Neoliberal*, Madrid: Catarata.

García Collado, F. and A. S. de M. C. Matos (2021), *Para Além da Biopolítica*, São Paulo: sobinfluencia.

Gebara, I. (1999), *Longing for Running Water: Ecofeminism and Liberation*, Minneapolis: Fortress.

Gentile, E. (2001), *Le Religioni della Politica: Fra Democrazia e Totalitarismi*, Roma/Bari: Laterza.

Gentili, D., M. Ponzi and E. Stimilli, eds. (2010), *Il Culto del Capitale: Walter Benjamin: Capitalismo e Religione*, Macerata: Quodlibet.

Gentili, D. (2020), *Il Tempo della Storia: Le Tesi* Sul Concetto di Storia *di Walter Benjamin*, Macerata: Quodlibet.

Ghamari-Tabrizi, B. (2016), *Foucault in Iran: Islamic Revolution After the Enlightenment*, Minneapolis: Minnesota University Press.

Girard, R. (2005), *Violence and the Sacred*, trans. P. Gregory, London: Continuum.

Gogarten, F. (1934), *Ist Volksgesetz Gottesgesetz? Eine Auseinandersetzung mit meinen Kritikern*, Hamburg: Hanseatische Verlagsanstalt.

Goizueta, R. S. (2019), 'Liberation Theology 1: Eduardo Gutiérrez', in W. T. Cavanaugh and P. Scott (eds.), *The Wiley Blackwell Companion to Political Theology*, 280–92, Oxford: Blackwell.

Goldmann, L. (1955), *Le Dieu Caché*, Paris: Gallimard.

Graham, E. (2019), 'Feminist Theology, Northern', in W. T. Cavanaugh and P. Scott (eds.), *The Wiley Blackwell Companion to Political Theology*, 210–26, Oxford: Blackwell.

Guerra, G. and T. Tagliacozzo (2020), *Felicità e Tramonto: Sul* Frammento Teologico-Politico *di Walter Benjamin*, Macerata: Quodlibet.

Gunjević, B. (2015), 'Virtudes Babilônicas: A Palavra da Minoria', in B. Gunjević and S. Žižek, *O Sofrimento de Deus: Inversões do Apocalipse*, trans. R. Bettoni, Belo Horizonte: Autêntica.

Gutiérrez, G. (1971), *Teología de la Liberación: Perspectivas*, Lima: CEP/Universitaria.

Gutiérrez, G. (1987), *On Job: God-Talk and the Suffering of the Innocent*, New York: Orbis.

Hall, D. J. (2013), *What Christianity Is Not: An Exercise in 'Negative' Theology*, Eugene: Cascade.

Haller, B. (1987), *Repräsentation: ihr Bedeutungswandel von der hierarchischen Gesellschaft zum demokratischen Verfassungsstaat*, Münster: Lit.

Han, B. (2003), 'L'*a Priori* Historique selon Michel Foucault: Difficultés Archéologiques', in E. da Silva (ed.), *Lectures de Michel Foucault. Vol. 2: Foucault et la Philosophie*, 23–38, Lyon: ENS Éditions.

Hardt, M. and A. Negri (2004), *Multitude: War and Democracy in the Age of Empire*, New York: Penguin.

Hardt, M. and A. Negri (2009), *Commonwealth*, Cambridge: Harvard University Press.

Hegel, G. W. F. (1976), *Frühe Schriften*, ed. E. Moldenhauer and K. M. Michel, Frankfurt am Main: Suhrkamp.

Hegel, G. W. F. (1986), *Wissenschaft der Logik I. Erster Teil. Die objektive Logik. Erstes Buch*, ed. E. Moldenhauer and K. M. Michel, Frankfurt am Main: Suhrkamp.

Heidegger, M. (1927), *Sein und Zeit*, Halle: Max Niemeyer.

Heidegger, M. (1933), *Die Selbstbehauptung der deutschen Universität*, Breslau: Korn.

Heidegger, M. (1954), 'Die Frage nach der Technik', in *Vorträge und Aufsätze*, 70–108, Pfullingen: G. Neske.

Heidegger, M. (1959), *Gelassenheit*, Pfullingen: Neske.

Heidegger, M. (1969), 'The Onto-Theo-Logical Constitution of Metaphysics', in *Identity and Difference*, trans. J. Stambaugh, New York: Harper & Row.

Heidegger, M. (1981a), *Aristoteles, Metaphysik IX [Theta] 1-3: von Wesen und Wirklichkeit der Kraft*, ed. H. Hüni, Frankfurt am Main: Vittorio Klostermann.

Heidegger, M. (1981b), 'Only a God Can Save Us', in T. Sheehan (ed.), *Heidegger: The Man and the Thinker*, 45–67, trans. W. J. Richardson, Chicago: Precedent.

Heidegger, M. (1988), *Zur Sache des Denkens*, Tübingen: Max Niemeyer.

Heidegger, M. (1991a), *Il Principio di Ragione*, trans. F. Volpi and G. Gurisatti, Milano: Adelphi.

Heidegger, M. (1991b), *Nietzsche. Vol. 3: The Will to Power as Knowledge and as Metaphysics. Vol. 4: Nihilism*, New York: HarperOne.

Heidegger, M. (1992), *Parmenides*, Frankfurt am Main: Vittorio Klostermann.

Heidegger, M. (1993a), 'Letter on Humanism', in D. F. Krell (ed.), *Basic Writings: From 'Being and Time' (1927) to 'The Task of Thinking' (1964)*, 213–45, ed. D. F. Krell, New York: Harper Collins.

Heidegger, M. (1993b), 'The End of Philosophy and the Task of Thinking', in D. F. Krell (ed.), *Basic Writings: From 'Being and Time' (1927) to 'The Task of Thinking' (1964)*, 427–49, New York: Harper Collins.

Heidegger, M. (1993c), 'What Is Metaphysics', in D. F. Krell (ed.), *Basic Writings: From 'Being and Time' (1927) to 'The Task of Thinking' (1964)*, 89–110, New York: Harper Collins.

Heidegger, M. (2003), *Beiträge zur Philosophie (Vom Ereignis)*, Frankfurt am Main: Vittorio Klostermann.

Heidegger, M. (2010), 'Introduction to the Phenomenology of Religion', in *The Phenomenology of Religious Life*, 1–111, trans. M. Fritsch and J. A. Gosetti-Ferencei, Bloomington: Indiana University.

Herrera, Abraham Cohen de Herrera. (2010), *La Porta del Cielo*, trans. Giuseppa Saccaro del Buffa, Vicenza: Neri Pozza.

Heron, N. (2008), *Liturgical Power: Between Economic and Political Theology*, New York: Fordham University.

Hervieu-Léger, D. (1993), *La Religion pour Memóire*, Paris: Cerf.

Higgs, J. (2012), *The KLF: Chaos, Magic and the Band Who Burned a Million Pounds*, London: Phoenix.

Hobbes, T. (1965), *Leviathan*, reprinted from the edition of 1651, Oxford: Oxford University Press.

Hofmann, H. (1974), *Repräsentation: Studien zur Wort- und Begriffsgeschichte von der Antike bis ins 19. Jahrhundert*, Berlin: Duncker & Humblot.

Hopkins, D. N. (2005), *Black Theology. USA and South Africa: Politics, Culture, and Liberation*, Eugene: Wipf & Stock.

Horkheimer, M. (1985–96), *Gesammelte Schriften*, 19 vols., Frankfurt am Main: Fischer.

Huici, G. (2016), *El Dios Ausente: Iconografía y Metafísica del Capitalismo*, Barcelona: Elba.

IBGE (2025), 'Panorama Censo 2022. Tema: Religião', August 2025, https://censo2022.ibge.gov.br/panorama/indicadores.html?localidade=BR&tema=10

ICL Notícias (2024), 'A Ameaça Michelle Bolsonaro: Teologia do Domínio I', 22 May 2024, https://iclnoticias.com.br/ameaca-michelle-bolsonaro-teologia-do-dominio-i/.

Instituto Humanitas Unisinos (2018), 'O Voto Evangélico Garantiu a Eleição de Jair Bolsonaro', 01 November 2018, https://www.ihu.unisinos.br/categorias/188-noticias-2018/584304-o-voto-evangelico-garantiu-a-eleicao-de-jair-bolsonaro.

Ipsos (2023), 'Religious Beliefs Across the World', May 2023, https://www.ipsos.com/sites/default/files/ct/news/documents/2023-05/Ipsos%20Global%20Advisor%20-%20Religion%202023%20Report%20-%2026%20countries.pdf.

Isasi-Diaz, A. M. (1993), *En la Lucha/In the Struggle: Elaborating a Mujerista Theology*, Minneapolis: Fortress.

Jacobson, E. (2003), *Metaphysics of the Profane: The Political Theology of Walter Benjamin and Gershom Scholem*, New York: Columbia University Press.

Jagessar, M. N. and A. Reddie, eds. (2014), *Black Theology in Britain: A Reader*, London: Routledge.

Jones, W. R. (1998), *Is God a White Racist? A Preamble to Black Theology*, Boston: Beacon.

Jongen, M., ed. (2007), *Der göttliche Kapitalismus: Ein Gespräch über Geld, Konsum, Kunst und Zerstörung mit Boris Groys, Jochen Hörisch, Thomas Macho, Peter Sloterdijk und Peter Weibel*, Brill/Fink: Munich.

Kafka, F. (2006), *Die Züraeur Aphorismen*, ed. R. Calasso, Frankfurt am Main: Suhrkamp.

Kairos Theologians (1986), *The Kairos Document: A Theological Comment on the Political Crisis in South Africa*, Grand Rapids: Eerdmans.

Kalyvas, A. (2018), 'Constituent Power', in J. M. Bernstein, A. M. Ophir and A. L. Stoler (eds.), *Political Concepts: A Critical Lexicon*, 87–117, New York: Fordham University Press.

Kantorowicz, E. H. (1946), Laudes Regiae*: A Study in Liturgical Acclamations and Medieval Ruler Worship*, Berkeley/Los Angeles: University of California Press.

Kantorowicz, E. H. (1951), '*Pro Patria Mori* in Medieval Political Thought', *The American Historical Review*, 56 (3): 472–92.

Kantorowicz, E. H. (1957), *The King's Two Bodies: A Study in Mediaeval Political Theology*, Princeton: Princeton University Press.

Katongole, E. (2011), *The Sacrifice of Africa: A Political Theology for Africa*, Grand Rapids: Eerdmans.

Kelsen, H. (1905), *Die Staatslehre des Dante Alighieri*, Wien/Leipzig: Franz Deuticke.

Kelsen, H. (1992), *Reine Rechtslehre*, 2. ed., Wien: Österreichische Staatsdruckerei.

Kelsen, H. (2004), *A New Science of Politics: Hans Kelsen's Reply to Eric Voegelin's 'New Science of Politics'. A Contribution to the Critique of Ideology*, Berlin: Walter de Gruyter.

Kelsen, H. (2012), *Secular Religion: A Polemic Against the Misinterpretation of Modern Social Philosophy, Science and Politics as 'New Religions'*, Wien/New York: Springer.

Kahn, P. W. (2011), *Political Theology: Four New Chapters on the Concept of Sovereignty*, New York: Columbia.

Khayati, M. (2009), *Captive Words: Preface to a Situationist Dictionary*, trans. K. Knabb, https://archive.org/details/al_Mustapha_Khayati_Captive_Words_Preface_to_a_Situationist_Dictionary_a4/mode/2up.

Klausen, J. C. and J. Martel (2011), *How Not to Be Governed: Readings and Interpretations From a Critical Anarchist Left*, London: Lexington.

Koch, A. M. (2011), 'Post-Structuralism and the Epistemological Basis of Anarchism', in S. Evren and D. Rousselle (eds.), *Post-Anarchism: A Reader*, 23–40, London: Pluto.

Kotsko, A. (2018), *Neoliberalism's Demons: On the Political Theology of Late Capital*, Stanford: Stanford University Press.

Kwok, P. L. (2019), 'Feminist Theology, Southern', in W. T. Cavanaugh and P. Scott (eds.), *The Blackwell Companion to Political Theology*, 194–209, Oxford: Blackwell.

Kyung, C. H. (1990), *Struggle to Be the Sun Again: Introducing Asian Women's Theology*, New York: Orbis.

Lafargue, P. (1916), *The Religion of Capital: A Satirical Exposure of Capital's Claims to Sanctity*, Ann Arbor: University of Michigan Library.

Laudani, R. (2011), *Disobedience in Western Political Thought: A Genealogy*, Cambridge: Cambridge University Press.

Lefort, C. (1981), *L'Invention Démocratique: Les Limites de la Domination Totalitaire*, Paris: Le Livre de Poche.

Leibholz, G. (1989), *La Rappresentazione nella Democrazia*, ed. Simona Fortini, Milano: Giuffrè.

Leibholz, G. (1996), *Das Wesen der Repräsentation und der Gestaltwandel der Demokratie im 20. Jahrhundert*, Berlin: Walter de Gruyter.

Lévi-Strauss, C. (1955), *Tristes Tropiques*, Paris: Plon.

Ley, M. (2003), *Politische Religion?* Munich: Wilhelm Fink.

Linhares, B. J. (2014), 'Princeton Theological Seminary and the Birth of Liberation Theology', *Reflexus*, 8 (2): 19–43.
Lloyd, V., ed. (2012), *Race and Political Theology*, Stanford: Stanford University Press.
Lloyd, V., ed. (2016), *Race and Secularism in America*, New York: Columbia University Press.
Løland, O. J. (2020), *Pauline Ugliness: Jacob Taubes and the Turn to Paul*, New York: Fordham University Press.
Loreto, C. (1994), *Coping With Poverty: Pentecostals and Christian Base Communities in Brazil*, Philadelphia: Temple University Press.
Lourenço, F. (2016), 'Introdução aos Quatro Evangelhos', in *Bíblia. Vol. I.: Novo Testamento: Os Quatro Evangelhos*, 21–38, trans. Frederico Lourenço, Lisboa: Quetzal.
Löwith, K. (1949), *Meaning in History: The Theological Implications of the Philosophy of History*, Chicago: University of Chicago Press.
Löwith, K. (1953), *Weltgeschichte und Heilsgeschehen: Die theologischen Voraussetzungen der Geschichtsphilosophie*, Stuttgart: Kohlhammer.
Löwy, M. (1996), *The War of Gods: Religion and Politics in Latin America*, London: Verso.
Lummis, C. D. (2016), *Radical Democracy*, Ithaca: Cornell University Press.
Macedo, E. and C. Oliveira (2008), *Plano de Poder: Deus, os Cristãos e a Política*, Rio de Janeiro: Thomas Nelson Brasil.
Macedo, E. (1990), *Vida com Abundância*, Rio de Janeiro: Universal Produções.
Macedo, E. (2002), *Orixás, Caboclos e Guias: Deuses ou Demônios?* Rio de Janeiro: Universal Produções.
Maier, H., ed. (1996–2003), *Totalitarismus und politische Religionen*, 3 vols., Paderborn: Ferdinand Schöningh.
Maimela, S. (1981), 'Man in "White" Theology', *Journal of Theology for Southern Africa*, 36: 64–78.
Maimonide, M. (2003), *La Guida dei Perplessi*, ed. M. Zonta, Torino: UTET.
Mansfield, N. (2010), *The God Who Deconstructs Himself: Sovereignty and Subjectivity Between Freud, Bataille, and Derrida*, New York: Fordham University Press.
Marder, M. (2010), *Groundless Existence: The Political Ontology of Carl Schmitt*, London: Continuum.
Mariano, R. (1996), 'Os Neopentecostais e a Teologia da Prosperidade', *Novos Estudos CEBRAP*, 44: 24–44.
Mariano, R. (2003), 'Guerra Espiritual: O Protagonismo do Diabo nos Cultos Neopentecostais', *Debates do NER*, 4 (4): 21–34.
Mariano, R. (2005), *Neopentecostais: Sociologia do Novo Pentecostalismo no Brasil*, São Paulo: Loyola.
Mariano, R. (2011), 'Laicidade à Brasileira: Católicos, Pentecostais e Laicos em Disputa na Esfera Pública', *Civitas*, 11 (2): 238–58.

Marion, J.-L. (2010), *Certitudes Négatives*, Paris: Grasset.

Marion, J.-L. (2013), *Dieu sans l'Être*, Paris: Presses Universitaires de France.

Mariz, C. (1999), 'A Teologia da Batalha Espiritual: Uma Revisão da Bibliografia', *Revista Brasileira de Informação Bibliográfica em Ciências Sociais*, 47 (1): 33–48.

Marramao, G. (1994), *Cielo e Terra: Genealogia della Secolarizzazione*, Roma/Bari: Laterza.

Marramao, G. (1996), 'Universalismo e Politiche della Differenza: La Democrazia come Comunità Paradossale', in G. de Finis and R. Scartezzini (eds.), *Universalità & Differenza: Cosmopolitismo e Relativismo nelle Relazioni tra Identità Sociali e Culture*, Milano: Franco Angeli.

Martel, J. R. (2011), *Textual Conspiracies: Walter Benjamin, Idolatry and Political Theory*, Michigan: University of Michigan Press.

Martel, J. R. (2012), *Divine Violence: Walter Benjamin and the Eschatology of Sovereignty*, London: Routledge.

Martel, J. R. (2020), 'The One Who Made the Lock also Made the Key: Thomas Hobbes on Encryption and Decryption in the Face of Sovereign Power and Authority', *Revista da Faculdade Mineira de Direito*, 23 (45): 34–48.

Martel, J. R. (Undated manuscript), *Deep Anarchism: Why the Solution to Anarchist Problems Is Always yet More Anarchism*.

Marx, K. (1956), 'Zur Kritik der Hegelschen Rechtsphilosophie. Einleitung', in F. Engels and K. Marx, *Werke*, vol. 1, 378–91, Berlin: Dietz.

Marx, K. (1968), 'Das Kapital', in F. Engels and K. Marx, *Werke*, vol. 23, Berlin: Dietz.

Mata, S. da (2020), 'A Teologia Política do Governo Bolsonaro', in V. Araujo, B. S. Klem and M. Pereira (eds.), *Do* Fake *ao Fato: (Des)Atualizando Bolsonaro*, 53–69, Vitória: Milfontes.

Matos, A. S. de M. C. and J. D. P. Matos (2023), '*Experimentum Linguae*: Da Língua Pura à Violência Pura', *VirtuaJus*, 8 (14): 44–59.

Matos, A. S. de M. C. (2013), 'Notes on a Political Atheology: A Reading of Hans Kelsen's *Secular Religion*', *Archiv für Rechts- und Sozialphilosophie*, 99 (2): 201–11.

Matos, A. S. de M. C. (2016), 'Walter Benjamin em Gotham City: Sobre a Violência Pura', *Sequência*, 74: 137–52.

Matos, A. S. de M. C. (2020), *Representação Política Contra Democracia Radical: Uma Arqueologia (A)Teológica do Poder Separado*, Belo Horizonte: Fino Traço.

Matos, A. S. de M. C. (2022), *A* An-Arquia *que Vem: Fragmentos de um Dicionário de Política Radical*, São Paulo: sobinfluencia.

Matos, A. S. de M. C. (2024a), 'A Teologia Político-Pornográfica de Pier Paolo Pasolini', in P. P. Pasolini, *Porno-Teo-Kolossal*, trans. A. S. de M. C. Matos, 6–33, São Paulo: sobinfuencia.

Matos, A. S. de M. C. (2024b), (A)Teologías Políticas Democrático-Radicales, trans. V. Nieto, *La Maleta de Portbou*, 65: 91–98.

May, T. (1994), *The Political Philosophy of Poststructuralist Anarchism*, Philadelphia: Penn University Press.
May, T. (2011), 'Is Post-Structuralist Political Theory Anarchist?', in S. Evren and D. Rousselle (eds.), *Post-Anarchism: A Reader*, 41–5, London: Pluto.
Mbembe, A. (2015), *Critique de la Raison Nègre*, Paris: La Découverte.
McVicar, M. J. (2015), *Christian Reconstruction: R. J. Rushdoony and American Religious Conservatism*, Chapel Hill: North Carolina Universith Press.
Meier, C. (1980), *Die Entstehung des Politischen bei den Griechen*, Frankfurt am Main: Suhrkamp.
Meier, H. (2006), *Leo Strauss and the Theologico-Political Problem*, New York: Cambridge University Press.
Meillassoux, Q. (2012), *Après la Finitude: Essai sur la Nécessité de la Contingence*, Paris: Seuil.
Metz, J. B. (1997), *Zum Begriff der neuen politischen Theologie (1967–97)*, Mainz: Matthias-Grünewald.
Meuter, G. (1994), *Der Katechon: Zu Carl Schmitts fundamentalistischer Kritik der Zeit*, Berlin: Duncker & Humblot.
Mignolo, W. D. (2011), *The Darker Side of Western Modernity: Global Futures, Decolonial Options*, Durham: Duke University Press.
Miller-McLemore, B. J. (2000), 'How Sexuality and Relationships Have Revolutionized Pastoral Theology', in S. Pattison and J. Woodward (eds.), *Blackwell Reader in Pastoral and Practical Theology*, 233–47, Oxford: Blackwell.
Moltmann, J. (1964), *Theologie der Hoffnung*, Munich: Kaiser.
Momigliano, A. (1975), *Il Conflitto tra Paganesimo e Cristianesimo nel Secolo IV*, Torino: Einaudi.
Monateri, F. (2023), *Katechon: Filosofia, Politica, Estetica*, Torino: Bollati Boringhieri.
Montaigne, M. (1958), *The Complete Essays of Montaigne*, trans. Donald M. Frame, Redwood: Stanford University Press.
Moreiras, A. (2004), 'A God Without Sovereignty. Political *Jouissance*. The Passive Decision', *The New Centennial Review*, 4 (3): 71–108.
Morgan, E. S. (1988), *Inventing the People: The Rise of Popular Sovereignty in England and America*, New York: Norton.
Mosala, I. J. (1989), *Biblical Hermeneutics and Black Theology in South Africa*, Grand Rapids: Eerdmans.
Mouffe, C., ed. (1999), *The Challenge of Carl Schmitt*, London: Verso.
Muller, J. Z. (2022), *Professor of Apocalypse: The Many Lives of Jacob Taubes*, Princeton: Princeton University Press.
Nadler, S. (2013), *A Book Forged in Hell: Spinoza's Scandalous Treatise and the Birth of the Secular Age*, Princeton: Princeton University Press.
Needham, R. (1980), 'Dual Sovereignty', in *Reconnaissances*, 63–106, Toronto: University of Toronto Press.

Negri, A. (2002), *Il Lavoro di Giobbe*, Roma: Manifestolibri.

Neubauer, S. (2012), 'Elements of a Critical Theory of Zionism: The Jewish State, the Disastrous History and the Changing Functionality of Antisemitism in the Late Thought of Max Horkheimer', *Constelaciones: Revista de Teoría Crítica*, 4: 119–32.

Newman, S. (2001), *From Bakunin to Lacan: Anti-Authoritarianism and the Dislocation of Power*, Lanham: Lexington.

Newman, S. (2011), 'Post-Anarchism and Radical Politics Today', in S. Evren and D. Rousselle (eds.), *Post-Anarchism: A Reader*, 46–68, London: Pluto.

Newman, S. (2015), *Post-Anarchism*, London: Polity.

Newman, S. (2018), *Political Theology: A Critical Introduction*, Cambridge: Polity.

Nicoletti, M. and L. Sartori, eds. (1991), *Teologia Politica*, Bologna: Edizioni Dehoniane Bologna.

Nicoletti, M. (1990), *Trascendenza e Potere: La Teologia Politica di Carl Schmitt*, Brescia: Morcelliana.

Nietzsche, F. (1961), *Thus Spoke Zarathustra*, trans. R. J. Hollingdale, London: Penguin.

Nietzsche, F. (1989), *Genealogy of Morals*, trans. C. Diers, New York: Vintage.

Nietzsche, F. (2008), *The Gay Science. With a Prelude in German Rhymes and an Appendix of Songs*, ed. B. Williams, trans. J. Nauckhoff and A. del Caro, Cambridge: Cambridge University Press.

North, G. (1982), 'The Intellectual Schizophrenia of the New Christian Right', in J. B. Jordan (ed.), *The Failure of the American Baptist Culture*, 1–40, Tyler: Geneva Divinity School Press.

North, G. (1986), *The Sinai Strategy: Economics and the Ten Commandments*, Tyler: Institute for Christian Economics.

North, G. (1989), *Political Polytheism: The Myth of Pluralism*, Tyler: Institute for Christian Economics.

Ober, J. (2008), 'The Original Meaning of Democracy: Capacity to Do Things, Not Majority Rule', *Constellations: An Internacional Journal of Critical and Democratic Theory*, 15 (1): 3–9.

Oduyoye, M. A. (1992), 'Women and Ritual in Africa', in M. R. A. Kanyoro and M. A. Oduyoye (eds.), *The Will to Arise: Women, Tradition, and the Church in Africa*, 9–24, New York: Orbis.

Origène (1992), *Commentaire sur Saint Jean*, ed. C. Blanc, Paris: CERF.

Oro, A. P. (1997), 'Neopentecostais e Afro-Brasileiros: Quem Vencerá esta Guerra?', *Debates do NER*, 1 (1): 10–37.

Oro, A. P. (2001), 'Neopentecostalismo: Dinheiro e Magia', *Ilha Revista de Antropologia*, 3 (1): 71–85.

Panotto, N. (2020), *Religiões, Política & Estado Laico: Novas Abordagens para o Contexto Latino-Americano*, trans. B. D. de Carvalho, São Paulo: Recriar.

Panotto, N., ed. (2016a), *Indecent Theologians: Marcella Althaus-Reid and the Next Generation of Postcolonial Activists*, Alameda: Borderless.

Panotto, N. (2016b), *Religión, Política y Poscolonialidad en América Latina: Hacia una Teología Posfundacional de lo Público*, Buenos Aires: Mino y Dávila.
Paravidini, J. L. L. and M. A. Gonçalves (2009), 'Neopentecostalismo: Desamparo e Condição Masoquista', *Revista Mal-Estar e Subjetividade*, 9 (4): 1173–202.
Pascal, B. (1962), *Pensées*, ed. L. Lafuma, Paris: Seuil.
Pasolini, P. P. (1964), *Il Vangelo Secondo Matteo*, Italy/France: Arco Film/Lux Compagnie Cinématographique de France, B&W, 137 min.
Passos, J. D. (2020), 'Uma Teocracia Pentecostal? Considerações a partir da Conjuntura Política Atual', *Horizonte*, 18 (57): 1109–36.
Pereira, E. (2023), 'Teologia do Domínio: Uma Chave de Interpretação da Relação Evangélico-Política do Bolsonarismo', *Projeto História*, 76: 147–73.
Peterson, E. (1994a), 'Das Buch von den Engeln: Stellung und Bedeutung der heiligen Engen im Kultus', in B. Nichtweiß (ed.), *Ausgewählte Schriften*, 195–243, Würzburg: Echter.
Peterson, E. (1994b), 'Der Monotheismus als politisches Problem: ein Beitrag zur Geschichte der politischen Theologie im Imperium Romanum', in B. Nichtweiß (ed.), *Ausgewählte Schriften*, 23–81, Würzburg: Echter.
Peterson, E. (1994c), 'Die Kirche', in B. Nichtweiß (ed.), *Ausgewählte Schriften*, 245–57, Würzburg: Echter.
Peterson, Erik (2012), *Εἷς Θεός: epigraphische, formgeschichtliche und religionsgeschichtliche Untersuchungen zur antiken 'Ein-Gott'-Akklamation*, ed. B. Nichtweiß, Würzburg: Echter.
Petrella, I. (2004), *The Future of Liberation Theology: An Argument and Manifesto*, Aldershot/Burlington: Ashgate.
Pew Research Center (2012), 'The Global Religious Landscape', 18 December 2012, https://www.pewresearch.org/religion/2012/12/18/global-religious-landscape-exec/.
Pew Research Center (2021), 'About Three-in-Ten U.S. Adults Are Now Religiously Unaffiliated', 14 December 2021, https://www.pewresearch.org/religion/2021/12/14/about-three-in-ten-u-s-adults-are-now-religiously-unaffiliated/.
Pew Reserch Center (2024), 'Religious 'Nones' in America: Who They Are and What They Believe', 24 January 2024, https://www.pewresearch.org/religion/2024/01/24/religious-nones-in-america-who-they-are-and-what-they-believe/.
Phillips, E. (2012), *Political Theology: A Guide for the Perplexed*, London: Bloomsbury.
Pierucci, A. F. (1989), 'Representantes de Deus em Brasília: A Bancada Evangélica na Constituinte', *Ciências Sociais Hoje*, 11: 104–32.
Pitkin, H. F. (1972), *The Concept of Representation*, Berkeley/Los Angeles: California University Press.
Plaskow, J. (1983), 'The Right Question is Theological', in S. Heschel (ed.), *On Being a Jewish Feminist: A Reader*, 223–33, New York: Schocken.
Plato (1966), *Plato in Twelve Volumes*, trans. H. N. Fowler, P. Shorey, R. G. Bury and W. R. M. Lamb, Cambridge: Harvard University Press; London: William Heinemann.

Poder 360 (2021), 'Bolsonaro Defende Tortura para Quem Ficar em Silêncio em CPI, em Maio de 1999', 18 May 2021, https://www.youtube.com/watch?v=VRzVMcOdK1I.

Podlech, A. (1978), 'Repräsentation', in O. Brunner, W. Conze and R. Koselleck (eds.), *Geschichtliche Grundbegriffe: Historisches Lexikon zur politisch-sozialen Sprache in Deutschland*, vol. 5, 509–47, Stuttgart: Klett-Cotta.

Preterossi, G. (2022), *Teologia Politica e Diritto*, Roma/Bari: Laterza.

Puech, H.-C. (1978), *En Quête de la Gnose*, Paris: Gallimard.

Py, F. (2020), *Pandemia Cristofascista*, São Paulo: Recriar.

Quijano, A. (1992), 'Colonialidad y Modernidad/Racionalidad', in H. Bonilla (ed.), *Los Conquistados*, 437–49, Bogotá: Tercer Mundo/FLACSO.

Rabinovich, S. (2023), *Notes for a Decolonial Political Theology*, London: Routledge.

Rancière, J. (2005), *La Haine de la Démocratie*, Paris: La Fabrique.

Raschke, C. (2019), *Neoliberalism and Political Theology: From Kant to Identity Politics*, Edinburgh: Edinburgh University Press.

Ratzinger, J. (2020), *Escatologia: Morte e Vida Eterna*, trans. R. Enderle. São Paulo: Molokai.

Raulet, G. (1997), *Le Caractère Destructeur: Messianisme, Politique et Esthétique chez Walter Benjamin*, Paris: Aubier.

Rausch, H., ed. (1968), *Zur Teorie und Geschichte der Repräsentation und Repräsentativverfassung*, Darmstadt: Wissenschaftliche Buchgesellschaft.

Rausch, H. (1977), 'Repräsentation: Wort, Begriff, Kategorie, Prozeß, Theorie', in K. Bosl (ed.), *Der moderne Parlamentarismus und seine Grundlagen in der ständischen Repräsentation*, 69–98, Berlin: Duncker & Humblot.

Reale, G. (1991), *Per una Nuova Interpretazione de Platone: Rilettura della Metafisica dei Grandi Dialoghi alla Luce delle 'Dottrine Non Scritte'*, Milano: Università Cattolica del Sacro Cuore.

Redell, P. C. (2014), *Mysticism as Revolt: Foucault, Deleuze and Theology Beyond Representation*, Aurora: The Davies Group.

Rivière, C. (1988), *Les Liturgies Politiques*, Paris: Presses Universitaires de France.

Rizzi, A. (1991), 'Esodo e Teologia Politica', in M. Nicoletti and L. Sartori (eds.), *Teologia Politica*, 109–19, Bologna: Edizioni Dehoniane Bologna.

Rizzi, M. (2002), 'Teologia Politica: La Rappresentazione del Potere e il Potere della Rappresentazione', in P. Bettiolo and G. Filoramo (eds.), *Il Dio Mortale: Teologie Politiche tra Antico e Contemporaneo*, 267–98, Brescia: Morcelliana.

Robbins, J. W. (2014), *Radical Democracy and Political Theology*, New York: Columbia University Press.

Roberts, J. D. (1974), *A Black Political Theology*, Louisville: Westminster John Knox.

Romeiro, P. (1993), *Supercrentes: O Evangelho Segundo Kenneth Hagin, Walnice Milhomens e os Profetas da Prosperidade*, São Paulo: Mundo Cristão.

Ruether, R. R. (1983), *Sexism and God-Talk: Toward a Feminist Theology*, London: SCM.

Sá, Alexandre Franco de (2024), 'Introdução', in C. Schmitt, *Teologia Política*, 29–51, trans. Alexandre Franco de Sá, São Luís: Livraria Resistência Cultural.

Said, E. (1993), *Culture and Imperialism*, London: Chatto & Windus.

Sanín-Restrepo, R. and M. Machado-Araujo (2020), 'A Teoria da Encriptação do Poder: Itinerário de uma Ideia', *Revista da Faculdade Mineira de Direito*, 23 (45): 1–17.

Sanín-Restrepo, R. and M. Machado-Araujo (2025a), 'A Prolific Paradox of Justice and Two Theses on the Encryption of the Hidden People', in R. Sanín-Restrepo, M. Machado-Araujo and S. J. Ndlovu-Gatsheni (eds.), *Decrypting Justice: From Epistemic Violence to Immanent Democracy*, 15–41, London: Bloomsbury.

Sanín-Restrepo, R. and M. Machado-Araujo (2025b), 'Conclusions', in R. Sanín-Restrepo, M. Machado-Araujo and S. J. Ndlovu-Gatsheni (eds.), *Decrypting Justice: From Epistemic Violence to Immanent Democracy*, 197–206, London: Bloomsbury.

Sanín-Restrepo, R. and Méndez-Hincapié, G. (2018), 'The Encrypted Constitution: New Ways of Emancipation From Global Power', in R. Sanín-Restrepo (ed.), *Decrypting Power*, 1–22, London: Rowman & Littlefield.

Sanín-Restrepo, R. (2016), *Decolonizing Democracy: Power in a Solid State*, London: Rowman & Littlefield.

Sanín-Restrepo, R. (2018), 'Introduction: The Meaning of the Encryption of Power as the Razor's Edge of Politics', in R. Sanín-Restrepo (ed.), *Decrypting Power*, ix–xxx, London: Rowman & Littlefield.

Sanín-Restrepo, R. (2021), *Contingency: Decrypting Heidegger's Terminology*, London: Rowman & Littlefield.

Scattola, M. (2009), *Teologia Política*, trans. J. J. C. Serra, Lisboa: Edições 70.

Schmitt, C. (1927), *Volksentscheid und Volksbegehren: ein Beitrag zur Auslegung der Weimarer Verfassung und zur Lehre von der unmittelbaren Demokratie*, Berlin: Walter de Gruyter.

Schmitt, C. (1996), *Politische Theologie: vier Kapitel zur Lehre von der Souveränität*, Berlin: Duncker & Humblot.

Schmitt, C. (1997), *Der Nomos der Erde im Völkerrecht des* Jus Publicum Europaeum, Berlin: Duncker & Humblot.

Schmitt, C. (2002), *Römischer Katholizismus und politische Form*, Stuttgart: Klett-Cotta.

Schmitt, C. (2008a), *Constitutional Theory*, trans. J. Seitzer, Durham: Duke University Press.

Schmitt, C. (2008b), *Politische Theologie II: die Legende von der Erledigung jeder politischen Theologie*, Berlin: Duncker & Humblot.

Schmitt, C. (2009), *Donoso Cortés in gesamteuropäischer Interpretation: Vier Aufsätze*, Berlin: Duncker & Humblot.

Schmitt, C. (2012), *Legalität und Legitimität*, Berlin: Duncker & Humblot.

Schmitt, C. (2017), *Political Romanticism*, trans. G. Oakes, London/New York: Routledge.

Schürmann, R. (1987), *Heidegger on Being and Acting: From Principles to Anarchy*, trans. C.-M. Gross in collaboration with the author. Bloomington: Indiana University Press.

Sedgwick, M. (2023), *Traditionalism: The Radical Project for Restoring Sacred Order*, Oxford: Oxford University Press.

Seminario di Studi Benjaminiani, ed. (2010), *Le Vie della Distruzione: A partire da* Il Carattere Distrutivo *di Walter Benjamin*, Macerata: Quodlibet.

Severino, E. (1989), *La Filosofia Futura*, Milano: Rizzoli.

Silva, A. A. da, ed. (1998), *Existe um Pensar Teológico Negro?* São Paulo: Paulinas.

Silva, J. P. da (2018), *Walter Benjamin e o Direito: Violência Pura como Estado de Exceção Efetivo*, Rio de Janeiro: Lumen Juris.

Silva, R. M. da (2019), *Paradoxos da Encarnação: Por uma Radicalização Democrática da Teologia Política*, Belo Horizonte: D'Plácido.

Silva, V. G. da (2005), 'Concepções Religiosas Afro-Brasileiras e Neopentecostais: Uma Análise Simbólica', *Revista USP*, 67: 150–75.

Silva, V. G. da, ed. (2007), *Intolerância Religiosa: Impactos do Neopentecostalismo no Campo Religioso Afro-Brasileiro*, São Paulo: Universidade de São Paulo.

Smith, A. (2000), *The Wealth of Nations: Books IV-V*, ed. A. Skinner, London: Penguin.

Soares, R. R. (1984), *Espiritismo: A Magia do Engano*, Rio de Janeiro: Graça.

Sobrino, J. (2008), *No Salvation Outside the Poor: Prophetic-Utopian Essays*, New York: Orbis.

Sölle, D. (1965), *Stellvertretung: ein Kapitel Theologie nach dem 'Tode Gottes'*, Stuttgart: Kreuz.

Sölle, D. (1971), *Politische Theologie: Auseinandersetzung mit Rudolf Bultmann*, Stuttgart: Kreuz.

Sölle, D. (1982), *Beyond Mere Obedience*, trans. L. W. Denef, New York: Pilgrim.

Sölle, D. (1990), *The Window of Vulnerability: A Political Spirituality*, trans. L. M. Maloney, Minneapolis: Fortress.

Sorel, G. (1908), *Réflexions sur la Violence*, Paris: Marcel Rivière.

Spegne, L. (2016), *Ascoltare il Futuro: Il Pensiero Apocalittico di Jacob Taubes*, Trapani: Il Pozzo di Giacobbe.

Spinoza, B. (2021), 'Trattato Teologico-Politico', in A. Sangiacomo (ed.), *Tutte le Opere. Testi Originali a Fronte*, 629–1136, trans. A. Dini, Milano: Bompiani.

Stimilli, E. (2019), *Jacob Taubes: Sovranità e Tempo Messianico*, Brescia: Morceliana.

Stimilli, E. (2020), *Il Debito del Vivente: Ascesi e Capitalismo*, Macerata: Quodlibet.

Sugirtharajah, R. S. (2012), *Exploring Postcolonial Biblical Criticism: History, Method, and Practice*, Chichester: Wiley Blackwell.

Sung, J. M. (1998), *Desejo, Mercado e Religião*, Petrópolis: Vozes.

Szaif, J. (2007), '*Doxa* and *Epistêmê* as Modes of Acquaintance in *Republic V*', *Études Platoniciennes*, 4: 253–72.

Tackels, B. (2012), *Walter Benjamin: Una Vida en los Textos*, trans. J. A. Codes and I. M. Arnao, València: Universitat de València.

Tamez, E. (1986), 'The Woman Who Complicated the History of Salvation', in J. S. Phobee and B. von Wartenberg-Potter (eds.), *New Eyes for Reading: Biblical and Theological Reflections by Women From the Third World*, 5–17, Oak Park: Meyer Stone.

Tanner, K. (1997), 'Social Theory Concerning the "New Social Movements" and the Practice of Feminist Theology', in R. Chopp and S. G. Daveney (eds.), *Horizons in Feminist Theology: Identity, Tradition, and Norms*, 179–97, Minneapolis: Fortress.

Taub, E. (2017), *Mesianismo y Redención: Prolegómenos para Una Teología Política Judía*, Buenos Aires: Miño y Dávila.

Taubes, J., H. Marcuse, R. Löwenthal, A. Schwan, D. Claessens, P. Furth, R. Dutschke and W. Lèfevre (1980), 'Moral und Politik in der Überflußgesellschaft: eine Podiumsdiskussion von Jacob Taubes mit Herbert Marcuse', in H. Marcuse, *Das Ende der Utopie: Vorträge und Diskussionen in Berlin 1967*, Frankfurt am Main: Neue Kritik.

Taubes, J., ed. (1987), *Teokratie*, Munich: Wilhelm Fink.

Taubes, J. (1991), *Abendländische Eschatologie*, München: Matthes & Seitz.

Taubes, J. (1996), *Vom Kult zur Kultur: Bausteine zu einer Kritik der historischen Vernunft. Gesammelte Aufsätze zur Religions- und Geistesgeschichte*, eds. A. Assmann, J. Assmann, W.-D. Hartwich and W. Menninghaus, München: Wilhelm Fink.

Taubes, J. (2007), *La Teología Política de Pablo*, trans. M. G.-B. López, Madrid: Trotta.

Taussig, M. (1987), 'O Batismo do Dinheiro e o Segredo do Capital', *Religião e Sociedade*, 14 (2): 18–31.

Taylor, M. C. (1987), *Erring: A Postmodern A/Theology*, Chicago: University of Chicago Press.

Teitelbaum, B. R. (2021), *War for Eternity: The Return of Traditionalism and the Rise of the Populist Right*, London: Penguin.

Terra Brasil (2024), 'Bolsonaro Defendeu Golpe sem Armas em Reunião Ministerial em 2022: "Não É Dar Tiro"', 09 February 2024, https://www.youtube.com/watch?v=1a9r6DEahak&ab_channel=TerraBrasil

Tödt, H. E. and T. Rendtorff (1968), *Theologie der Revolution: Analysen und Materialien*, Frankfurt am Main: Suhrkamp.

Townes, E. M. (1989), 'Christian Ethics and Theology in Womanist Perspective', *Journal of Feminist Studies in Religion*, 5 (2): 83–112.

Treml, M. (2012), 'Reinventing the Canonical: The Radical Thinking of Jacob Taubes', in E. Goebel and S. Weigel (eds.), *Escape to Life. Jewish Intellectuals in New York: A Compendium on Exile After 1933*, 457–78, Berlin: De Gruyter.

Trevisan, J. (2013), 'A Frente Parlamentar Evangélica: Força Política no Estado Laico Brasileiro', *Numen*, 16: 29–57.

Tribunal Superior Eleitoral do Brasil (2022), 'Lula É Eleito Novamente Presidente da República do Brasil', 30 October 2022, https://www.tse.jus.br/comunicacao/noticias/2022/Outubro/lula-e-eleito-novamente-presidente-da-republica-do-brasil.

Vaccari, G., ed. (1969), *Teologia della Rivoluzione: I Testi Inediti della Rivolta Sociale e Politica della Chiesa Latinoamericana*, Milano: Feltrinelli.

Vallauri, L. L., ed. (1981), *Cristianesimo, Secolarizzazione e Diritto Moderno*, Milano: Giuffrè.

Varro, M. T. (1976), *Antiquitates Rerum Divinarum*, 2 vols., ed. B. von Cardauns, Wiesbaden: Steiner.

Vattimo, G. (2002), *After Christianity*, trans. L. D'Isanto, New York: Columbia University Press.

Veja (2022), '"Não Vejo Nada Demais" em Pedir para Fechar Congresso e STF, Diz Bolsonaro', 23 August 2022, https://veja.abril.com.br/coluna/radar/nao-vejo-nada-demais-em-pedir-para-fechar-congresso-e-stf-diz-bolsonaro.

Villacañas, J. L. (2016), *Teología Política Imperial y Comunidad de Salvación Cristiana: Una Genealogía de la División de Poderes*, Madrid: Trotta.

Villacanãs, J. L. (2020), *Neoliberalismo como Teología Política: Habermas, Foucault, Dardot, Laval y la Historia del Capitalismo Contemporáneo*, Barcelona: NED.

Villacañas, J. L. (2024), 'Una Constante Histórico-Evolutiva de la Humanidad', *La Maleta de Portbou*, 65: 81–90.

Voegelin, E. (1939), *Die politischen Religionen*, Stockholm: Bermann-Fischer.

Volpi, F. (2010), *Heidegger e Aristotele*, Bari-Roma: Laterza.

Volpi, F. (2011), *La Selvaggia Chiarezza: Scritti su Heidegger*, Milano: Adelphi.

Vondey, W. (2013), *Pentecostalism: A Guide for the Perplexed*, London: Bloomsbury.

Walsh, C. (2009), *Interculturalidad, Estado, Sociedad: Luchas (De)Coloniales de Nuestra Época*, Quito: Universidad Andina Simón Bolívar/Abya-Yala.

Weber, M. (2013), *Die protestantische Ethik und der Geist des Kapitalismus*, ed. D. Kaesler, München: C. H. Beck.

Weigel, S. (2019), 'In Paul's Mask: Jacob Taubes Reads Walter Benjamin', in W. Styfhals and S. Symons (eds.), *Genealogies of the Secular: The Making of Modern German Thought*, 193–216, Albany: New York State University Press.

Weil, S. (1949), *L'Enracinement: Prélude à Une Déclaration des Devoirs Envers l'Être Humain*, Paris: Gallimard.

Weil, S. (1957), 'La Personne et le Sacré', in *Écrits de Londres et Dernières Lettres*, 11–44, Paris: Gallimard.

West, C. (1982), *Prophesy Deliverance! An Afro-American Revolutionary Christianity*, Louisville: Westminster John Knox.

West, G. (2008), 'Doing Postcolonial Biblical Interpretation @Home: Ten Years of (South) African Ambivalence', *Neotestamentica*, 42 (1): 147–64.

Wiedenhofer, S. (1976), *Politische Theologie*, Stuttgart: Kohlhammer.

Withy, K. (2022), *Heidegger on Being Self-Concealing*, Oxford: Oxford University Press.

Wohlfarth, I. (1986), '«Immer radikal, niemal konsequent...» Zur theologisch-politischen Standortsbestimmung Walter Benjamin', in N. Bolz and R. Faber (eds.), *Antike und Moderne: zu Walter Benjamins 'Passagen'*, 116–37, Würzburg: Königshausen & Neumann.

Woodcock, G. (1998), 'Introdução Histórica', in G. Woodcock (ed.), *Os Grandes Escritos Anarquistas*, 11–52, trans. J. Tettamanzi and B. Becker, Porto Alegre: L&PM.

Woodhead, L. (1997), 'Spiritualising the Sacred: A Critique of Feminist Theology', *Modern Theology*, 13 (2): 191–212.

Zinn, H. (1970), *The Problem Is Civil Obedience*, https://www.howardzinn.org/collection/the-problem-is-civil-obedience.

Zohar (2003), *The Zohar: Pritzker Edition*, trans. D. C. Matt, Redwood: Stanford University Press.

Index

Note: Page numbers followed by "n" refer to notes.

www.ingramcontent.com/pod-product-compliance
Ingram Content Group UK Ltd.
Pitfield, Milton Keynes, MK11 3LW, UK
UKHW020213290926
15470UKWH00001B/151

9 781666 978650